Register Now for Online Access to Your Book!

Your print purchase of *Social Work Capstone Projects: Demonstrating Professional Competencies Through Applied Research* **includes online access to the contents of your book**—increasing accessibility, portability, and searchability!

Access today at:
http://connect.springerpub.com/content/book/978-0-8261-8636-2
or scan the QR code at the right with your smartphone. Log in or register, then click "Redeem a voucher" and use the code below.

6UT4M4BR

Scan here for quick access.

Having trouble redeeming a voucher code?
Go to https://connect.springerpub.com/redeeming-voucher-code

If you are experiencing problems accessing the digital component of this product, please contact our customer service department at cs@springerpub.com

The online access with your print purchase is available at the publisher's discretion and may be removed at any time without notice.

Publisher's Note: New and used products purchased from third-party sellers are not guaranteed for quality, authenticity, or access to any included digital components.

SPRINGER PUBLISHING

Social Work Practice
A Competency-Based Approach

John Poulin PhD, MSW | Selina Matis PhD, LCSW

This primary social work practice text, built around the nine core CSWE competencies, is the only book available that provides the benefits of a fully integrated competency-based approach. Engaging vignettes, chapter objectives that outline key concepts, abundant case examples, critical-thinking questions, and a detailed case summary with discussion questions in each chapter, help students deepen their understanding of practical applications of the nine core competencies.

Copyright 2021 | 9780826178527
480 pp | Paperback

The Social Work Field Placement
A Competency-Based Approach

John Poulin PhD, MSW
Heather Witt PhD, LMSW
Selina Matis PhD, LCSW

This unique core text helps BSW and MSW students structure their field placement learning around the nine CSWE professional social work competencies. Empowering students to go beyond merely completing tasks, the book facilitates mastery and integration of these competencies by elucidating key concepts and applying them to realistic competency-based case scenarios.

Copyright 2019 | 9780826175526
360 pp | Paperback

SOCIAL WORK CAPSTONE PROJECTS

John Poulin, PhD, MSW, is a professor emeritus and adjunct professor at Widener University's Center for Social Work Education, where he has taught generalist practice, research, and policy courses for 32 years. As an adjunct professor he is currently teaching the foundation field seminar in Widener's online master's degree program (MSW). He received a bachelor's degree from the University of Southern Maine, an MSW from the University of Michigan, and a PhD from the University of Chicago's School of Social Service Administration. The former director of Widener's BSW program, he founded its MSW program and served as the dean and director for 13 years. He also served for 10 years as the executive director of Social Work Consultation Services (SWCS), an innovative community-based field placement agency developed by the school of social work in collaboration with a local community human service organization. SWCS provides a wide range of free social work services to low-income community residents as well as free capacity-building services to underresourced community-based human service organizations, and served as field placement site for hundreds of BSW and MSW students. Dr. Poulin has published numerous journal articles and book chapters and five social work textbooks.

Stephen Kauffman, PhD, is a professor at Widener University's Center for Social Work Education, where he has taught community practice, program evaluation, research, and policy since 1991. Since receiving his PhD from Bryn Mawr College and his MSW from Washington University in St. Louis, his research and practice have focused on citizen participation and community and organizational responses to global problems, such as environmental decay, poverty (in all its dimensions), and education. With this focus, major research projects have included program evaluations of U.S. Department of Justice (DOJ) violence prevention programs, U.S. Health and Human Services housing programs, Century 21 school performance studies, lead abatement, and teenage pregnancy prevention. The programs (and evaluations) have received funding from the U.S. DOJ, the U.S. Department of Housing and Urban Development, the state of Pennsylvania, and several private foundations. Most recently, his work has targeted the relationship between universities and their surrounding environments. He has published in *Social Work, Journal of Social Work Education, Journal of Community Practice, Journal of Baccalaureate Social Work,* and elsewhere.

Travis Sky Ingersoll, PhD, MSW, MED, is an associate professor of social work at West Chester University. He received his PhD in human sexuality and two master's degrees, one in social work and the other in education, at Widener University. Dr. Ingersoll weaves important sexual health information into every class he teaches, from race relations to social policy. His course "Sexuality Concepts for Social Workers" focuses on training social work students to be competent and comfortable addressing the sexual health concerns of their clients. Outside of his role as a college professor, Dr. Ingersoll has guest-lectured and facilitated interactive workshops in person and through distance-learning technologies, domestically and internationally, on a variety of topics. His presentations have educated groups about how to teach sensitive topics, cross-cultural sexuality, sexual health, sexuality throughout the life span, sexually transmitted infections, sexual orientation, intimate relationship violence, media's role in the promotion of sexual violence among men, trans-realities and the gender spectrum, how to utilize the Fear of Intimacy Scale in clinical settings, and to recognize the myriad opportunities for producing sexuality scholarship. Dr. Ingersoll's academic publications include the textbook *Sexuality Concepts for Social Workers*, international studies examining the fear of intimacy, sexual anxiety, gender roles, and implementing clinical interventions to residents of elderly communities. To contact or learn more about the author, visit www.travisskyingersoll.com

SOCIAL WORK CAPSTONE PROJECTS

Demonstrating Professional Competencies Through Applied Research

John Poulin, PhD, MSW

Stephen Kauffman, PhD

Travis Sky Ingersoll, PhD, MSW, MED

Copyright © 2022 Springer Publishing Company, LLC
All rights reserved.

No part of this publication may be reproduced, stored in a retrieval system, or transmitted in any form or by any means, electronic, mechanical, photocopying, recording, or otherwise, without the prior permission of Springer Publishing Company, LLC, or authorization through payment of the appropriate fees to the Copyright Clearance Center, Inc., 222 Rosewood Drive, Danvers, MA 01923, 978-750-8400, fax 978-646-8600, info@copyright.com or on the Web at www.copyright.com.

Springer Publishing Company, LLC
11 West 42nd Street, New York, NY 10036
www.springerpub.com
connect.springerpub.com/

Acquisitions Editor: Kate Dimock
Compositor: S4Carlisle Publishing Services

ISBN: 978-0-8261-8635-5
ebook ISBN: 978-0-8261-8636-2
DOI: 10.1891/9780826186362

SUPPLEMENTS:
Instructor Materials:
Qualified instructors may request supplements by emailing textbook@springerpub.com
Faculty Resources ISBN: 978-0-8261-8638-6
Student Materials:
Student Resources ISBN: 978-0-8261-8637-9

21 22 23 24 / 5 4 3 2 1

The author and the publisher of this Work have made every effort to use sources believed to be reliable to provide information that is accurate and compatible with the standards generally accepted at the time of publication. The author and publisher shall not be liable for any special, consequential, or exemplary damages resulting, in whole or in part, from the readers' use of, or reliance on, the information contained in this book. The publisher has no responsibility for the persistence or accuracy of URLs for external or third-party Internet websites referred to in this publication and does not guarantee that any content on such websites is, or will remain, accurate or appropriate.

Library of Congress Cataloging-in-Publication Data
LCCN number: 2021022584

Contact sales@springerpub.com to receive discount rates on bulk purchases.

Publisher's Note: **New and used products purchased from third-party sellers are not guaranteed for quality, authenticity, or access to any included digital components.**

Printed in the United States of America.

We dedicate this book to social work field instructors who teach and mentor our students in developing their professional social work competencies and show the importance of applied research to our future leaders.

—John Poulin and Stephen Kauffman

Thank you to everyone who has supported my emotional, intellectual, and spiritual growth throughout the years. I am grateful for the support and love of my partner Melinda, for the radiating life force that is my daughter Freya, and for JP for being a great mentor.

—Travis Sky Ingersoll

CONTENTS

Preface   xiii

Part I. Getting Started

1. **Capstone Projects, Professional Competencies, and Ethical Applied Research   3**
   Capstone Projects   3
   Professional Social Work Competencies   4
   Holistic Competency   9
   Competency Model of Social Work Practice   10
   Social Work Values and Ethics   12
   Ethical Standards   12
   Institutional Review Boards   13
   Applied Research   15
   Competency Log: Capstone Project, Paper, and Presentation   18
   Practice Activities   22
   Technology Exercises   22
   References   22

2. **Strategies for Effective Writing   25**
   Getting Organized   25
   Writing Your Paper   29
   Practice Activities   38
   Technology Exercises   39
   References   39

3. **Identifying a Research Topic   41**
   Identifying a Research Problem   41
   Information Technology—Your New Best Friend   44
   Biases in Research: Sources and Prevention Strategies   45
   Reviewing the Literature   47
   Getting Your Capstone Project Approved   52
   Practice Activities   54
   Technology Exercises   54
   References   54

4. **Data Collection   59**
   Sources of Data   59
   Data Collection Methods   63
   Sampling   64
   Quantitative Data Collection   66
   Qualitative Data Collection   75

Practice Exercises 78
Technology Exercises 79
References 79

Part II. Applied Research Designs

5. Program Evaluations: Policies, Process, and Outcome Assessments 83
Evaluation of Programs and Policies 83
Purposes 84
Policy Evaluation 85
Program Evaluation 89
Formative Evaluations 89
Summative Evaluations 93
Practice Activities 100
Technology Exercises 101
References 101

6. Needs Assessments 103
Needs Assessment 103
Needs Defined 104
Organizational Needs Assessment 108
Community Needs Assessment 113
Methods 117
Practice Activities 119
Technology Exercise 120
References 120

7. Qualitative Concepts, Approaches, and Processes 121
Qualitative Descriptive Studies 121
Qualitative Data Analysis Approaches 130
Practice Activities 138
Technology Exercise 138
References 139

8. Practice Effectiveness Evaluations 143
Role of Evaluation in Social Work Practice 143
Formal Practice Evaluation: Single-System Designs 146
Ethical and Social Justice Issues 155
Practice Activities 159
Technology Exercises 159
References 159

Part III. Data Collection and Analysis

9. Quantitative Data Analysis 163
Quantitative Data Analysis 163
Variables 164
The Function of Variables in Quantitative Analysis 165
Descriptive Statistics 168

Inferential Statistics   175
Data Management and Presentation   178
Your Analysis Plan   179
Practice Activities   180
Technology Exercises   180
References   180

10. Beginning Phases of Qualitative Research   183
The Qualitative Research-Planning Stage   184
Practice Activities   193
Technology Exercise   194
References   194

11. Qualitative Research: Data Coding, Analysis, Interpretation, and Reporting Results   197
Qualitative Research Data Analysis   197
Qualitative Data Analysis Software   214
Practice Activities   215
Technology Exercise   215
References   216

Part IV. Writing and Presentations

12. Writing Your Capstone Paper   221
Introduction   221
Literature Review   224
Methods   227
Results   230
Discussion   230
Additional Components of the Capstone Paper   232
Practice Activity   233
Technology Exercises   236
References   236

13. Presenting Your Capstone Project   237
Project Presentations   238
Poster Presentations   244
Oral Presentations   247
Practice Activities   255
Technology Exercise   256
References   256

Index   259

PREFACE

This textbook targets BSW and MSW programs that require students to conduct capstone research projects and/or research projects tied to their field placements. The focus is on designing, implementing, and reporting research projects aimed at improving programs and services. Although this book reviews some content typically provided in social work research and/or generalist practice courses, it is not intended to compete with existing social work research or practice textbooks. This book is the only one available in social work that focuses on students' capstone research projects.

This book provides students with a structured approach to designing, implementing, and reporting capstone research projects. The aim is to help students develop capstone projects that demonstrate the skills and cognitive–affective process dimensions of the professional social work competencies (Council for Social Work Education [CSWE], 2015). The book is designed to help students conduct applied research projects tied to their social work field placements. It can also be used in nonfield-based capstone research projects.

Most capstone projects provide students an opportunity to demonstrate their competency on all nine of the professional competencies. The applied research approaches described in this book help students develop capstone projects that are particularly well suited to assessment of the research and policy competencies. The research and policy competencies are often challenging for students in direct-service field placements to demonstrate due to the lack of learning opportunities related to these two competencies. Research and policy practice experiences are often not intrinsic components of the social work students' learning experiences in direct service field placements. Special projects and assignments must be created for these competencies. The quality of these field placement–level special projects and assignments varies widely. Creating a program-level capstone assignment ensures a more consistent approach and learning experiences for the assessment of the research and policy competencies as well as the other professional competencies.

CSWE also requires that at least one assessment measure be based upon real or simulated practice situations. Most programs used students' field placements to satisfy this requirement. Currently, there are no social work textbooks that focus on conducting applied capstone research projects that can satisfy this requirement for the research and policy competencies. Additionally, the student capstone projects generated from this book will provide BSW and MSW programs with data that can be used to assess the social work competencies. To help facilitate competency assessment this textbook comes with two rubrics—a skills dimension rubric and a cognitive–affective process dimension rubric. Each rubric assesses the student's capstone project on all nine of the professional social work competencies. The data sources for both rubrics are the Capstone Competency Log (CCL) and the student's capstone paper and presentation. The CCL is described in the book and a copy is available to students electronically on the Springer Publishing Company website. The CCL documents the student's cognitive-affect process and skills throughout the project from idea generation to final oral presentation. The rubrics are also designed to do competency assessments of the products of the student's capstone research project—the final paper or report and oral presentation.

For many social work students, conducting a research project is a new experience and most are unfamiliar with the research process and protocols. This book takes them through the process step by step. Our aim is to help students conceptualize and carry out applied research projects designed to improve social work programs/services by providing descriptions of the quantitative and qualitative applied research methodologies that can be used to improve social work programs and services. The applied research chapters cover data collection methods, program evaluation, organization and community needs assessments, qualitative research approaches, practice effectiveness studies, quantitative data analysis, and qualitative data analysis. The book also helps students complete their research projects with chapters on identifying a research topic, strategies for effective writing, writing a capstone paper, and oral and poster presentations.

As part of their applied capstone research, this book helps students conduct a policy analysis related to a program or service. As with the research process, most social work students are inexperienced in conducting policy analyses. A component of the capstone research project is an analysis of the program's or service's policies and procedures. This book provides students with helpful guidelines on how to conduct a policy analysis and write-up and present the findings in a professional manner. Completing this component of the capstone project provides students with an opportunity to demonstrate their policy practice competency. Overall, the book's objectives are to help students do the following:

- Demonstrate their social work practice competencies
- Make the connection between the National Association of Social Workers (NASW) *Code of Ethics* and the importance of conducting applied research to improve social work services
- Make the connection between the CSWE social work competencies and the importance of conducting research to improve social work services
- Research the literature and write a problem statement on a social service issue
- Write quantitative and qualitative research questions
- Select research quantitative or qualitative methodologies appropriate for their identified research questions and problem statements
- Carry out a capstone research project designed to improve a program or service
- Develop professional writing skills
- Strengthen their communication and professional presentation skills

Key Features

A key feature of this book is its tie-in to the NASW *Code of Ethics* and the CSWE professional competencies. The benefit to students of all levels is that it helps them place their proposed research with a larger professional context.

Another key feature of this book is that it contains extensive information on professional writing and the dos and don'ts of writing research reports. The benefit for students, especially BSW and many MSW students, is that it will provide concrete examples of effective professional writing that will help them in preparing their own capstone projects.

An additional key feature of this book is that it contains information on quantitative and qualitative research approaches. This information will benefit students at all levels by providing in one place a detailed summary of the major research approaches that could be used to improve social work programs and services. This will help students identify a research approach appropriate to their chosen research questions. Additional key features are the following:

- Focus on applied research to improve social work programs and services
- Content on professional presentations
- Coverage of major quantitative and qualitative applied research methodologies
- Detailed descriptions of all written components of capstone research projects
- Step-by-step guide on designing, implementing, and presenting capstone applied research projects
- QR codes to online resources
- Case examples provided throughout the book to help students apply the theory to practice and to understand the material in the chapter
- Practice activities for each chapter to help students apply knowledge and chapter content to their capstone projects
- Technology exercises at the end of every chapter help students use the internet and other sources for conducting research
- Capstone project checklist
- Capstone Competency Log
- Competency rubric—skills dimension
- Competency rubric—cognitive/affective process dimension
- Sample measures for student use

John Poulin, Stephen Kauffman
and Travis Sky Ingersoll

Reference

Council on Social Work Education. (2015). *Educational policy and accreditation standards.* https://www.cswe.org/getattachment/Accreditation/Standards-and-Policies/2015-EPAS/2015EPASandGlossary.pdf.aspx

Qualified instructors may request a faculty resources supplement, which includes a capstone competency log, capstone paper checklist, capstone project cognitive affective processed rubric, capstone project skills rubric, group exercises, and sample capstone project syllabus, by emailing textbook@springerpub.com

Student resources, including a behavioral observation form, capstone competency log, capstone paper checklist, capstone writing plan template, general rating scales, individualized rating scale, and sample participant log, are available from connect.springerpub.com/content/book/978-0-8261-8636-2

I

GETTING STARTED

1

CAPSTONE PROJECTS, PROFESSIONAL COMPETENCIES, AND ETHICAL APPLIED RESEARCH

This chapter discusses capstone research projects' purposes, the Council on Social Work Education (CSWE, 2015) professional competencies, the National Association of Social Workers (NASW, 2017) *Code of Ethics*, ethical research principles and standards, institutional review boards, informed consent, and different types of applied research.

By the end of the chapter, you will be able to do the following:

- Describe the purpose of capstone projects and learning pathways.
- List nine professional social work competencies.
- Describe the concept of holistic competency.
- Describe the NASW Research and Evaluation ethical standards.
- Determine if a research project requires Institutional Review Board (IRB) approval.
- Create an informed consent form.
- Describe five approaches to applied social work research.

▪ Capstone Projects

A capstone project is a multifaceted assignment that serves as a culminating academic and intellectual experience for students (The Glossary of Educational Reform, 2016). Capstone projects in social work are typically designed to foster critical thinking and to develop written and oral communication skills as well as research skills. They are also used as a vehicle for Bachelor of Social Work (BSW) and Master of Social Work (MSW) students to demonstrate mastery of the professional social work competencies. Capstone projects tied to students' field placements can also be used to foster organizational and/or community change to promote social justice and improved social work services.

Capstone projects are often viewed as learning pathways that expand the educational experience beyond the courses offered (The Glossary of Educational Reform, 2013). They allow students to apply the knowledge acquired in individual courses to research projects that help create integrated learning experiences that go beyond individual courses. Capstone projects are also learning pathways to students' ongoing development as professional social workers. They help students see the interconnections among the professional competencies and to view social work practice from a holistic perspective.

Capstone projects are similar in some ways to standard research papers but in many ways very different. A standard research paper has a particular format that sequentially describes each component of a research project. Capstone projects in social work have a different format. They are designed to cover a number of discreet topics such as the research process, policy issues and recommendations, social problem analysis, as well as coverage of a range of social work competencies. The end products of capstone projects typically include a written report as well as an oral component with some type of electronic visual presentation, such as PowerPoint, Keynote, or Prezi.

Professional Social Work Competencies

For social work education programs in the United States, the accrediting body is the CSWE Commission on Accreditation (COA). The CSWE's Commission on Educational Policy (COEP) creates educational policy for social work education and the COA creates accreditation standards. The educational policy and accreditation standards together form the Educational Policy and Accreditation Standards (EPAS) that guide the accreditation of baccalaureate- and master-level social work educational programs (Poulin & Matis, 2015).

ACCREDITATION AND SOCIAL WORK COMPETENCIES: EPAS 2015

Each of the nine professional competencies describes the knowledge, values, skills, and cognitive and affective processes that make up the competency at the generalist level of practice, followed by a set of behaviors that integrate these components. These behaviors represent examples of observable components of the competencies, while the preceding statements represent the underlying content and processes that inform the behaviors (CSWE, 2015).

Competency 1: Demonstrate Ethical and Professional Behavior

Social workers understand the value base of the profession and its ethical standards, as well as relevant laws and regulations that may impact practice at the micro, mezzo, and macro levels. Social workers understand frameworks of ethical decision-making and how to apply principles of critical thinking to those frameworks in practice, research, and policy arenas. Social workers recognize personal values and the distinction between personal and professional values. They also understand how their personal experiences and affective reactions influence their professional judgment and behavior. Social workers understand the profession's history, its mission, and the roles and responsibilities of the profession. Social workers also understand the role of other professions when engaged in interprofessional teams. Social workers recognize the importance of lifelong learning and are committed to continually updating their skills to ensure they are relevant and effective. Social workers also understand emerging forms of technology and the ethical use of technology in social work practice. Social workers:

- make ethical decisions by applying the standards of the NASW *Code of Ethics*, relevant laws and regulations, models for ethical decision-making, ethical conduct of research, and additional codes of ethics as appropriate to context;
- use refection and self-regulation to manage personal values and maintain professionalism in practice situations;
- demonstrate professional demeanor in behavior; appearance; and oral, written, and electronic communication;
- use technology ethically and appropriately to facilitate practice outcomes; and
- use supervision and consultation to guide professional judgment and behavior.

Competency 2: Engage Diversity and Difference in Practice

Social workers understand how diversity and difference characterize and shape the human experience and are critical to the formation of identity. The dimensions of diversity are understood as the intersectionality of multiple factors including but not limited to age, class, color, culture, disability and ability, ethnicity, gender, gender identity and expression, immigration status, marital status, political ideology, race, religion/spirituality, sex, sexual orientation, and tribal sovereign status. Social workers understand that, as a consequence of difference, a person's life experiences may include oppression, poverty, marginalization, and alienation as well as privilege, power, and acclaim. Social workers also understand the forms and mechanisms of oppression and discrimination and recognize the extent to which a culture's structures and values, including social, economic, political, and cultural exclusions, may oppress, marginalize, alienate, or create privilege and power. Social workers:

- apply and communicate understanding of the importance of diversity and difference in shaping life experiences in practice at the micro, mezzo, and macro levels;
- present themselves as learners and engage clients and constituencies as experts of their own experiences; and
- apply self-awareness and self-regulation to manage the influence of personal biases and values in working with diverse clients and constituencies.

Competency 3: Advance Human Rights and Social, Economic, and Environmental Justice

Social workers understand that every person regardless of position in society has fundamental human rights such as freedom, safety, privacy, an adequate standard of living, healthcare, and education. Social workers understand the global interconnections of oppression and human rights violations and are knowledgeable about theories of human need and social justice and strategies to promote social and economic justice and human rights. Social workers understand strategies designed to eliminate oppressive structural barriers to ensure that social goods, rights, and responsibilities are distributed equitably, and that civil, political, environmental, economic, social, and cultural human rights are protected. Social workers:

- apply their understanding of social, economic, and environmental justice to advocate for human rights at the individual and system levels; and
- engage in practices that advance social, economic, and environmental justice.

Competency 4: Engage in Practice-Informed Research and Research-Informed Practice

Social workers understand quantitative and qualitative research methods and their respective roles in advancing a science of social work and in evaluating their practice. Social workers know the principles of logic, scientific inquiry, and culturally informed and ethical approaches to building knowledge. Social workers understand that evidence that informs practice derives from multidisciplinary sources and multiple ways of knowing. They also understand the processes for translating research findings into effective practice. Social workers:

- use practice experience and theory to inform scientific inquiry and research;
- apply critical thinking to engage in analysis of quantitative and qualitative research methods and research findings; and
- use and translate research evidence to inform and improve practice, policy, and service delivery.

Competency 5: Engage in Policy Practice

Social workers understand that human rights and social justice, as well as social welfare and services, are mediated by policy and its implementation at the federal, state, and local levels. Social workers understand the history and current structures of social policies and services, the role of policy in service delivery, and the role of practice in policy development. Social workers understand their role in policy development and implementation within their practice settings at the micro, mezzo, and macro levels and they actively engage in policy practice to effect change within those settings. Social workers recognize and understand the historical, social, cultural, economic, organizational, environmental, and global influences that affect social policy. They are also knowledgeable about policy formulation, analysis, implementation, and evaluation. Social workers:

- identify social policy at the local, state, and federal levels that impacts well-being, service delivery, and access to social services;
- assess how social welfare and economic policies impact the delivery of and access to social services; and
- apply critical thinking to analyze, formulate, and advocate for policies that advance human rights and social, economic, and environmental justice.

Competency 6: Engage With Individuals, Families, Groups, Organizations, and Communities

Social workers understand that engagement is an ongoing component of the dynamic and interactive process of social work practice with, and on behalf of, diverse individuals, families, groups, organizations, and communities. Social workers value the importance of human relationships. Social workers understand theories of human behavior and the social environment, and critically evaluate and apply this knowledge to facilitate engagement with clients and constituencies, including individuals, families, groups, organizations, and communities. Social workers understand strategies to engage diverse clients and constituencies to advance practice effectiveness. Social workers understand how their personal experiences and affective reactions may impact their ability to effectively engage with diverse clients and constituencies. Social workers value principles of relationship-building and interprofessional collaboration to facilitate engagement with clients, constituencies, and other professionals as appropriate. Social workers:

- apply knowledge of human behavior and the social environment, person-in-environment, and other multidisciplinary theoretical frameworks to engage with clients and constituencies; and
- use empathy, reflection, and interpersonal skills to effectively engage diverse clients and constituencies.

Competency 7: Assess Individuals, Families, Groups, Organizations, and Communities

Social workers understand that assessment is an ongoing component of the dynamic and interactive process of social work practice with, and on behalf of, diverse individuals, families, groups, organizations, and communities. Social workers understand theories of human behavior and the social environment, and critically evaluate and apply this knowledge in the assessment of diverse clients and constituencies, including individuals, families, groups, organizations, and communities. Social workers understand methods of assessment with diverse clients and constituencies to advance practice effectiveness. Social workers recognize the implications of the larger practice context in the assessment process and value the importance of interprofessional collaboration in this process. Social workers understand how their personal experiences and affective reactions may affect their assessment and decision-making. Social workers:

- collect and organize data, and apply critical thinking to interpret information from clients and constituencies;
- apply knowledge of human behavior and the social environment, person-in-environment, and other multidisciplinary theoretical frameworks in the analysis of assessment data from clients and constituencies;
- develop mutually agreed-on intervention goals and objectives based on the critical assessment of strengths, needs, and challenges within clients and constituencies; and
- select appropriate intervention strategies based on the assessment, research knowledge, and values and preferences of clients and constituencies.

Competency 8: Intervene With Individuals, Families, Groups, Organizations, and Communities

Social workers understand that intervention is an ongoing component of the dynamic and interactive process of social work practice with, and on behalf of, diverse individuals, families, groups, organizations, and communities. Social workers are knowledgeable about evidence-informed interventions to achieve the goals of clients and constituencies, including individuals, families, groups, organizations, and communities. Social workers understand theories of human behavior and the social environment, and critically evaluate and apply this knowledge to effectively intervene with clients and constituencies. Social workers understand methods of identifying, analyzing, and implementing evidence-informed interventions to achieve client and constituency goals. Social workers value the importance of interprofessional teamwork and communication in interventions, recognizing that beneficial outcomes may require interdisciplinary, interprofessional, and interorganizational collaboration. Social workers:

- critically choose and implement interventions to achieve practice goals and enhance capacities of clients and constituencies;
- apply knowledge of human behavior and the social environment, person-in-environment, and other multidisciplinary theoretical frameworks in interventions with clients and constituencies;
- use interprofessional collaboration as appropriate to achieve beneficial practice outcomes;
- negotiate, mediate, and advocate with and on behalf of diverse clients and constituencies; and
- facilitate effective transitions and endings that advance mutually agreed-on goals.

Competency 9: Evaluate Practice With Individuals, Families, Groups, Organizations, and Communities

Social workers understand that evaluation is an ongoing component of the dynamic and interactive process of social work practice with, and on behalf of, diverse individuals, families, groups, organizations, and communities. Social workers recognize the importance of evaluating processes and outcomes to advance practice, policy, and service-delivery effectiveness. Social workers understand theories of human behavior and the social environment, and critically evaluate and apply this knowledge in evaluating outcomes. Social workers understand qualitative and quantitative methods for evaluating outcomes and practice effectiveness. Social workers:

- select and use appropriate methods for evaluation of outcomes;
- apply knowledge of human behavior and the social

Reflection Questions

1. In which competency do you feel you have progressed the most in terms of your professional development? Why?
2. In which competency do you feel least confident in terms of your professional development? Why? How might you strengthen your knowledge about the substantive content of the competency and your skills in implementing the competency?

environment, person-in-environment, and other multidisciplinary theoretical frameworks in the evaluation of outcomes;
- critically analyze, monitor, and evaluate intervention and program processes and outcomes; and
- apply evaluation findings to improve practice effectiveness at the micro, mezzo, and macro levels (CSWE, 2015).

Holistic Competency

McKnight (2013) proposes that competence is an "ongoing ability" to "integrate knowledge, skills, judgment, and professional attributes in order to practice safely and ethically" within one's professional scope (p. 460). The CSWE defines holistic competence as the demonstration of knowledge, values, skills, and cognitive and affective processes that include the social worker's critical thinking, affective reactions, and exercise of judgment in regard to unique practice situations (CSWE, 2015, p. 6).

KNOWLEDGE

The knowledge dimension is your mastery of the substantive content of the competency. Social work curricula are constructed to provide students with course work that provides readings, assignments, and discussions that educate students on the current knowledge related to each competency. Students also increase their competency knowledge through their own research on the topics that compose the underlying content and processes of each competency. A prerequisite of one ability to demonstrate competence is a solid understanding and knowledge of the literature that makes up the competency (Poulin & Matis, 2020).

VALUES

The values dimension is less clear than the knowledge dimension. Although competency #1 is about values and professional behavior, the other eight competencies all have social work values dimensions as well. The values dimensions can have knowledge (social work values) as well as skill (ethical behavior and decision-making) components. Understanding the values and ethics associated with the application of the different social work competencies in unique practice situations is a fundamental aspect of ethical decision-making and professional social work competence (Poulin & Matis, 2020).

SKILLS

The skills dimension refers to your ability to apply social work knowledge and values in your social work practice. There are numerous skills associated with each professional competency. Your field placement experience provides you with an opportunity to apply, refine, and learn social work skills in practice situations. Your skill is your ability to apply social work theories, concepts, and techniques in your practice with clients and/or constituents (Poulin & Matis, 2020).

COGNITIVE AND AFFECTIVE PROCESSES

This dimension has three associated subdimensions—critical thinking, affective reactions, and professional judgment. Critical thinking is the open-minded search for understanding. It is a process focused on explaining the "why." The process includes "providing evidence, examining the implications of the evidence, recognizing any potential contradictions and examining alternative explanations" (Heron, 2006, p. 221). The CSWE (2015) defines critical thinking as "an intellectual, disciplined process of conceptualizing, analyzing, evaluating, and synthesizing multiple sources of information generated by observation, reaction, and reasoning" (p. 20). Critical thinking is a crucial component of professional competence because it ensures that your social work practice is reasoned and thoughtful and not the rote application of social work techniques.

Affective reaction, on the other hand, generally refers to the affective component of social work practice with clients (Rubaltelli & Slovic, 2008). It is the worker's emotional response to the client's presentation and situation. It is tied to empathy and other affective processes. Affective reaction has relevance for social work competency in that effective social work practice requires affective understanding of the client as well as one's own feelings, emotions, and reactions (Poulin & Matis, 2015).

Professional judgment is about decision-making in social work practice. A key issue debated in relation to decision-making in social work is the extent to which social workers use analytical versus intuitive reasoning styles (Collins & Daly, 2011). Thus, professional judgment is reasoned decision-making based on evidence, knowledge, analytical reasoning, and practice wisdom. It is a process of examining all facets of the case and making a reasoned decision supported by both objective and subjective evidence. Exercising informed professional judgment is a critical component of professional social work competence (Poulin & Matis, 2015).

> **Reflection Questions**
> 1. How could you assess the cognitive and affective reactions dimensions of a competency related to designing and implementing a capstone research project?
> 2. What affective reactions do you anticipate in conducting your capstone research project? How will you manage your affective reactions?

Competency Model of Social Work Practice

The nine social work competencies and the associated dimensions are the interrelated components of professional social work practice. The competencies are interconnected. They do not stand alone. Holistic competency is the practice of social work utilizing multiple professional competencies in each practice activity or client interaction. Figure 1.1 shows a conceptualization of the interrelationships among the nine professional social work competencies. The competencies with the two outer bands are those that apply broadly to all practice situations. The ethical and professional behavior, diversity and difference, and social, economic, and environmental justice competencies are fundamental components of effective social work practice at all levels (Poulin & Matis, 2020).

The competencies in the middle band of the figure are the two areas of social work practice that are not client based—policy practice and research. These competencies are

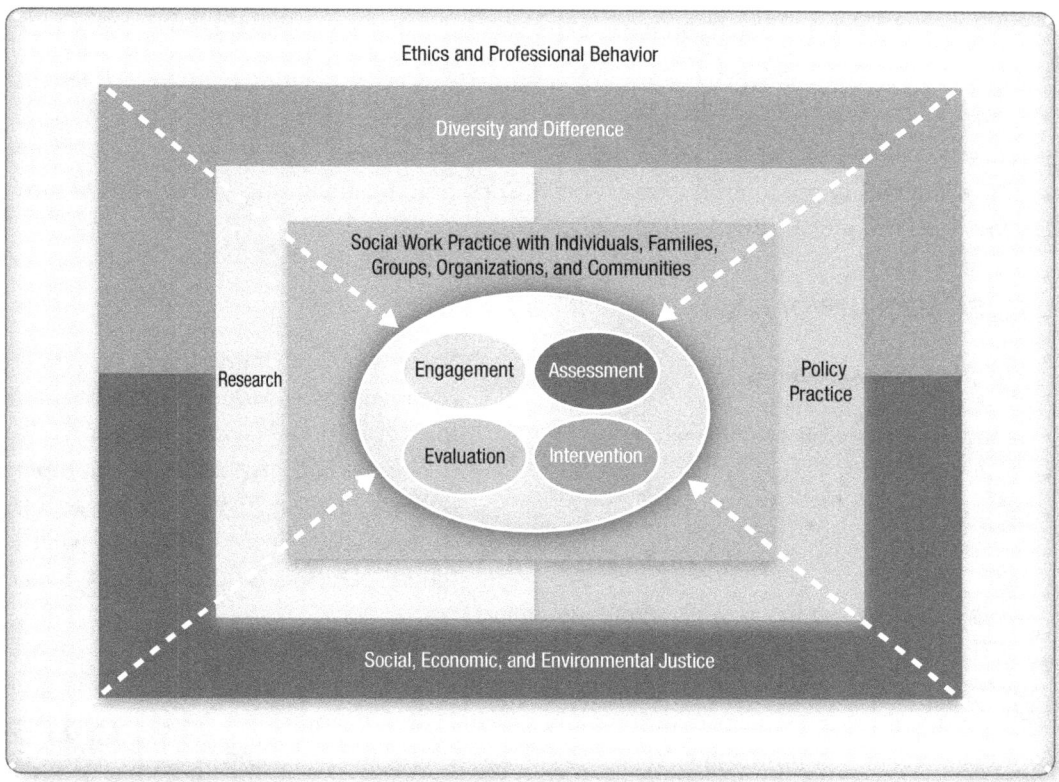

FIGURE 1.1 Interrelationships of social work competencies.

informed by the ethical behavior, diversity, and justice competencies and in turn inform social work practice with client and constituency competencies. The center component represents the engagement, assessment, intervention, and evaluation competencies in social practice with individuals, families, groups, organizations, and communities. Thus, the ethical behavior, diversity, social justice, policy practice, and research competencies all inform the practice competencies of engagement, assessment, intervention, and evaluation with individuals, families, groups, organizations, and communities (Poulin & Matis, 2015).

Thus, the nine professional competencies are interconnected in the delivery of social work practice with clients and constituencies. For example, a social worker's ability to engage with an individual client is influenced by their ethical and professional behavioral competency; diversity and difference competency; social, economic, and environmental justice competency; and possibly their policy practice and research competencies. In short, most social work practice situations require the use of all or most of the nine professional competencies. Thus, to be a competent social work practitioner you must develop knowledge, values, skill, cognitive process, and affective processes competency for each professional competency and be able to apply multiple competencies in a variety of practice situations (Poulin & Matis, 2020).

Social Work Values and Ethics

The practice of social work is based on a number of value positions and principles that guide the work with clients irrespective of the approach used, the presenting client problem, the client population, or the setting in which services are provided. These values and principles apply to all forms of social work practice including policy and research practice (Poulin et al., 2019).

CORE SOCIAL WORK VALUES

> **Reflection Questions**
> 1. How are your personal values and professional social work values similar? How do they differ?
> 2. How do you manage and regulate any differences between your personal values and the professional values of social work?

Social work is a value-based profession (Reamer, 2013). Values provide the basis for professional social work practice (Congress & McAuliffe, 2006; Gumpert & Black, 2006). They guide the actions we take and our evaluations of what is "good" (DuBois & Miley, 2014). Social work has a rich tradition of principles and beliefs.

The heart of these is reflected in the NASW *Code of Ethics* (NASW, 2017) that identifies core social work values, which are referred to as "ethical principles." The core professional values are: service to others; social justice; dignity and worth of the person; and importance of human relationships, integrity, and competence. These values and their associated ethical standards all play a critical role in social work practice. The NASW *Code of Ethics* is available online at https://www.socialworkers.org/About/Ethics/Code-of-Ethics/Code-of-Ethics-English

Ethical Standards

The core social work values and ethical principles embody the ideals to which all social workers should aspire. The *Code of Ethics* sets specific standards and explains how the core values and principles influence the actions of professional social workers. The standards spell out social workers' ethical responsibilities to clients, to colleagues, in practice settings, as professionals, to the social work profession, and to the broader society (NASW, 2017). They are detailed, comprehensive guidelines for professional behavior. The NASW *Code of Ethics* (NASW, 2017) identifies the six areas of professional behavior: responsibilities to clients, to colleagues, to practice settings, and as professionals, to the profession, and to the broader society. Each area of responsibility includes a number of subareas. It is important that you carefully review the detailed descriptions of the standards found in the NASW *Code of Ethics* available online at https://www.socialworkers.org/About/Ethics/Code-of-Ethics/Code-of-Ethics-English

The NASW Ethical Standards cover a very broad range of behaviors from interactions with clients to participation in larger societal change. Thus, as a social worker it is your ethical responsibility to have these standards of behavior guide your professional behavior in all aspects of your professional life. Without a doubt, doing so will create challenges when different ethical standards are in conflict in your practice with clients, experiences with colleagues, and at your agency or field placement. The ethical standards related to being a professional, the social work profession, and society are more under your own control and the choices you make. Nevertheless, conflicts are possible among and between the areas of professional responsibilities (Poulin & Matis, 2020).

The NASW *Code of Ethics* (2017) standard on Evaluation and Research has 17 subsections related to applied research on evaluating organizational and community interventions and outcomes. The *Code of Ethics* subsections address social workers' ethical responsibilities to do the following:

- Evaluate the programs and practice interventions.
- Promote and facilitate evaluation of programs and services.
- Develop guidelines for protecting evaluation participants.
- Obtain voluntary and informed consent.
- Provide participants the right to withdraw from the evaluation.
- Ensure access to supportive services.
- Protect participants from harm.
- Ensure confidentiality.
- Report finding accurately.
- Avoid conflicts of interest.
- Use responsible research practices.

In sum, social workers have an ethical responsibility to evaluate program implementation and outcomes using appropriate research practices that protect human subjects. Social workers also have an ethical responsibility to avoid conflicts of interest in conducting evaluation of social work programs and interventions and to disseminate accurate evaluation findings.

Institutional Review Boards

An IRB is a committee that reviews the methods proposed for research to ensure that they are ethical. Federal regulations require that research projects involving human participants be approved or be determined exempt prior to the start of the research (U.S. Food and Drug Administration, 2019). The main goal of IRBs is the protection of human subjects. Most colleges, universities, and medical facilities have IRBs and require proposed research projects conducted by persons affiliated with their institution be reviewed and approved by the IRB. The purpose of the review is to ensure that appropriate steps are taken to protect the rights and welfare of humans participating as subjects in a research study. The review assesses the ethics of the research to ensure the protection of the human participants in the study.

The *Belmont Report*, published in 1979 by the National Commission for the Protection of Human Subjects of Biomedical and Behavioral Research, provides the ethical foundation for the federal regulations for the protection of human research subjects. The major ethical principles guiding the protection of human subjects are respect for persons, beneficence, and justice. As described in the *Belmont Report*, respect for persons includes participants' rights to make decisions for themselves. This requires that human subjects must freely provide informed consent to participate in the research study. Participation in the research is acknowledged as voluntary and is free from cohesion or undue influence by the researcher. The principle of beneficence refers to maximize possible benefits of the study and minimize potential risks. The risks to study participants must be reasonable compared to the potential to subjects and/or society. The principle of justice refers to an equal distribution of benefits among the research subjects. All IRBs use the ethical principles outlined in the *Belmont Report* in their assessment and review of research studies.

DETERMINING IF YOUR PROJECT REQUIRES IRB APPROVAL

There are three types of IRB reviews. A full board review is used when there is potential serious harm or the subject population is considered vulnerable. An expedited review is done when there is minimal risk for the study participants. Expedited reviews are usually done by two or three IRB members with approval by the full committee. The third type of review is exempt. The IRB does not approve an exempt application; they just determine if the project should be exempt. Before beginning your proposed capstone research project, you should first determine if your project requires IRB approval or an exempt review.

The federal regulation [45 CFR 46.102(l)] specifies that IRB review and approval is required for projects that meet the definition of research, involve human subjects, and involve an interaction or intervention with human subjects (Department of Health and Human Services, 2016). Research is defined as a systematic investigation designed to develop or contribute to *generalized* knowledge. "*Contribute to generalizable knowledge* means that the purpose or intent of the project is to test or to develop scientific theories or hypotheses, or to draw conclusions that are intended to be applicable and/or shared beyond the populations or situations being studied" (Boston University, 2020, para. 5). If your applied research project does not meet the federal government's definition of research then IRB approval is not required. However, most IRBs require an exempt review in which the IRB determines if your project has met the federal definition for being exempt.

Research projects that do not require IRB approval include data collected for administrative purposes, program evaluations, quality assurance and quality improvement projects, and single case studies. Also, course projects are often exempt from IRB approval. Most applied research projects as well as course projects do not meet the knowledge generalization criteria of the federal definition of research. However, we recommend that you check with your course professor and your university IRB about whether or not an exempt IRB application is required. Regardless, it is imperative that you protect any human subjects involved in your research and that you follow the research and evaluation ethical standards.

INFORMED CONSENT

If you are planning on using human subjects in your capstone research project, then you will need to obtain informed consent from your participants. All of your study participants will have to voluntarily agree to participate in your research. To do so they will need to understand the purpose of the research, the potential risks and benefits, and what will be expected. Your research participants will need to read or have read to them an informed consent form and indicate that they voluntarily agree to participate. The informed consent form should be written in a language and at a reading level appropriate to the subject population. Even for college-educated participants the language should be keep as simple and jargon free as possible. It should also be written from the prospective of the participant, that is, "I volunteer to participate."

The following information should be included on your consent form:

- That you are a student researcher
- The name of your faculty advisor
- The activities involving research
- The purposes of the research
- The procedures to be performed
- Participation is voluntary
- The time involved for study participation
- How confidentiality of data is maintained
- Risks of participating in the study
- Benefits of participating in the study (if any)
- Name and contact information for the investigator (Boston University, n.d.)

Reflection Questions

1. What are the potential risks to the participants of a possible capstone research project conducted at your field placement agency?
2. What are the potential benefits?

Sample informed consent letters can be found on the internet and at many university IRB websites. A fairly straightforward example that would be appropriate for many capstone research projects can be found on the Stanford University IRB website at https://web.stanford.edu/group/ncpi/unspecified/student_assess_toolkit/pdf/sampleinformedconsent.pdf

Applied Research

"Applied research" in social work typically focuses on finding solutions to organizational, community, and service-delivery problems. Applied research addresses practical issues encountered in the provision of social work services to clients and constituents. "Basic research," on the other hand, tends to focus on generalizations and theory development. Basic social science research seeks understanding of social phenomena. Thus, the major difference between applied and basic research is in their purposes. The purpose of applied research is to solve problems while the purpose of basic research is to generate new knowledge or add to the existing body of knowledge.

All types of research methods can be used to conduct applied research studies. It is the purpose and not the methods that makes it applied research. A common way to group research methods is quantitative versus qualitative approaches. Mixed-methods approaches combine both quantitative and qualitative data collection strategies.

TABLE 1.1 TYPES OF APPLIED RESEARCH AND DATA TYPES

TYPE	QUANTITATIVE	QUALITATIVE	MIXED METHOD
Program evaluation	Yes	Yes	Yes
Needs assessment	Yes	Yes	Yes
Case studies	No	Yes	No
Qualitative descriptive studies	No	Yes	No
Practice effectiveness studies	Yes	No	No

Quantitative approaches involve collecting numerical data and using various statistical methods to analyze the collected data. A variety of data collection methods can be used with quantitative applied social work research. They include survey questionnaires, interview schedules, recording direct observations, and other approaches to collecting numerical data.

Qualitative approaches, on the other hand, are subjective and descriptive. Data collection is based on words or observations and the data analysis seeks to describe or interpret whatever is being researched. Instead of numbers, qualitative research collects information in the form of words. It relies on observation or participants' answers to open-ended questions (Melanson, 2020).

This book reviews five types of research that are often used in conducting applied social work research projects. The five types covered are (a) program evaluations, (b) organizational and community needs assessments, (c) case studies, (d) qualitative descriptive studies, and (e) practice effectiveness studies. Table 1.1 lists the five approaches and their data types (quantitative, qualitative, and/or mixed methods). This classification shows that program evaluations and needs assessment can be either quantitative or qualitative or employ both types of data. On the other hand, case studies and qualitative descriptive studies collect only qualitative data while practice effectiveness studies collect only quantitative type data.

ACTION RESEARCH

One of the best ways you can protect yourself from burnout in the field is by helping create positive change through action research (Schuyler et al., 2018). Imagine that your social work program's capstone project involves you assisting the neighborhood walk-in-clinic where you are interning in order to help evaluate its service-delivery system. Or, what if the Veteran's Administration field placement to which you are assigned is interested in assessing the effectiveness of its posttraumatic stress disorder (PTSD) treatment program? The actual problems, limitations, and challenges may not be known to the agency, so you will need to conduct a careful initial assessment.

You need to be aware that developing a thorough understanding of an agency's day-to-day operations, as well as discovering clients' experiences, needs, challenges, and responsibilities, will slowly emerge during the course of your project. Let us assume that you, your field supervisor, and the agency sponsoring your research have all agreed that it is vital to include client-based perspectives in your study, for it is not enough just to know whether the agency is operating effectively, it is imperative to know how well it works for the people it manages and serves (Lune & Berg, 2017). This emphasis on the experiences, thoughts, opinions, and suggestions of those an agency or organization serves is a cornerstone of action research.

Action research is a developing process of inquiry that integrates theory and action to connect scientific knowledge with existing organizational knowledge. Action research also aims to address actual organizational problems with participation from the people who are part of the system being examined (Coghlan, 2011). It is a type of collaborative qualitative research that seeks action to improve organizational practice and then study the outcomes of the action that was taken. The primary purpose of action research is to improve or change what it seeks to study. When conducting this type of research, you stand with and alongside the participants of your study (Berg, 2007), engaging in collaborative and transparent relationships in order to create a space for open and honest dialogues (Reason & Bradbury, 2008). Important themes in action research are the importance of practice effectiveness, client life experiences, the web of relationships, community building, and social change (Rutman et al., 2005).

According to Lune and Berg (2018), action research progresses through three basic phases. Those phases are looking, thinking, and taking action:

> **Looking**—During this initial phase you assess the situation and create a general picture of what is going on. This involves collecting information and seeing who the stakeholders are and what their interests may be. When conducting your evaluation, you want to define and describe the problems or issues that need investigation, as well as the context in which they are found. You should also consider, and without judgment, what all the stakeholders have been doing. Stakeholders can contribute to this process by guiding you through your study's setting. Stakeholders can also inform you of previous efforts to address identified problems.
>
> **Thinking**—This phase involves formulating interpretations and offering some explanation about issues or problems being faced. During your evaluation, you need to analyze the data you have collected, while simultaneously interpreting any problems as they currently exist. Next, you want to reflect on what your participants have been doing. You will accomplish this by having conversations with participants and reflecting on the issue or problem together. It is a good idea to take notes and/or record the conversations. These conversations will provide you with a means for further assessment of areas of success, as well as any deficiencies, issues, or problems that may confront the agency or any of its stakeholders. You will be responsible for interpreting the findings, but do not do it in isolation. Make sure others (e.g., your field supervisor or your seminar professor) assist you in this process.

Action—This final phase of the process is what action research is all about, which is to resolve issues and problems by taking action toward improving the lives of your participants (stakeholders). Your evaluation report should offer considerations regarding which actions might result in the most positive changes in the agency and/or in the lives of its staff, interns, volunteers, and clients. The considerations you present should be framed within the lines of the value of any changes or interventions you propose, the appropriateness and potential effectiveness of your suggestions, and the probable outcomes of any action to be made toward the changes you propose. Working alongside an agency's stakeholders, you will work to formulate plans for solutions to problems that have been mutually identified. You then take the action plans you create back to the stakeholders so that you can further discussion and elaboration. Ultimately, and in line with the concept of participant empowerment, it will be the stakeholders themselves who will choose a new plan of action.

Although there are a number of action research paradigms that are antioppressive, deconstructionist, and revolutionary in nature (e.g., participatory action research, community-based action research, and antioppressive research), those approaches are beyond the scope and applicability of this chapter. If you are interested in knowing more about those approaches, read George and Syrja-McNally's (2015) work titled *Social Enquiry and Action Research for Social Workers*. The most useful ways for social work field interns to engage in action research, particularly in relation to their time-limited Research-Based Capstone Project, will be in the form of needs assessments and program evaluations.

> **Reflection Question**
> Of the many areas of social work practice (e.g., child welfare, domestic violence, transitional housing, veterans' affairs, school social work), in what area would you like to see more Action Research take place? What are your reasons?

Competency Log: Capstone Project, Paper, and Presentation

The capstone competency log (CCL) is designed to help you keep track of your activities and cognitive processes in carrying out your capstone project that are related to the social work professional competencies (CSWE, 2015). See Table 1.2. Your completed CCL will provide data that will document the professional competencies you demonstrated in completing your capstone research project, writing your final paper, and giving your oral presentation.

Each professional competency, as defined by the CSWE, is described in the CCL. The narrative descriptions of the competencies define them. The competencies are complex with multiple components and practice behaviors. The CSWE identified five competency dimensions—knowledge, values, skills, affective reactions, and cognitive processes. The CCL covers the knowledge, skills, and cognitive process dimensions. These are the competency dimensions that are best captured by an applied research project. The practice behaviors listed after the competency descriptions are examples of the skill dimension for that competency. The number of practice behaviors for each competency has been expanded beyond the examples listed in the CSWE 2015 EPAS. The practice behaviors were expanded in an attempt to capture more of the content items identified in the competency descriptions. Some of the competencies and many of the practice behaviors will not be relevant to your capstone project.

We recommend that as you research your study topic, design and implement your project, and prepare your capstone paper and presentation, you make ongoing entries in your CCL. Keep your CCL current and up to date. Review each competency each week and reflect upon your project activities related to the competencies. Date and describe the activity, reflect upon how it relates to the competency, and then summarize your

TABLE 1.2 CAPSTONE COMPETENCY LOG

ACTIVITY	KNOWLEDGE	SKILLS	COGNITIVE PROCESS
Date and describe the capstone research, paper, or presentation activity related to the ethical and professional behavioral competency.	Summarize your knowledge of ethical and professional behavior and describe how you demonstrate that knowledge in the activity.	Identify the ethical and professional practice behavior(s) you used with the activity and reflect upon your effectiveness in implementing the skill.	Describe your cognitive processes and how your critical thinking influenced your project decisions.
Date: 9/12/21: Reviewed the NASW *Code of Ethics* ethical standards on Evaluation and Research (5.02).	After reviewing ethical standards 5.02 I identified seven standards that had particular relevance for the initial stages of my research project. They were: (d) consider possible consequences, (e) voluntary and written informed consent, (i) right to withdraw, (j) access to supportive services, (k) protection from harm, (m) confidentiality, and (p) avoiding conflict of interest and dual relationships. I understand and am knowledgeable about the meaning of these ethical standards.	The competency practice behaviors related to this activity are (a) adhere to the core social work values and NASW ethical principles, and (b) follow ethical standards in conducting research studies. At this point, I have identified the practice behaviors but it is too early in my project to evaluate my effectiveness in implementing these skills.	In reviewing the relevant ethical standards, I concluded that (e) voluntary and written informed consent, (k) right to withdraw, and (m) ensuring confidentiality will be handled with the informed consent form. However, identifying (d) possible consequences, (j) access to support services, (k) protection from harm, and (p) avoid conflict of interest and dual relationships will require additional research and reflection to be comprehensively addressed in my research.

(continued)

TABLE 1.2 CAPSTONE COMPETENCY LOG (*continued*)

ACTIVITY	KNOWLEDGE	SKILLS	COGNITIVE PROCESS
Date: 9/14/21: Identified the procedures I will need to employ to avoid the conflict of interest ethical standard with my study participants.	Since I cofacilitate the Peer Support Group, my personally asking the participants to fill out the study questionnaires is a potential conflict of interest. I would be asking the participants to evaluate a program that I run. This could be viewed as a conflict of interest.	The applicable practice behavior is: Follow ethical standards in conducting research studies. I believe that my plan to avoid conflict of interest demonstrates my competency in applying the practice behavior to my capstone research project.	To help minimize the potential for conflict of interest, I decided to: (1) make sure the informed consent form clearly states that participation is voluntary, that participation has no bearing on receiving program services, participation is completely confidential, and that people can withdraw without penalty at any time; (2) I have decided to have another intern introduce the study, obtain informed consent, distribute and collect the study questionnaire. I will be absent from the room during this process.
Date:			
Date:			
Summary: Describe your ethical and professional behavioral competencies for the knowledge, skills, and cognitive process dimensions in completing your capstone research project, paper, and presentation. Identify your strengths and your challenges for each dimension.	Knowledge:	Skills:	Cognitive Processes:

competency knowledge, skills, and cognitive processes related to the activity. Box 1.1 is a sample CCL for Competency #1. An electronic copy of the CCL can be found online in the Student Toolbox provided by Springer Publishing Company at www.springerpub.com/capstone. The online CCL covers all nine of the professional social work competencies.

BOX 1.1

SAMPLE COMPETENCY LOG

Student Name: Jessica Jones
Course Number and Name: SW621—Capstone Research

Brief Description of Capstone Project: A quantitative evaluation of the Teens Together Program that serves homeless LGBTQ teenagers. The evaluation focuses on the participants' overall satisfaction with the program and with the Peers Together support group component. In addition to participant satisfaction, the evaluation will assess the impact the Peers Together program has on the participants' self-esteem, perceived social support, and family relationships.

Competency 1: Demonstrate Ethical and Professional Behavior

Social workers understand the value base of the profession and its ethical standards, as well as relevant laws and regulations that may impact practice at the micro, mezzo, and macro levels. Social workers understand frameworks of ethical decision-making and how to apply principles of critical thinking to those frameworks in practice, research, and policy arenas. Social workers recognize personal values and the distinction between personal and professional values. They also understand how their personal experiences and affective reactions influence their professional judgment and behavior. Social workers understand the profession's history, its mission, and the roles and responsibilities of the profession. Social workers also understand the role of other professions when engaged in interprofessional teams. Social workers recognize the importance of lifelong learning and are committed to continually updating their skills to ensure they are relevant and effective. Social workers also understand emerging forms of technology and the ethical use of technology in social work practice.

- Adhere to the core social work values and NASW ethical principles.
- Make ethical decisions by applying the ethical standards of the NASW *Code of Ethics*, relevant laws and regulations.
- Use ethical decision-making models to resolve ethical dilemmas.
- Follow ethical standards in conducting research studies.
- Use refection and self-regulation to manage personal values and maintain professionalism.
- Use reflection to understand how affective reactions influence practice decisions and professional judgment.
- Demonstrate professional behavior and appearance in oral communication.
- Demonstrate professional behavior in written, and electronic communication.
- Demonstrate understanding of the roles and responsibilities of all disciplines when engaged in interprofessional teams.
- Use technology ethically and appropriately to facilitate practice outcomes.
- Participate in professional development and trainings.
- Use supervision and consultation to guide professional judgment and behavior.

PRACTICE ACTIVITIES

1. Create an informed consent form for a hypothetical applied research capstone project that you think could be conducted at your field placement agency. Make sure your consent form covers all of the information listed earlier and that it has a reading level no higher than 10.0. Its reading level can be calculated in Microsoft Word under the spell check function. It calculates the Flesch-Kincaid Grade level of a whole document or any select portion of a document.
2. Identify all the potential ethical issues associated with your hypothetical research project and list the possible ways each ethical issue could be addressed.

TECHNOLOGY EXERCISES

1. Access your college or university IRB website and review the IRB policies and application procedures to determine if your hypothetical student research project requires an IRB application. As a nonstudent project, would your hypothetical research study need a full board, expedited, or exempt review?
2. Research the internet to identify a free IRB certification–training course. Complete the online course.

REFERENCES

Berg, B. L. (2007). *Qualitative research methods for social sciences* (6th ed.). Pearson Education.

Boston University. (2020). *Determination of research and research involving human subjects.* http://www.bu.edu/researchsupport/compliance/human-subjects/determining-if-irb-approval-is-needed

Boston University. (n.d.). *Tips for creating a consent document.* http://www.bu.edu/researchsupport/compliance/human-subjects/tips-for-creating-a-consent-document

Coghlan, D. (2011). Action research: Exploring perspectives on a philosophy of practical knowing. *Academy of Management Annals, 5*(1), 53–87. https://doi.org/10.1080/19416520.2011.571520

Collins, E., & Daly, E. (2011). *Decision making and social work in Scotland: The role of evidence and practice wisdom.* Institute for Research and Innovation in Social Sciences. https://www.iriss.org.uk/resources/reports/decision-making-and-social-work-scotland

Congress, E., & McAuliffe, D. (2006). Social work ethics: Professional codes in Australia and the United States. *International Social Work, 49,* 151–164. https://doi.org/10.1177/0020872806061211

Council on Social Work Education. (2015). *Educational policy and accreditation standards.* https://www.cswe.org/getattachment/Accreditation/Standards-and-Policies/2015-EPAS/2015EPASandGlossary.pdf.aspx

Department of Health and Human Services. (2016). *45 CFR subtitle A (10–1–16 edition).* https://www.govinfo.gov/content/pkg/CFR-2016-title45-vol1/pdf/CFR-2016-title45-vol1-part46.pdf

DuBois, B., & Miley, K. K. (2014). *Social work: An empowering profession* (8th ed.). Pearson.

George, P., & Syrja-McNally, D. (2015). Social enquiry and action research for social work. In J. D. Wright (Ed.), *International encyclopedia of the social & behavioral sciences* (2nd ed., pp. 269–274). Elsevier.

Gumpert, J., & Black, P. (2006). Ethical issues in group work: What are they? How are they managed? *Social Work with Groups*, *29*(4), 61–74. https://doi.org/10.1300/J009v29n04_05

Heron, G. (2006). Critical thinking in social care and social work: Searching student assignments for the evidence. *Social Work Education*, *25*, 209–224. https://doi.org/10.1080/02615470600564965

McKnight, S. E. (2013). Mental health learning needs assessment: Competency-based instrument for best practice. *Issues in Mental Health Nursing*, *34*, 459–471. https://doi.org/10.3109/01612840.2012.758205

Lune, H., & Berg, B. (2017). *Qualitaive research methods for the social sciences* (9th ed.). Pearson.

Melanson, G. (2020). *What are the different kinds of research?* Wisegeek. https://www.wisegeek.com/what-are-the-different-types-of-research.htm#

National Association of Social Workers. (2017). *Code of ethics.* https://www.socialworkers.org/about/ethics/code-of-ethics

Poulin, J., & Matis, S. (2015). Social work competencies and multidimensional assessment. *Journal of Baccalaureate Social Work*, *20*, 117–135. https://doi.org/10.18084/1084-7219.20.1.117

Poulin, J., & Matis, S. (2020). *Social work practice: A competency-based approach.* Springer Publishing Company.

Poulin, J., Matis, S., & Witt, H. (2019). *The social work field placement: A competency-based approach.* Springer Publishing Company.

Reamer, F. G. (2013). *Social work values and ethics* (4th ed.). Columbia University Press.

Reason, P., & Bradbury, H. (2008). Introduction to grounding. In W. K. Caroll (Ed.), *SAGE handbook of action research: Participative inquiry and practice* (2nd ed., pp. 11–14). SAGE Publications.

Rubaltelli, E., & Slovic, P. (2008). Affective reaction and context-dependent processing of negations. *Judgement and Decision Making*, *3*, 607–618. http://journal.sjdm.org

Rutman, D., Hubberstey, C., Barlow, A., & Brown, L. (2005). Supporting young people's transitions from care: Reflections on doing participatory action research with youth from care. In L. Brown & S. Strega (Eds.), *Research as resistance: Critical, indigenous & anti-oppressive approaches* (pp. 153–180). Canadian Scholars' Press/Women's Press.

Schuyler, K. G., Taylor, M. O., & Wolberger, O. M. (2018). Bringing mindfulness and joy to work: Action research on organizational change. In J. Neal (Ed.), *Handbook of personal and organizational transformation* (pp. 1193–1217). Springer.

The Glossary of Educational Reform. (2013). *Learning pathway.* https://www.edglossary.org/learning-pathway

The Glossary of Educational Reform. (2016). *Capstone project.* https://www.edglossary.org/capstone-project

The National Commission for the Protection of Human Subjects of Biomedical and Behavioral Research. (1979). *The Belmont Report: Ethical principles and guidelines for the protection of human subjects of research.* https://www.hhs.gov/ohrp/regulations-and-policy/belmont-report/index.html

U.S. Food and Drug Administration. (2019, April). *Code of Federal Regulations, Title 21.* https://www.accessdata.fda.gov/scripts/cdrh/cfdocs/cfCFR/CFRSearch.cfm?CFRPart=56&showFR=1&subpartNode=21:1.0.1.1.22.3

2

STRATEGIES FOR EFFECTIVE WRITING

This chapter focuses on strategies and guidelines for writing a professional-quality capstone report. The chapter is organized into two main sections—preparing to write a professional paper and the dos and don'ts of professional writing. The focus is on writing tips and guidelines in general. Chapter 12 is devoted to the actual writing of your capstone project paper.

By the end of this chapter, you will be able to do the following:

- Identify the kind of writing environment that works best for you.
- Develop an outline for writing an academic paper.
- Create a writing plan.
- Describe four traits associated with academic or professional writing.
- Incorporate bias-free writing in your academic papers.
- Follow the American Psychological Association (APA) documentation and reference list guidelines.
- Describe six proofreading strategies.

▪ Getting Organized

Becoming an effective writer is difficult for most and it takes practice. The more you write, the better you get and the easier it becomes. Fortunately, there are now a lot of resources available to help with the writing process. We strongly recommend the *Publication Manual of the American Psychology Association, 7th Edition* (APA, 2020a) for two reasons. First, the APA style manual is an excellent source for detailed information on all aspects of professional writing. It is an excellent reference source to use when writing your professional and/or academic papers. Second, professional writing in social work follows the APA style guidelines. Thus, you need to learn and become proficient in using the APA style guidelines. The *Publication Manual* is your reference for formatting academic social work papers and most professional social work writing.

A second very helpful resource on writing and APA style is the *Purdue Online Writing Lab* (OWL). The website provides a wealth of information on writing academic papers, correct grammar and word use, and up-to-date information on the latest versions of the APA *Publication Manual*. It covers all of the APA requirements in an easy-to-retrieve electronic format. The *Purdue OWL* and web pages related to APA guidelines can be accessed at https://owl.purdue.edu/owl/purdue_owl.html.

TIME AND SPACE

A first step in getting organized to write is to do a self-assessment of what works best for you. Is there a time of day when you prefer for writing? Are you best in the morning or late night? Where do you prefer to do your writing? At home? In a coffee shop? At the library? Do you like to listen to music or do you prefer quiet? Figure out the type of writing environment that is optimal for your writing and then structure your writing and environment based on your preferences. Set a specific time aside for your writing in a space that is comfortable and conducive to writing. The key is to be structured and consistent in your approach to writing.

We also recommend that you set a minimum amount of time for each writing session and that you stick with it. The amount of time can vary based on your needs and obligations, but set a specific timeframe for writing and commit to it. Whether you write one sentence or five pages, stay with it until your time commitment has expired. It is also probably best to limit your distractions during your writing session. Avoid checking your email, reading or responding to text messages, watching YouTube videos, or checking your various social media apps while you are trying to write. We can pretty much guarantee that none of these activities will help you get your paper written.

> **Reflection Questions**
> 1. What kind of writing environment works best for you?
> 2. What distracts you when you are writing? How can you eliminate your distractions?

OUTLINING

Before you begin writing a professional or academic paper, you need to have some idea about what you want to cover in your paper and figure out a beginning, logical structure for the contents of the paper. Fortunately, professional writing typically follows a fairly standard format in terms of the major sections of the paper. The same goes for academic or class papers. Assignments in social work usually specify the different sections of the paper that you are required to cover. What you need to determine is the specific content that will go in each section of the paper. Organizing the content is one of your main tasks before you begin writing. Very few people can just write academic or professional social work papers without some form of outlining before they begin writing. Developing an outline might help you avoid writer's block and it definitely helps you stay organized and focused in your writing.

There are two common types of outlines—topic and sentence (Wrench et al., 2012). Topic outlines use single words for headings and subpoints. Sentence outlines use full sentences for each heading and subheading. Both approaches typically use an alphanumeric structure for the various levels of the outline. Often, the first level is represented by Roman numerals (I, II, III, etc.); the second level is represented by capital

TABLE 2.1 EXAMPLE OF TWO TYPES OF OUTLINES

TOPIC OUTLINE	SENTENCE OUTLINE

I. Capstone project definition
   A. Purpose
      1. Critical thinking
      2. Professional competencies
   B. Learning pathways
   C. Capstone versus research paper
	I. Capstone projects are multifaceted assignments that serve as a culminating academic experience.
	   A. Capstone projects serve two major purposes.
	      1. They develop critical thinking skills.
	      2. They can be used to demonstrate professional competencies.
	   B. Capstone projects are learning pathways for ongoing professional development.
	   C. Capstone projects differ from a standard research paper.

letters (A, B, C, etc.); the third level is represented by numbers (1, 2, 3, etc.); and the fourth level is represented by lowercase letters (a, b, c, etc.). The type of outline you choose does not matter nor does how you choose to label your outline levels. What is important is that you identify your content and the structure of your paper. Table 2.1 shows an abbreviated example of a topic and a sentence outline.

Also, note that while your completed outline might appear rigid and fixed, it is not. In practice it is an ever-changing document. In our experiences as academic writers, the outline is the beginning point for organizing the paper. Once the writing process begins and as one becomes immersed in the topic, a different logical structure usually emerges as well as changes in the topics covered in the paper. Sometimes topics or levels are added. Sometimes they are eliminated. Almost always they are reordered in one way or another. We recommend that before you deviate from your outline, think through the changes by revising your outline. Review your revised outline to see if the new order or changes make sense. The point here is to keep your outline up-to-date as the structure of your paper changes and make changes to the structure thoughtfully. Development of your paper and outline go hand in hand.

> **Reflection Questions**
> 1. What type of outline works best for you? Why?
> 2. What are the advantages of using an outline? What keeps you from using an outline?

DEVELOPING A WRITING PLAN

A writing plan basically sets your goals for completing your paper (Weisman & Zornado, 2018). We recommend developing a writing plan for a couple of reasons. First, it makes completing the project less overwhelming by breaking it down into manageable parts. It becomes a compilation of many smaller parts instead of one potentially daunting task. A second reason we recommend writing plans is that in doing so you set manageable goals and deadlines, which help you stay on task. Realistic goals and deadlines can also help you not fall into the procrastination trap of putting your writing off until the last minute. Last minute papers are usually poorly written papers.

Creating a writing plan is fairly straightforward. We suggest using the level one heading of your outline for your writing plan. Setting due dates for the subsections under a level-one heading is difficult if not impractical. The tricky part is selecting realistic due dates for the major sections of your paper. The best approach is to work backward from the paper's due date. The time frame for each section should include time for editing and revising. Your goal should be to have a fairly clean copy of the section before moving on to the next major section. Build in time in your writing plan for that to happen.

We also recommend that your writing plan include a three-step revision process. Review the first draft for structure and content. After completing your edits, we suggest having a peer or a friend read your paper to see if it is clear and understandable. The final revision is a careful proofreading of your paper looking for spelling and grammar errors, APA-formatting mistakes, and documentation errors (in-text citations and reference list). Table 2.2 shows a sample writing plan for a capstone research paper. The timetable in the sample writing plan assumes that all the necessary research and data gathering has been completed and that writing the paper is all that remains to be done.

TABLE 2.2 SAMPLE WRITING PLAN

TASK COMPLETED	DUE DATE
Title page	December 15
Draft introduction	December 20
Draft literature review	January 30
Draft policy issues	February 15
Draft theoretical framework	February 28
Draft methods	March 4
Draft findings	March 10
Draft recommendations	March 15
Draft competency self-evaluation and assessment	March 20
References	March 20
Content and structure edit and revision—(Edit first draft for the organization and structure of the overall paper and the content, organization, and sentence structure of each paragraph.)	April 1
Peer feedback and revision—(Have a peer read your second draft for clarity and understanding.)	April 15
Proofreading edit and revision—(Proofread your third draft for spelling, grammar, APA formatting, and documentation of in-text citations and references.)	April 29
Paper due date	**April 30**

Writing Your Paper

This section summarizes some dos and don'ts of writing your paper. The topics covered are writing style for professional papers, bias-free writing, APA-formatting guidelines, and proofreading strategies. This chapter does not cover the rules of grammar, the mechanics of style, or how to format tables and figures as described in detail in the APA *Publication Manual* (2020a).

The Purdue OWL (Purdue University, n.d.-a, Purdue OWL, "Grammar") and a number of other websites and books cover the correct use of grammar. We recommend that before you begin writing you review the grammar rules on the OWL website, or any other website devoted to the rules of grammar. If you struggle using correct grammar in your writing, we recommend that you have your paper reviewed by someone at your school's writing center or similar writing-support service. If needed, you should build time into your writing plan for an additional grammar review and edits.

WRITING STYLE

This section describes some of the commonly accepted style norms for writing a professional or academic research paper in social work. The APA *Publication Manual* (2020a) provides detailed descriptions of current writing-style guidelines. The guidelines summarized here cover those that we consider essential for effective professional or academic writing in social work.

First Person

The use of the first person in professional writing is a fairly recent change in writing practices and that change has been incorporated into the 7th edition of the APA *Publication Manual* (2020a). The use of the first-person pronouns is now the preferred way to refer to yourself in your writing. Referring to yourself as the author or researcher is no longer recommended. In your writing, refer to yourself using the pronoun *I* or *we* if you have a coauthor(s). "I interviewed 10 participants" is the preferred style. Writing "the researcher interviewed 10 participants" or "10 participants were interviewed" is no longer recommended. The current norm is to avoid using terms like "this author," "the researcher" and instead refer to yourself in the first person. Doing so helps the reader feel more connected to your writing.

The use of "I" also applies when you are expressing your own views in the paper. "I believe the participants understood the purpose of my research project" is preferred to a third-person statement such as "the participants understood the purpose of the research project." If you are going to state your opinion, take ownership of it and clearly state that it is your opinion.

Short Paragraphs

It is generally recommended that two fairly short paragraphs are preferred to one longer paragraph. Using short paragraphs helps keep the readers' attention. They are easier to read and for some reason a lot of people seem to prefer shorter paragraphs to longer ones. Try to avoid paragraphs that take up a full page. You should try to have between two and three paragraphs per page.

Shorter paragraphs also help make your writing clear and concise. A new paragraph indicates a new idea (APA, 2020a). Each paragraph should focus on one major point. Generally, it is recommended that the paragraph begin with your major point and be followed by sentences that elaborate on the major point. Purdue OWL recommends three to five sentences after your introductory sentence (Purdue University, n.d.-b, Purdue OWL, "Paragraphs and Paragraphing," para. 1). They also recommend balancing your paragraphs on the page (Purdue University, n.d.-c, Purdue OWL, "Paragraphs and Paragraphing," para. 2). "Balancing" refers to having approximately equal length paragraphs on the page; ideally, two or three paragraphs per page. Having unequal sized paragraphs gives more weight or importance to the longer paragraph.

Concise and Clear Sentences

As with your paragraphs, your sentences should also be clear and concise. "Concise" refers to writing only what needs to be said to make your point. Do not add extra words to your sentences. Try to be as economical as possible in what you write. Strive to eliminate wordiness, redundancies, and jargon (APA, 2020a). Doing so makes your paper easier to follow and readable. Short sentences that are to the point increase your accuracy in conveying your meaning. Long complicated sentences tend to be confusing for the reader and are counterproductive to effective communication. However, a paper full of very short sentences is choppy and lacks flow from one sentence to another. We recommend that you try to vary the length and complexity of your sentences. You still need to avoid overly complex sentences, but some variety in your sentences will increase the flow and make your paper a more interesting read.

"Transitions" between sentences are also important to improve continuity and flow. Transitions help smooth out what would be choppy sentences. Pronouns can be transitional when they refer to a noun in the preceding sentence (APA, 2020a). In addition, there are many transitional words or phrases that can be used to improve the flow of your sentences. Transitional words can be additive, adverse, causal, or sequential (Fleming, 2020). *Additive* transitions indicate that you are adding to an idea or that the ideas are similar. *Adversative* transitions are used to signal conflict, contradiction, concession, and dismissal. *Causal* transitions indicate a cause-and-effect relationship between two ideas and *sequential* transition an ordering or time frame (Fleming, 2020).

> **Reflection Questions**
> 1. What are your strengths as a writer?
> 2. What are your challenges as a writer?
> 3. What do you need to do to strengthen your writing?

The following examples shown in Table 2.3 are just a few of the many possible transitional words for each category. A comprehensive list of transitional words can be found at the ThoughtCo website: https://www.thoughtco.com/list-of-transition-words-1857002

Another key to writing concise sentences is using the active voice in your writing. The opposite of this is to avoid using the passive

TABLE 2.3 EXAMPLES OF TRANSITIONAL WORDS

ADDITIVE	ADVERSATIVE	CAUSAL	SEQUENTIAL
• Indeed, • And, • Or, • Too, • Moreover, and • Furthermore	• But, • However, • On the other hand, • In contrast, • While, and • Whereas	• Accordingly, • As a result, • Consequently, • Hence, • Therefore, and • Thus	• In the (first, second, third, etc.) place, • To begin with, • Initially, • Next, • Before, and • Afterward

voice. "Voice" refers to the relationship between a verb and a subject. Active voice means that a sentence has a subject that acts upon its verb. Passive voice means that a subject is a recipient of a verb's action. Active voice sentences are declarative with the subject coming before the verb. The opposite occurs with the passive voice. An example of the active voice is "Social workers value the importance of the helping relationship." The subject "social worker" acts upon the verb "value" that is associated with the object "helping relationship." The same subject, verb, and objective in the passive voice is "The importance of the helping relationship is valued by social workers." The preference in professional writing is the active voice. The use of the passive voice is acceptable but avoid its overuse.

Headings and Subheadings

Headings and subheadings are used to organize your paper by identifying topics that will be covered in various sections of your paper. They are one word or concise phrases that describe what the section is about. They help the reader find information and assist the reader by breaking your paper into manageable parts. Headings and subheadings are organized hierarchically into levels. Topics of equal importance should have the same level headings (APA, 2020a). Each section should start with the highest level heading with up to four levels of subheadings. Your headings and subheadings should be concise and clearly distinguishable from the text (APA, 2020a).

The introduction to your paper does not have a heading. It is assumed that the beginning of your paper is your introduction. Subheadings within your introduction begin with a level-two heading and are followed with level-three and lower subheadings as needed. Each major section of your paper begins with a level one heading and follows a top-down progression for the section's subheadings. The number of headings and subheadings of your paper will depend upon the length and complexity of the sections. The number of subheading levels within your paper may vary. However, avoid having just one subheading in a section. The minimum number of subheadings per section is two (APA, 2020a).

In the 7th edition of the *Publication Manual* there are five levels of headings and subheadings (APA, 2020a). See Box 2.1. Headings and subheadings are never given an alphanumeric number. The different levels are distinguished by the format of the heading or subheading. The formatting components are combinations of bold, italic, page position (centered, flush left, or indented), punctuation (period vs. no period), and the position of the text relative to the heading. APA level one headings are **Centered, Boldface, and**

> **BOX 2.1**
>
> **EXAMPLE OF AN APA STYLE PAPER WITH FIVE HEADING LEVELS**
>
> <div align="center">Strategies for Effective Writing (<i>Level 1</i>)</div>
>
> There are a number of.....
>
> ### Getting Organized *(Level 2)*
> Being organized is a key ....
>
> #### *Time and Space* (*Level 3*)
> Timelines are very helpful and ....
> **Control your Environment.** *(Level 4)* Find a comfortable ....
> ***Create a Routine.*** *(Level 5)* Many writers follow ....
>
> ### Outlining *(Level 2)*
> The next step is to ....

Title Case and the text starts a new paragraph. Level two is **Flush Left, Boldface, and Title Case** and the text starts a new paragraph. Level three is ***Flush Left, Boldface, Italic, and Title Case*** and the text starts a new paragraph. Level four is **Indented, Boldface, Title Case ending with a period,** and the text continues on the same line as the heading. Level five is ***Indented, Boldface, Italic, Title Case ending with a period,*** and the text continues on the same line as the heading.

BIAS-FREE WRITING

The National Association of Social Workers (NASW) Code of Ethics (2017) applies to your professional writing. You need to beware of potential bias in your word choices and strive to use language that is free of bias. Doing so is always important but as a social work student doing a capstone project that, more likely than not, involves research with marginalized and oppressed populations, it is especially important to value the dignity and worth of the people about whom you are writing. We believe that bias-free writing is an important component of being a culturally competent social worker.

Cultural Competence

Cultural competence is an end product. It is the ability to interact effectively with persons from different cultures and backgrounds. NASW (2015) defines cultural competence as:

> ... *the process by which individuals and systems respond respectfully and effectively to people of all cultures, languages, classes, races, ethnic backgrounds, religions, spiritual traditions, immigration status, and other diversity factors in a manner that recognizes, affirms, and values the worth of individuals, families, and communities and protects and preserves the dignity of each.* (p. 13)

We believe that your writing can be viewed from a cultural competency lens. Your word choices and the language you choose are actions that convey your cultural competency as a writer.

Cultural Humility

Cultural humility is a related concept and an important component of social work practice with diverse populations. While being culturally competent refers to an end state, cultural humility is more about process. Specifically, cultural humility is your willingness to suspend what you know or think you know about a person based upon generalizations. It involves being open and learning from the person how they view themselves and their culture, beliefs, and values. The concept of cultural humility has an important role in your capstone research project, especially if you are gathering data from your agency's client population. However, this chapter is about effective writing, which is an end product. Hence, the concept of cultural competency applies here.

Intersectionality

In writing your capstone report you should also be sensitive to the multiple ways your research participants' identities are formed and shaped by various cultural, socioeconomic, race, ethnicity, gender, sexuality, and social contexts. A person's multiple social identities are referred to as "intersectionality" and the concept is usually associated with their oppression and discrimination resulting from the overlap of the various social identities (APA, 2017). Intersectionality also can include experiences and social identities associated with privilege. Thus, intersectionality is the intersecting systems of both privilege and oppression (Boyer, 2016, para. 2).

The APA *Publication Manual* states that

> *to address intersectionality in a paper, identify individuals' relevant characteristics and group memberships (e.g., ability and/or disability status, age, gender, gender identity, generation, historical as well as ongoing experiences of marginalization, immigrant status, language, national origin, race and/or ethnicity, religion or spirituality, sexual orientation, social class, and socioeconomic status, among other variables), and describe how their characteristics and group memberships intersect in ways that are relevant to the study.* (APA, 2020a, p. 149)

> **Reflection Questions**
> 1. How can you incorporate intersectionality in your papers?
> 2. How can cultural humility strengthen your writing?

For example, in describing your study participants' race and gender, do not report each characteristic separately using specific terms, such as "African American females" or "Caucasian men." Take into account the interactions among your participants' multiple social identities. The experiences of someone who is African American, female, and low income is very different than someone who is African American, female, and wealthy. Your writing needs to convey the differences by taking intersectionality into account.

Bias-Free Writing Guidelines

Two key components of bias-free writing are inclusivity and respect (APA, 2020a). The APA *Publication Manual* provides detailed general and specific guidelines on the use of bias-free language. The APA guidelines can be reviewed on their website at https://apastyle.apa.org/style-grammar-guidelines/bias-free-language (APA, 2020b).
The general guidelines include level of specificity, relevant characteristics, and sensitivity to labels. Avoid generalizations and be specific in your descriptions of the people about whom you are writing. For example, "Mexican immigrants" is more specific than "Hispanic immigrants." In addition, describe the relevant characteristics of those about whom you are writing. Do not describe characteristics that are not pertinent to that about which you are writing. For example, if you are writing about people who are homeless, referencing their sexual identity most likely would not be warranted. If sexual identity intersects with homelessness within the context of your writing, then it would be appropriate. However, if it does not intersect, referencing their sexual identity may communicate bias or have prejudicial connotations (APA, 2020a).

Also, be sensitive about labels you choose. Use language that people use to describe themselves (APA, 2020a). You may need to research how people refer to themselves or ask them if you can do so. Language preferences change, so when you begin writing about the subjects who participated in your capstone project, make sure you are using their preferred labels. Another component of selecting sensitive labels is choosing ones that respect their humanity. Do not use adjectives as nouns (APA, 2020a). For example, avoid labels such as "the poor" or "the elderly." Instead use terms such as "people in poverty" or "older adults." Also, avoid labels that equate people with their condition, such as "addicts" or "drug users." In addition to providing general guidelines for bias-free writing, the APA *Publication Manual* has language recommendations for reducing bias in writing about age, disability, gender, race and ethnicity, sexual orientation, and socioeconomic status. The following briefly describes the dos and don'ts for each category.

Age

The guideline for reporting the age of your study participants is to be specific and use age ranges instead of open-ended descriptions such as "over 21" or "under 65." In describing age groups use the language individuals use to describe themselves. Also, refer to a person's age only when it is relevant to the context of what you are writing and avoid generalizations that reinforce stereotypes about age. Similarly, do not use patronizing adjectives when referring to a person's age such as the "sweet little old lady." Overall, in writing your capstone report be specific in describing the age of your study participants and avoid age-related generalizations or stereotypes.

Disability

There are a lot of different terms used to describe a person with a disability. Different groups prefer different terms. The general guideline is to use the language preferred by those about whom you are writing. In doing so you communicate respect by honoring their perceived social identity. Also, it is preferable to use person-first language (APA, 2020a). Put the emphasis on the person and not on the individual's disability. For example, "persons with substance additions" is preferable to "addicts" or "substance abusers." However, some people with disabilities prefer identity-first language. This allows them to claim the disability and choose their identity (APA, 2020a). If your capstone project includes participants with disabilities, it is important for you to clarify how they want to be described and if they prefer person-first or identity-first language.

In your writing include disability references only if doing so is relevant to the context and avoid language that portrays people with disabilities in overly negative or overly positive terms as well as euphemisms, such as "special needs" (APA, 2020a). Finally, when the context of your writing includes both people with and without disabilities do not refer to those without disabilities as "normal" or "able-bodied." Doing so implies that those with disabilities are abnormal or unable to compensate for their disability.

Gender

Gender and sex are different constructs and need to be differentiated in your writing to avoid bias (APA, 2020a). Traditionally, both terms referred to a person's assigned sex at birth. More recently, the definition of gender has expanded beyond male/female categories, and the use of the term "sex" is now used mainly to describe sexual activity or sexual organs. Thus, it is recommended that you use the term "gender" rather than "sex" in your writing and that you be inclusive in your gender descriptions or labels. Use terms such as "male cisgender," "transgender female," or "gender-fluid people."

As noted for other categories, in writing your capstone paper use language that your participants use to refer to themselves. This includes your use of pronouns. It is now generally accepted to use gender-neutral pronouns in academic writing. APA now recommends using the singular "they" for a person who uses "they" as their pronoun as well as when referring to a person whose gender is unknown (APA, 2020a). The use of "they" is preferable to using combinations such as "he or she" or "he/she." Such combinations imply a binary view of gender and exclude those who do not use those pronouns. Finally, avoid nouns that imply a gender binary such as "waiter/waitress." Instead choose a gender-neutral noun such as "server" or "waitperson."

Race and Ethnicity

As with gender, the terms used to describe racial and ethnic groups evolve and change over time. Therefore, it is important that you research the preferences of your capstone research project participants and/or ask them about their preferences. The general guidelines of being specific and sensitive to labeling issues also apply to writing about race and ethnicity using bias-free language.

"Race" refers to physical differences that are considered socially significant (APA, 2020a). "Ethnicity," on the other hand, refers to shared cultural characteristics and beliefs. In your writing, avoid identifying people by race or ethnicity unless it is relevant to the context of your capstone report. We also recommend that you avoid the term "non-White," which implies that a White culture is the standard by which other cultures are compared. The use of person-first identity is preferred. Use terms such as "members of minority groups," or, better yet, be specific in your descriptions such as "members of the Native American community." Racial and ethnic terms should be capitalized and not hyphenated if they contain multiple names (APA, 2020a).

Sexual Orientation

Sexual orientation refers to a person's sexual and emotional attraction to another person (APA, 2020a). As with the other topic areas discussed here, the language for sexual orientation is evolving. Nevertheless, the term "sexual orientation" is now used instead of "sexual preference," which implies a choice. People choose their partners. They do not choose their sexual orientation. Sexual orientation should not be confused with gender identity. For example, someone who identifies as transgendered may be attracted to similarly gendered, differently gendered, or people who have other gender identities.

There are a number of terms for different sexual orientations. LGBTQ is an acronym for lesbian, gay, bisexual, transgender, and queer, as well as others who do not identify as straight (Barbaw, 2019). The following briefly describes the four sexual orientation components (LGBQ) of the acronym.

Gay and Lesbian

The word "gay" is used to describe persons sexually and emotionally attracted to persons of the same gender. It could apply to both males and females, but it is predominantly used to refer to men. Many gay women prefer the term "lesbian" although some may prefer gay or gay women. Using the term "homosexual" is outdated and currently viewed as derogatory and offensive by most gay people (Barbaw, 2019). If you are unsure about the preferences of those about whom you are writing, it is probably safest to use the term gay for men and lesbian for women. In writing it is appropriate to just use the terms "lesbians" or "lesbian women" and "gay men" or "gay people" but not the term "gays" (APA, 2020a).

Bisexual

The term "bisexual" is used to describe persons who are sexually and emotionally attracted to persons of the same gender and those of another gender. Sometimes the word "bi" is used to refer to people who are bisexual. We recommend that you use the term "bisexual" in your professional writing for clarity.

Queer

The term "queer" has many different meanings within the LGBTQ community. Broadly speaking, it simply means that the person is not heterosexual and/or cisgender (Higgins, 2019). It is also used in a general sense to refer to belonging to the LGBTQ community. It allows one to connect with the LGBTQ community without having to choose one orientation. It allows for fluidity of sexual orientation and acknowledges that sexual and emotional attraction can exist inside and outside the existing labels (Higgins, 2019).

CITATION GUIDELINES

Professional writing in social work requires that you follow the APA citation guidelines described in detail in the APA *Publication* Manual (2020a). The citation guidelines are the rules for acknowledging how others have contributed to your work. You must give credit for ideas you have borrowed from someone else's work and have paraphrased or quoted directly, both in your text and your reference list. This includes print and electronic materials. Not properly citing others who have directly contributed to your work is plagiarism, which is a serious ethical violation that results in severe consequences in most academic institutions. In addition to citing published works, you also need to credit written and personal correspondences that you include in your capstone research paper. The APA *Publication Manual* provides detailed information on the correct formats for various in-text citations and how to correctly format those sources in the reference section of your paper. Use the manual to make sure you are correctly formatting your citations and references as you write your paper. Also, make sure that reference list and in-text citations match. Everything cited in the text needs to be included in your reference list and vice versa.

PROOFREADING TIPS

As noted earlier, proofreading your capstone paper is a critical last step in the writing process. Do not skip this step. We can pretty much guarantee that every paper will have some spelling, grammar, APA formatting, in-text citation, reference list, word omissions, incorrect words or word usage, and/or some other type of errors. The quality of your final product is dependent upon your doing a careful proofreading. A paper full of mistakes is unprofessional and is less likely to be viewed positively than the same paper without mistakes. In developing the work plan section of this chapter, we listed proofreading as a single step in the writing process. Here we are recommending that the proofreading step be broken down into multiple steps, with each step focusing on a single type of error. For example, proofread for APA errors. Then proofread for spelling errors, and so on. During each pass through the paper focus on only one type of error. We believe that this type of approach will improve your chances of catching mistakes. The following outlines other proofreading strategies that will increase the effectiveness of your proofreading and ultimately your writing.

Give It a Rest

Put your paper aside for a day or two before you begin proofreading. If you come at it with fresh eyes you are more likely to pick out errors and mistakes. You know what you wanted to write and if you have just finished the paper you are more susceptible to seeing what you thought you wrote and not what is actually there.

Use Your Spellchecker

Most word-processing programs have fairly robust spellcheckers. Use yours. Spellcheckers will help you identify incorrect spellings, repeated words, missing words, and punctuation errors. They are not fool-proof, but they will flag most simple errors. However, do not assume that your paper is error free if your spellchecker shows no mistakes.

Read Backward

Begin with the last word of your paper and read your entire paper word for word backward. Doing so helps you spot spelling errors. Your focus is on the individual words and not the sentences. Often it is hard to spot spelling errors reading from front to back because your mind automatically corrects wrong or misspelled words in your sentences.

Read Out Loud

Another strategy is to read your paper out loud. Hearing your sentences helps identify awkward sentences, missing words, abrupt transitions, and wrong word choices. When you read a paper to yourself that you have written, your mind tends to see what you intended to write and not what is actually on the paper.

Printed Version

Reading on a computer screen is different from reading a printed copy of the same document. Rereading your work in a different format may help you catch errors. We recommend doing preliminary edits on your computer and then doing a final proofreading on a hardcopy.

Get Someone Else to Proofread Your Paper

Having someone read your paper should be part of your writing plan and timetable. Doing so serves two important functions. First, someone unfamiliar with your content and purpose can provide helpful feedback on the organization of your paper, its flow, and if the content is clear. Second, someone unfamiliar with your paper may have an easier time to identify errors and mistakes because their mind will not automatically skip them over. Not knowing what is coming in this case is an advantage.

Double and Triple Check Your References and Hyperlinks

APA mistakes in terms of the formatting of references are common. It is easy to get the exact formatting wrong for all the different types of material cited in your capstone research paper. We recommend that you carefully review each citation in your reference list. Check for formatting including spaces, periods, italics, parentheses, and other formatting components. You should also double check the spelling of the author's name and the year of publication. Finally, check all hyperlinks to DOIs, websites, and other electronic sources. Make sure all your hyperlinks are active and take you where you want to go.

PRACTICE ACTIVITIES

1. Conduct a self-inventory of your writing preferences. What works best for you in terms of your writing environment, time of day, and other factors that might contribute to or hinder your writing?
2. Develop a tentative writing plan for a capstone project you would be interested in undertaking.

3. Using a classroom paper that you have completed, analyze your work on the following: use of first person, length of paragraphs, clarity of sentences, use of transitions, headings and subheadings, bias-free language, as well as spelling and grammar errors.
4. Proofread the paper you analyzed in the foregoing practice exercise. Check for spelling, grammar, and punctuation errors.

TECHNOLOGY EXERCISES

1. Research spelling and grammar applications that are free downloads from the internet. Select one that has good reviews and then use it to proof the classroom paper you analyzed in the foregoing practice activity. Compare the results.
2. Conduct a library search for peer-reviewed journal articles on bias-free professional writing. Download at least one article and make a list of the main ideas and/or recommendations suggested in the article.

REFERENCES

American Psychological Association. (2017). *Multicultural guidelines: An ecological approach to context, identity, and intersectionality.* https://www.apa.org/about/policy/multicultural-guidelines.aspx

American Psychological Association. (2020a). *The publication manual of the American Psychological Association: The official guide to APA style* (7th ed.). Author.

American Psychological Association. (2020b). *Bias-free language.* https://apastyle.apa.org/style-grammar-guidelines/bias-free-language

Barbaw, K. (2019). *Allosexual, demisexual, bicurious & other sexualities you need to know.* Refinary29. https://www.refinery29.com/en-us/sexual-orientation-types-of-sexualities

Boyer, K. (2016). *Intersectionality 101: Your privilege and oppression: Explaining the misunderstood concept of intersectionality.* Odyssey. https://www.theodysseyonline.com/intersectionality-101-understanding-your-privilege-oppression

Fleming, G. (2020). *Complete list of transition words.* Thought Company. https://www.thoughtco.com/list-of-transition-words-1857002

Higgins, M. (2019). *What does queer mean? 5 things to know about the Q in LGBTQ.* Bustle. https://www.bustle.com/articles/175470-what-does-queer-mean-5-things-to-know-about-the-q-in-lgbtq

National Association of Social Workers. (2015). *Standards and indicators for cultural competence in social work practice.* https://www.socialworkers.org/LinkClick.aspx?fileticket=PonPTDEBrn4%3d&portalid=0

National Association of Social Workers. (2017). *Code of ethics.* National Association of Social Workers. https://www.socialworkers.org

Purdue University. (n.d.-a). *Purdue online writing lab: Grammar.* https://owl.purdue.edu/owl/general_writing/grammar/index.html

Purdue University. (n.d.-b). *Purdue online writing lab: Paragraphs and paragraphing.* https://owl.purdue.edu/owl/general_writing/academic_writing/paragraphs_and_paragraphing/index.html

Purdue University. (n.d.-c). *Purdue online writing lab: Introduction. APA headings and seriation.* https://owl.purdue.edu/owl/research_and_citation/apa_style/apa_formatting_and_style_guide/apa_headings_and_seriation.html

Weisman, D., & Zornado, J. (2018). *Professional writing for social work practice* (2nd ed.). Springer Publishing Company.

Wrench, J. S., Goding, A., Johnson, D. I, & Attias, B. A. (2012). *Public speaking: Practice and ethics* (v.1.0). Creative Commons. https://2012books.lardbucket.org/pdfs/public-speaking-practice-and-ethics.pdf

3

IDENTIFYING A RESEARCH TOPIC

This chapter discusses some of the very first steps in your capstone project. It begins with a discussion of identifying a research topic. This includes understanding what makes a good problem to be studied, how to use information technology, what is meant by bias and how it might affect your study, and how to prevent bias. This is followed by a discussion on how to do a literature review before and after you have selected your problem, and developing your theoretical and conceptual framework. The final section of this chapter focuses on getting your applied capstone research approved by your instructor and field placement agency. This includes writing a problem statement and developing research questions.

By the end of this chapter, you will be able to do the following:

- Identify what makes a good research problem.
- Identify the kinds of issues you will need to examine as you select your problem.
- Describe how to do a literature review both before and after you identify your problem.
- Identify what the theoretical or conceptual framework is, and learn how to write one.
- Write a problem statement.
- Develop research questions for your applied capstone research project.

■ Identifying a Research Problem

All research projects require some sort of plan. This means you have to think about every aspect of your capstone project. The process is often gradual. The first step, however, is identification of your research problem. All of the effort that follows, including your literature, your theoretical or conceptual framework, the specific questions that you examine, and your methodology and analysis depend on your research problem (Sacred Heart University, 2020a). The following describes some issues that you should take into consideration as you examine possible research problems to be addressed in your capstone research project.

WHAT IS A GOOD PROBLEM TO STUDY?

So, what do I study? What do we mean by a "research problem"? A research problem is an area of interest. The research problem is the overarching theme, phenomena, or concept of interest (Bryman, 2007; Tran et al., 2017). The research problem helps to clarify the study's significance, context, and framework (Sacred Heart University, 2020a).

You may start with a general topic, influenced by your education, life experiences, interests, and career goals. Opportunities also play a role. Sometimes things fall into your lap because of the work you do or the people you know. Commonly, it might arise from something you have seen in practice. Alternatively, it might come from your family experiences. For example, many social workers come from a background of childhood trauma and this led to an interest in social work concerns (Gilin & Kauffman, 2015).

Thus, the research problem often arises from simply wanting to know more about what you have seen or experienced. By the way, the term "problem" is generic. It refers to any area of interest, not just those things that we as social workers consider "problems." The problem might be something causing or resulting in distress such as poverty, environmental injustice, or mental health. Likewise, it might just as appropriately focus on service utilization, staffing levels in an organization, or competing theories about community trauma. They are all "problems" in the sense that they cause or result in suffering. In research, the term "problem" refers to an issue that we find puzzling.

Almost anything can make for a good research problem. Very often, our practice and context are a good source. Think about just some of the questions that you need to address as you or your colleagues work with a client. Needs, treatment goals, effective interventions, skills, knowledge, theory or values of practice, and the contexts of both you and the client all may be wonderful research problems. Furthermore, any systemic level, from the individual to the nation may provide important puzzles. Often, innovative practices, for example, are underresearched (Atkins & Frederico, 2017).

Research can also have as a purpose the application of knowledge. You may find some types of applied research, or "practice-informed research," of interest. This, among other things, means the direct relationship between what we do (practice) and understanding it through research (Rowan et al., 2018).

ISSUES TO CONSIDER FOR ASSESSING A PROBLEM AND STUDY

There are other issues beyond interest and purpose that you may want to consider as they are important general guides for your project. These include feasibility, ethics, scientific soundness, and interest and importance.

Feasibility

Not all research problems are feasible to examine. First, research requires resources. At the least, it requires time. As a student, time is constrained by formal deadlines. Your project needs to fit into those constraints, whether it is a semester, a year, or at most a few years. Furthermore, time allotments are unequal. There may be weeks where little happens, but there also might be weeks where you can do little else but your research. The more sources of data you engage, the longer the data collection and/or the analysis will take. One possible solution is using secondary sources, which are widely used (Chudagr & Luschei, 2016; Hughes et al., 2020; Lee, 2005; Martinez et al., 2020; Sherif, 2018). Your field placement may have data sets for you to study. These sources are low cost (Sherif, 2018) and are often unobtrusive (Johnston, 2014). They might not, however, be appropriate for several reasons (Rew et al., 2000) such as unobtrusiveness and the timeliness of data.

Second, research may be quite expensive (Matei et al., 2015). Costs like mailing, transcription, or compensation for participants can quickly mount. Money also always has conditions, even questionable motives and requirements (Steele et al., 2019). There may be ethical issues, such as compensation. Compensation may influence participants (Cantinotti et al., 2016), especially for marginalized populations (Davidson & Page, 2012; Smith et al., 2007). The U.S. Food & Drug Administration Office of the Commissioner, et al. (2018) provide a good discussion and list of suggestions about this.

Finally, are data accessible? Many research questions may be addressed by agencies with which we are familiar, and agencies may be happy to have at least certain kinds of questions investigated. Yet some agencies keep their clients or data fairly "close to the vest." Sometimes, government data are held tightly (Piché, 2011; Spivakovsky, 2011; Taualii et al., 2011). You need to investigate permission as early as possible. You may also have to undergo an institutional review board (IRB) review at both your school and the agency where the clients/data are found. The two reviews may take quite a long time.

Ethics

The study you choose includes a number of ethical decisions that apply to social work research. First, many problems are ethically complex (Rowan et al., 2018). We often address very intimate aspects of our client's lives that involve at least some risk. Generally, the riskier a study is, the more rigorous the review will be (National Research Council, 2014). Consider a study that withholds treatments. Withholding treatment in the name of science has a long history (Emanuel et al., 2020). Doing so restricts client autonomy (Williamson, 2020) and must be balanced by the need for scientific certainty. There are many complexities to this issue that you may want to consider (Resnik, 2008).

A further ethical consideration, and one that ties into the problem of bias (discussed in what follows) comes from the power imbalance between researcher and subjects, agencies, or agency employees. You want to do good research, but how will you report findings that might not be favorable to the agency? While social work ethics should be enough for us, the pressure to please those persons who give us access to their clients is strong. This is hard for clinicians (Buchbinder & Eisikovits, 2004) as well as researchers. You must consider the balance between scientific and clinical value, scientific validity, fear of offending the agency, subject selection, favorable risk–benefit ratios, independent review, informed consent, and respect for potential and enrolled participants (Emanuel et al., 2020).

Scientific Soundness

A good social work research problem should be scientifically sound. Thyer (2009) suggests that it is affected by a number of parameters that include realism and acceptance of determinism, rationalism, positivism, naturalism, parsimony, scientific skepticism, and empiricism. Similarly, it should reject metaphysical explanations, nihilism, circular reasoning, scientism, and radical rationalization—meaning nothing can be really known. This last concept comes from a philosophical position that everything we know is a product of thought. In the extreme, thought cannot be validated by empirical evidence.

Interest and Importance

Interest is also very important. As a researcher, I find that research is most engaging and fun with problems that I find interesting. Of course, often problems that initially seem uninteresting become interesting. What you find interesting may be a social issue like climate change, or a population such as transsexual youth, or a specific community or place. It may also be a particular theory or research methodology, intervention, or policy. The list is extensive.

Finally, we get to the importance of the problem. Selecting a good research problem need not require you to save the world, end poverty, eliminate racism or climate change, or prove or disprove Karl Marx. However, a good research problem may contribute to any of these topics. Asking a new question or an old question in a new way, or applied to a new population or setting, make most research studies important. But always try to find some new twist.

▪ Information Technology—Your New Best Friend

Many of the themes discussed in the previous section may seem overwhelming. Technology may be a valuable support. A brief overview of the subject has identified many ways technology can assist you in the process (Atkinson-Bonasio, 2013). Following are just a few of these possibilities:

- *Literature databases*. Use your library! See what others have done and then build on it. Academia and government publish reams of useful information each year in journal articles, books, and reports. Examining these can help you find information on variables, methods, questions answered and unanswered, problem characteristics, demographics, theories and models, and more.
- *Special-purpose databases*. While still technically literature databases, there are a few that provide special types of information. There are databases on grant funding if you wish to pursue grant support. Many researchers also publish their data for others to use in new ways. There are also data sets that include research measures and instruments. Finally, there are databases that produce local and geographic information. Again, use your library.
- *Data collection*. The costs of collecting data are much reduced if you use the online tools at your disposal. Many of these tools are free of cost or low cost, and some will even help with data management and analysis. Some of these are publicly available, and some are found at your school.
- *Data storage*. Data takes a lot of space. However, cloud-based applications, as well as high-density local systems, can store huge amounts of information. This includes both data and literature. Such tools can keep all of your information readily available.
- *Smartphone platforms*. Many people have access to a smartphone. For many, it is their primary source of information and communication (Pew Research

Center, 2019). These are now common and widely used for a variety of research purposes, such as Health Care (Dorsey et al., 2017). You may use these for quite sophisticated data-collection methods.
- *Data-analysis software.* There are many useful data-analysis software programs, both qualitative and quantitative. Most schools have at least some available for your use.
- *Opening up your results to greater review.* Many of us have a world of new videos, podcasts, and websites that we review regularly. Such methods are quite useful for disseminating results. Collaboration with others (Cuff, 2014) and the crowd sourcing of your study are also easier.

Reflection Questions
1. What forms of technology do you often use in the classroom? Do you believe these would be adaptable to a research project? Why or why not?
2. Have you ever answered an online survey on your smartphone? How much information did you provide, and what did you not provide?

Biases in Research: Sources and Prevention Strategies

SOURCES OF BIAS

Selecting your problem of study opens you up to a critical concern—the problem of bias. "Bias" is any process that introduces error into research (Pannucci & Wilkins, 2010). At the highest level of analysis, bias results from "randomness" and human limitations. Bias may occur in a study at several points. It may be intentional, but it is more often unintentional. Some sources of bias are very controllable by a researcher, whereas others are less so. One useful way of identifying sources is to understand that bias can slip into a project because of actions by the researcher, the participant, or the methodology (Farnsworth, 2020).

Researcher Bias—Epistemological, Social, and Economic Context

At its most complex level, bias is rooted in the fact that knowledge and the creation of knowledge is not value or context free. We are humans. We think. Thought filters our experience. This is a characteristic of human experience, perhaps a characteristic of reality itself. Although science has long believed the world can be studied in a purely objective way, the affective, cognitive, social, economic, and political processes of the researcher cannot be removed completely. Most scientists have largely (if not completely) accepted this human limitation. How this has changed is fascinating but beyond the scope of this book.

Sometimes researcher bias can be intentional (Turkheimer et al., 2017), though not the "fault" of the researcher.

Consider the questions the researcher examines. Funders may prioritize certain research questions while ignoring others. Funding may be easy to obtain for noncontroversial issues, but more difficult for other problems. Researchers may also experience pressure to report findings that please their funders. Findings that show no (or sometimes opposite) outcomes may affect the ability of the agency/funder to obtain future funding.

> **Reflection Questions**
> 1. Do you trust the information you find on the internet? What criteria do you use to determine if information is credible?
> 2. How serious do you think the problem is of information being changed because of outside influences?

Methodological Bias

There are several sources of bias in methodologies; these are the places where a researcher should pay particular attention. Pannucci and Wilkins (2010) suggest that bias can occur because of study design, implementation, and analysis/interpretation.

Bias in Study Design

Design may influence a study's findings. For example, samples may be biased. It is the normal tendency of a sample to differ from its population due to random error. The smaller the sample relative to the population in terms of size, the larger the effect of a bias may be. To limit this effect, use the largest feasible sample. Statistical tools such as *power calculations* can at least help you estimate the likelihood of the bias.

A related problem is difference from the population. The closer the characteristics of the sample, the lesser the possible effect. Subject assignment is a related issue. Participants in a study can be channeled to influence results (Pannucci & Wilkins, 2010). This is "creaming" of subjects, most likely to show a change or benefit from an intervention. Creaming has a sense of intention to it, but it may be very subtle and unrecognized.

The key is to use samples that (a) are as close to the population in characteristics as possible, (b) use random assignment of subjects to research groups whenever possible and appropriate, and (c) are as large as feasible.

Measurement too can introduce bias. Social work research uses predominately observation or asking questions for measurement. Each type of measurement has different possible bias issues. *Observation* typically requires interpretation of the observed. Interpretation from the observed (what you see, hear, taste, touch) to the abstract (the variable concept) has that slippery human problem of "thinking." Similarly, *asking questions* can introduce bias by the way a question is asked or even the order of questions in a questionnaire.

Bias in Implementation

Bias can slip in with research implementation. For example, how an interviewer asks a question may influence the answers a subject provides. The best way to handle this effect is to standardize the questions and the questioning process as much as possible (Pannucci & Wilkins, 2010).

Participants in the research process too can contribute to bias. People may answer questions in ways that they think they should answer. This problem of social desirability may be particularly complex in some situations (Farnsworth, 2020). Participants such as prisoners, the socially isolated, and children may require special consideration.

Furthermore, recording information may introduce bias. Time filters

> **Reflection Questions**
> 1. What are some of the ways that you can think of to reduce bias in a research study?
> 2. How serious do you think the problem is of respondents' bias? How would you control it?

memory. Thus, many researchers attempt some kind of immediate recording as well as process to check information, such as logging or member checking. Similarly, avoid retrospective questions.

Bias in Analysis and Interpretation

Another place where bias may slip in comes at the point of analysis. How certain we are with a study's results is a complex issue. Selection of the most restrictive probability level in quantitative research is often desirable. Even then, however, the problem is far from resolved. Bias in interpretation has its roots in the same sources as other types. The difference, however, is findings from a study are accepted. What those findings mean or imply may, however, be misinterpreted.

For example, a study using 100 college student volunteers might yield interesting results, but claiming that the results apply to an entire population is inappropriate. Likewise, a finding from a qualitative study of 10 individuals in a focus group may not be transferable to other, even similar groups.

This kind of problem is common today. Thousands of research studies are published each year. Selecting those of most interest or importance is difficult, particularly because there are thousands of news organizations that want to capture the attention of the public. At the moment this book is being written, the Coronavirus problem is not controlled, and even treatments for complicated cases are at best in the early stages. The researcher who finds and the news source that first reports the "magic bullet" treatment will earn significant fame and accolades. The pull to say more about results than may be accurate is strong.

Finally, the problem of confounding or misinterpretation occurs. A variable outside the study may affect or confound the information. Most human problems are very complex and rarely will a single or even a couple of causes lead to an effect. One way that people often talk about this is the confusion between correlation and causation. To claim that a relationship has a definite cause and effect when it is just two things happening together may be confusing, as well as incorrect.

CONTROLLING BIAS

Controlling bias in your research has been introduced earlier. There are other methods and processes that are invaluable. Table 3.1 shows some commonly used strategies. Most simply, controlling bias means asking the right questions, of the right people, in a sound, consistent way, without misinterpreting what you find (Survey Monkey, 2020). Moreover, do not claim more than the study actually shows. Even simple findings can be important.

Reviewing the Literature

One of the very first steps in any research study process, and one that may inform much of what you do, is

Reflection Questions

1. Have you ever read a study and heard a media report about that study? Were the results the same? Or do they say different things?
2. What do you think makes for a good study report?

TABLE 3.1 STRATEGIES TO CONTROL BIAS

SOURCE OF BIAS	STUDY COMPONENT	PREVENTION METHOD
Researcher/researcher context	Epistemology (value system of knowledge acquisition)	Recognize personal values
	Ideology of funding sources	Examine priorities of source
	Publication bias against negative findings	Locate journals that accept negative findings
	Academic system of rewards	Advocate for more equitable determination of output
Methodological	Study designs	<ul><li>Use adequate sample size with power calculations for estimations</li><li>Avoid channeling/creaming in group selection</li></ul>
	Measurement	<ul><li>Use measures with established reliability/validity</li><li>Standardize interviewing</li></ul>
	Recording	Record information immediately
	Analysis	Do not change research criteria after research begins
Participants	Social desirability	<ul><li>Ask questions in neutral settings</li><li>Avoid threat</li><li>Build relationships</li></ul>
	Recall	<ul><li>Try to avoid memory information</li><li>Member checking</li></ul>

the literature review. You may look at almost any published research study and most of the first few pages comprises literature, typically the research of others. One way to think about what the literature review does is that it provides background for all aspects of the research study. This background may address almost any part of the research project, from the findings of previous research studies by other authors, to the methods used in previous research, to unanswered questions and disputes across researchers. The section also, importantly, places the current project in the quest for knowledge on the topic.

A literature review does not contain everything on the subject (Hart, 1998). You shape it to the conceptual and practical aspects of a project. Previous research has very useful material for you to build upon and use. We may break this down into three parts. What goes into a well-written literature review? Second, what kinds of information should you consider? Third, we provide some tips that make the literature search easier.

COMPONENTS OF THE LITERATURE REVIEW

So, what goes into the literature review? Of course, the answer is literature and information, though selectively applied. Selection criteria include both the sources/quality of the information and the content.

Sources/Quality of Information

Not all information is equally accurate, timely, or even truthful. Not all information is equally valid. Therefore, the process of selection of information should be a sifting process, where the information that is included is as strong as possible, and information of questionable truthfulness should be left out or treated with suspicion.

So what makes for good information? At a minimum, it should be understandable (Holosko, 2006). Then, ask, does the information come from a trustworthy source? What is a trustworthy source? Here are some of the questions you should ask of a data source as you review it.

1. Who sponsors/hosts the information?
2. Who wrote the information? Who reviewed it?
3. When was the information written?
4. What is the purpose of the source?

You may also ask how old the information is. Older information might be quite important. But the development of new knowledge is an ongoing process. Thus, what is current or recent is likely also aware of the older studies. New findings may supplement and build on older research.

Second, you want to consider the power of the information. This again is not a hard-and-fast concept, but it addresses the quality of the methods, findings, and analysis. You should ask if the study has been "peer reviewed." Has the study, at both the developmental stage (through an IRB or similar review) and then later on at the time of publication been examined by experts? Studies that have been reviewed are more soundly created and interpreted.

In addition, studies based on large samples, randomly drawn, are desirable if you hope to build your study on generalizable information. Now, this is less relevant if you want very specialized information. In the case of qualitative evidence, this point is even less important.

> **Reflection Questions**
> 1. There are very many studies that are done with small samples. How do you know if those studies are truly representative or just very good descriptive studies?
> 2. What are some of the components of the literature review that you would find difficult to write? Why?

Third, several studies that have support and replication from diverse sources (and different researchers) with similar findings are more powerful. Nevertheless, research studies that yield different results may also be useful. This leaves an opening for new research and for you to add to the knowledge base.

Finally, not all of the information in a literature review must be research studies. Conceptual papers or literature review articles that otherwise follow the rules just mentioned are also useful. Literature from a scholarly journal is usually desirable. Likewise, respected theorists (often in book form) may be valuable too.

To get at some of the deeper issues of quality, there are tools you may use to access and separate information. One way to do this, particularly if you are looking at lots of information, is the SQ3R method—Survey, Query, Read, Recite, and Review—a technique designed to help you judge the usefulness of a study (Robinson, 1978; Vacca & Vacca, 2005).

Content—What to Include in the Literature Review

On the basis of the criteria discribed earlier, with one limited exception, use primarily peer-reviewed literature review and/or data from trustworthy sources. Peer-reviewed data are typical for articles that have been published in academic journals—but not all academic journals. Other trustworthy sources usually include government data, such as census data. The one major exception to the issue of peer-reviewed information lies with your conceptual framework and/or the theories you plan to test (if any). Theories, by their very nature, are not directly testable, and you will find theories and even models that have not been validated. You may be moving into uncharted territory, so be careful, but it may be a necessary inclusion.

There is flexibility in the structure of the review, but be intentional about the way you organize the material in your write-up. Try to organize the write-up by common themes. For example, variables examined, variable measurement, findings supporting/not supporting your question, methods used to collect data, competing theoretical explanations, and unanswered questions can be useful themes for grouping your study. Even chronological order can be used, if appropriate. Remember, one of the most important parts of the literature review is to provide guidance. The logic here can help structure your study later.

Further, based on your reading so far, identify the major unanswered questions and controversies. Are there important disagreements between studies? What does the literature point to as areas needing further investigation?

Keep the literature review as tight and concise as possible. Following are 10 steps that may be useful (Pautasso, 2013):

1. Define your topic and the purposes for the review period clearly.
2. Search and research literature.
3. Take notes and keep track of what you find.
4. Choose and be clear about the purpose of the review period.
5. Be focused but interesting.
6. Be critical of what you find.
7. Present what you find in a logical way.
8. Accept feedback from others.
9. Be objective.
10. Use up-to-date sources.

IDENTIFYING A THEORETICAL OR CONCEPTUAL FRAMEWORK

As part of your literature review, you will also need to identify a theoretical or conceptual framework for your capstone research project. This is where you identify the intellectual context for your research. It is where you come up with an interpretation of why you suspect you will find what you will find and/or what kinds of things might be important to consider about your research problem.

This component of your literature review ties your research to the formal construction of knowledge. Why is it important? Although there are different competing and valuable ways of knowing the world (e.g., qualitative vs. quantitative approaches), the basis of Western science is commonly linked to a philosophy called "positivism." Positivism has been widely accepted by the social work community since the earliest days of Mary Richmond (Agnew, 2004). The basic assumptions of positivism are as follows:

1. The universe and everything we observe in it are guided by unchanging laws.
2. These laws may be learned.
3. To learn these laws, we apply two human tools or attributes: observation and logic.
4. The formal application of these tools can be systematized, and the result is what we call "science."
5. The more completely we separate the influence of the thinker/observer from what is observed, the better and more accurate our understanding of those laws will be.

These statements appear simple enough, but immediately, significant problems arise of such importance that entirely different and competing ways of knowing have developed. Perhaps the most important of these difficulties is that observation and logic are believed to be entirely different realities. Specifically, observation focuses on the materiality of the universe (the universe is made up of stuff that can be seen, touched, tasted, etc.). Logic, however, is made up of thoughts. And in this worldview, thought does not equal stuff.

What? Huh? Well, look at it this way. Suppose you like lollipops. You can think about lollipops all day long, and you can create in your mind the perfect lollipop in various shapes and colors. However, those lollipops you envision will never be held in your hand, tasted by your tongue, or stuck in your hair. This is the ultimate issue in positivism, the gulf that exists between our thinking about the lollipop and the lollipop itself.

This type of example is exactly what makes the theoretical framework difficult to work with for some people. In identifying your conceptual framework, you have to link your thinking about the research problem with what you hope to observe. For this, the process involves a thought strategy known as "deductive logic." Deductive logic is a tool that we use to move from the general statements that a theory makes to specific, presumably observable aspects of the real world that we call "hypotheses." As you may remember, a hypothesis is a statement that should be testable, refutable, and true if the theory from which it comes is correct.

Now, not all research follow this process. If the problem you want to study does not yield itself to a theory, you can create a conceptual framework as an alternative. The conceptual framework does not use deductive logic to move from a specific theory to a specific hypothesis, but rather allows you to take concepts from (even competing) theories, models, and ideas from others who have studied the problem. You then put the concepts together in a new way. This can then

Reflection Questions
1. Are you aware of any theories that you would find useful for your research project? What are they? How might they be useful to you?
2. What do you think makes a good theory? Why?

yield a model—a proposed set of concepts that, when overlaid over what you observe, will yield two invaluable tools for you. First, it will provide guidance about what variables are important to include, and, second, it will give you a way to interpret the data you find.

Following are the kinds of information that can be used in a theoretical framework, or a conceptual framework if that is the direction that you choose. At a minimum it should contain the following (Sacred Heart University, 2020b; University of Southern California, 2020a):

- Your research question
- The theories that give you a possible way for understanding your question as well as the possible answers you might find (this can give way to your hypothesis)
- The important constructs and ideas from your theory or theories that inform your thinking
- Identification of any other influences on your research problem or what you might think of as context or confounding variables

Getting Your Capstone Project Approved

OBTAINING AGENCY PERMISSION

Before beginning your capstone research project, we recommend that you review your research ideas with your field instructor and/or site supervisor. As agency staff, they will have knowledge about service delivery and organizational and community challenges that could become the focus of your applied research project. It is also helpful to ask other social workers employed at your field agency about areas that they think could be improved or assessed. In addition to demonstrating your professional competence, a major benefit of capstone projects tied to your field placement agency is improved services for clients and/or organizational functioning. Supervisors and social workers who work with the clients, manage programs, or have administrative duties in the agency are excellent sources of ideas for your capstone project. They know what works well and what needs to be improved.

> **Reflection Questions**
> 1. What will you need to do to obtain agency permission for your capstone project?
> 2. What obstacles or challenges do you anticipate in obtaining agency permission for your capstone project?

After you have brainstormed with your supervisor and staff members, we recommend that you prepare a short but very clear problem statement summarizing the proposed capstone research project. Your proposed project should be reviewed and approved by your instructor and field placement supervisor/administrator. Also, your proposed project should be reviewed by an agency administrator for approval and/or feedback.

WRITING A PROBLEM STATEMENT

Once your problem is selected, your literature is found and reviewed, and you have a theory or conceptual framework to guide your thinking, you are ready to write the problem statement. It serves as the transition between the literature and your specific, focused study. A very practical set of steps, or components, includes an introduction of the topic, the questions you hope to answer, and/or any hypotheses, some context, and some general information about your methods and analysis (University of Southern California, 2020b).

In a very real way, everything up to this section has been other people's work. But this section makes a major movement from what others have done to what you will do. You are now the owner of your project! As such, it typically contains four sections. They are as follows:

- *A summary of the observed problem.* First, you describe the observed problem you are interested in examining. Now, this does not mean "I saw people sleeping on the streets" (although, stylistically and for impact, such a statement may be included and is appropriate). Rather, it means summarizing and providing a definition and context for the problem. This section may use both quantitative and qualitative data. Quantitative data usually (but not always) means using statistical entities that characterize the problem. You might include prevalence data (how many people are affected), incidence (how rapidly the problem is growing), impact data (the effects of the problem), comparative data (showing the relative impacts on different groups), service utilization data (how many services are used), and needs estimates. The section can also include qualitative evidence, such as descriptions and quotations from affected persons.
- *A summary of the literature.* Second, you summarize what the literature has said about the problem. Are there important studies that have made important observations about the problem? What variables have been included, and importantly what is not yet known (as identified in the literature).
- *A summary of the theoretical or conceptual frameworks.* Third, in addition to (or expanding) the literature just discussed, what theories appear to adequately explain the problem? What major theoretical questions or debates need examination?
- *Gaps in the research and your study purpose.* Fourth, building on the previous bullet points, what will your study do? What major question(s) will it hope to answer? And upon conclusion of the study, what will your contribution to science, to social work, and to the service population be.

In addition to the above components we also suggest that, for the purposes of getting your capstone research project approved, you include in your problem statement your research questions or hypotheses, methods, benefits of the research, and potential risks to participants.

- *Research questions/hypotheses.* List the specific research questions or hypotheses that your capstone project will address. Your research questions may come to you before you get to the point of completing all of these previous steps. You know what you want to study, and you know what has been studied. You also have a pretty good idea of the areas needing further investigation. Now it is time to take all that information and convert it into a question or set of specific questions that you will apply and hopefully answer with your methodology. Hypotheses are similar to research questions but are worded in the form of statements instead of questions.

- *Methods.* Provide a brief description of how the study will be conducted, your applied research approach, study participants, data collection methods, approximate amount of time required for each participant, and a time frame for the project.
- *Risks and benefits of the research.* Describe potential risks to study participants, how human subjects will be protected, and what you will do to correct any harm incurred by your participants. Also indicate that if approved you will provide an informed consent form for review and approval.

PRACTICE ACTIVITIES

1. Write down a list of all of the problem areas that you might find an interest in researching. In a column next to it, try to identify a research method that will help you investigate the problem. Then in a third column, write down the fears or issues you would need to overcome to conduct that research.
2. Using the same set of items from the previous list, see if you are already aware of at least one theory that would be useful for understanding the problem. Try to identify one research question for each item that you would personally like to investigate.
3. Look back over the papers that you have written as a student and examine the literature you use to write those papers. From this, begin to develop your own database. Try to organize those literature sources in a logical way such that you may draw on some of that information in your capstone project.

TECHNOLOGY EXERCISES

1. Go to your library's website and look up its online databases. Without actually conducting a full search, select as many terms as you can that might be useful for identifying useful research studies.
2. Now, think about the social problem that you might be interested in examining. Identify the populations that might be affected by that problem. Examine the internet site Fedstats.gov and search that problem among the populations of interest. What statistics do you find that might be useful to you? Write those down for later use.

REFERENCES

Agnew, N. E. (2004). *From charity to social work: Mary Richmond and the creation of an American profession.* University of Illinois Press.

Atkins, P., & Frederico, M. (2017). Supporting implementation of innovative social work practice: What factors really matter? *British Journal of Social Work, 47*(6), 1723–1744. https://doi.org/10.1093/bjsw/bcx091

Atkinson-Bonasio, A. (2013). *Nine views on how technology can transform research and open up science.* Elsevier. https://www.elsevier.com/connect/9-views-on-how-technology-can-transform-research-and-open-up-science

Bryman, A. (2007). The research question in social research: What is its roll? *International Journal of Social Research Methodology, 10,* 5–20. https://doi.org/10.1080/13645570600655282

Buchbinder, E., & Eisikovits, Z. (2004). Reporting bad results: The ethical responsibility of presenting abused women's parenting practices in a negative light. *Child & Family Social Work, 9*(4), 359–367. https://doi.org/10.1111/j.1365-2206.2004.00336.x

Cantinotti, M., Leclerc, B.-S., Brochu, P., Jacques, C., Sévigny, S., & Giroux, I. (2016). The effect of research compensation in the form of cheques on gamblers' cash-in behaviour. *Journal of Gambling Issues, 32,* 1–10. https://doi.org/10.4309/jgi.2016.32.1

Chudagr, A., & Luschei, T. F. (2016). The untapped promise of secondary data sets in international and comparative education policy research education. *Education Policy Analysis Archives, 24*(113) 1–15. https://doi.org/10.14507/epaa.24.2563

Cuff, E. (2014). The effect and importance of technology in the research process. *Journal of Educational Technology Systems, 43*(1), 75–97. https://doi.org/10.2190/ET.43.1.f

Davidson, P., & Page, K. (2012). Research participation as work: Comparing the perspectives of researchers and economically marginalized populations. *American Journal of Public Health, 102*(7), 1254–1259. https://doi.org/10.2105/AJPH.2011.300418

Dorsey, E. R, Chan, Y., McConnell, M., Shaw, S., Trister, A., & Friend, St. (2017). The use of smartphones for health research. *Academic Medicine, 92*(2),157–160. https://doi.org/10.1097/ACM.0000000000001205

Emanuel, E., Adobler, E., & Stunkel, L. (2020). *Research ethics: How to treat people who participate in research.* National Institutes of Health; Clinical Center Department of Bioethics. https://bioethics.nih.gov/education/FNIH_BioethicsBrochure_WEB.PDF

Farnsworth, B. (2020). *What is bias? A field guide for scientific research.* https://imotions.com/blog/what-is-bias

Gilin, B., & Kauffman, S. (2015). Strategies for teaching about trauma to social work students. *Journal of Teaching in Social Work, 35*(4), 378–396. https://doi.org/10.1080/08841233.2015.1065945

Hart, C. (1998). *Doing a literature review: Releasing the social science research imagination.* Sage.

Holosko, M. J. (2006). *Primer for critiquing social research: A student guide.* Brooks/Cole.

Hughes, K., Hughes, J., & Tarrant, A. (2020). Re-approaching interview data through qualitative secondary analysis: Interviews with internet gamblers. *International Journal of Social Research Methodology, 23*(5), 565–579. https://doi.org/10.1080/13645579.2020.1766759

Johnston, M. P. (2014). Secondary data analysis: A method of which the time has come. *Qualitative and Quantitative Methods in Libraries, 3,* 619–626. http://www.qqml-journal.net/index.php/qqml/article/view/169

Lee, K. (2005). Effects of experimental center-based child care on developmental outcomes of young children living in poverty. *Social Service Review, 79*(1), 158–180. https://doi.org/10.1086/426721.

Martinez, Y. C., Ellington, L., Vadaparampil, S. T., Heyman, R. E., & Reblin, M. (2020). Concordance of cancer related concerns among advanced cancer patient–spouse caregiver dyads. *Journal of Psychosocial Oncology, 38*(2), 143–155. https://doi.org/10.1080/07347332.2019.1642285

Matei, M., Calipsoana, C. V., & Azoicai, D. (2015). A review on cancer research funding. *Social Research Reports, 27,* 3–25. https://www.researchreports.ro/a-review-on-cancer-research-funding

National Research Council. (2014, March 31). *Proposed revisions to the common rule for the protection of human subjects in the behavioral and social sciences.* National Academies Press;

Determining Minimal Risk in Social and Behavioral Research. https://www.ncbi.nlm.nih.gov/books/NBK217976

Pannucci, C. J., & Wilkins, E. G. (2010). Identifying and avoiding bias in research. *Plastic and Reconstructive Surgery, 126*(2), 619–625. https://doi.org/10.1097/PRS.0b013e3181de24bc

Pautasso, M. (2013). Ten simple rules for writing a literature review. *PLoS Computational Biology, 9*(7), e1003149. https://doi.org/10.1371/journal.pcbi.1003149

Pew Research Center. (2019). *Mobile connectivity in emerging economies.* https://www.pewresearch.org/internet/2019/03/07/mobile-connectivity-in-emerging-economies

Piché, J. (2011). "Going public": Accessing data, contesting information blockades. *Canadian Journal of Law & Society/Revue Canadienne Droit et Societe, 26*(3), 635–643. https://doi.org/10.3138/cjls.26.3.635

Resnik, D. B. (2008). Randomized controlled trials in environmental health research: Ethical issues. *Journal of Environmental Health, 70*(6), 28–30. https://www.ncbi.nlm.nih.gov/pmc/articles/PMC2653276

Rew, L., Koniak-Griffin, D., Lewis, M. A., Miles, M., & O'Sullivan, A. (2000). Secondary data analysis: New perspective for adolescent research. *Nursing Outlook, 48*(5), 223–229. https://doi.org/10.1067/mno.2000.104901

Robinson, F. P. (1978). *Effective study* (6th ed.). Harper & Row. .

Rowan, D., Richardson, S., & Long, D. (2018). Practice informed research: Contemporary challenges and ethical decision-making. *Journal of Social Work Values and Ethics, 15*(2), 15–22. https://jswve.org/download/15-2/articles15-2/15-Practice-informed-research-JSWVE-15-2-2018-Fall.pdf

Sacred Heart University. (2020a). *Organizing academic research papers: The research problem/question.* https://library.sacredheart.edu/c.php?g=29803&p=185918

Sacred Heart University. (2020b). *Organizing academic research papers: The theoretical framework.* https://library.sacredheart.edu/c.php?g=29803&p=185919

Sherif, V. (2018). Evaluating preexisting qualitative research data for secondary analysis forum. *Qualitative Social Research, 19*(2), 26–42. https://www.qualitative-research.net/index.php/fqs/article/view/2821

Smith, Y. R., Johnson, A. M., Newman, L. A., Greene, A., Johnson, T. R., & Rogers, J. L. (2007). Perceptions of clinical research participation among African American women. *Journal of Women's Health, 16*(3), 423–428. https://doi.org/10.1089/jwh.2006.0124

Spivakovsky, C. (2011). The need for flexible and adaptive research in an environment of diverse barriers to accessing data. *Canadian Journal of Law & Society/Revue Canadienne Droit et Societe, 26*(3), 607–612. https://doi.org/10.3138/cjls.26.3.607

Steele, S., Ruskin, G., McKee, M., & Stuckler, D. (2019). "Always read the small print." A case study of commercial research funding, disclosure and agreements with Coca-Cola. *Journal of Public Health Policy, 40*(3), 273–285. https://doi.org/10.1057/s41271-019-00170-9

Survey Monkey. (2020). *Leading types of bias in research and how to prevent them from impacting your survey.* https://www.surveymonkey.com/mp/dont-let-opinions-sneak-survey-4-ways-avoid-researcher-bias/?program=7013A000000mweBQAQ&utm_bu=CR&utm_campaign=717000000059189235&utm_adgroup=58700005410222821&utm_content=39700049736551248&utm_medium=cpc&utm_source=adwords&utm_term=p49736551248&utm_kxconfid=s4bvpi0ju&gclid=CjwKCAjwx9_4BRAHEiwApAt0zpDmUKVY3UEidsKVyvS1Z5PvD05RpnZv0IMFhZqjyzTJh4y063dAYxoCCMgQAvD_BwE&gclsrc=aw.ds

Taualii, M., Quenga, J., Samoa, R., Samanani, S., & Doverry, D. (2011). Liberating data: Accessing Native Hawaiian and other Pacific Islander data from national data sets. *Asian Americans and Pacific Islanders Nexus, 9*(1/2), 249–255. https://doi.org/10.36650/nexus9.1-2_249-255_TaualiiEtAl

Thyer, B. (2009). *The handbook of social work research methods* (2nd ed.). Sage.

Tran, T. V., Rhee, S., & Shen, C. (2017). *Research methods & data analysis for multicultural social work and human services* (2nd ed.). Cognella Academic.

Turkheimer, E., Harden, K. P., & Nisbett, R. E. (2017). *Charles Murray is once again peddling junk science about race and IQ*. https://www.vox.com/the-big-idea/2017/5/18/15655638/charles-murray-race-iq-sam-harris-science-free-speech

U.S. Food & Drug Administration Office of the Commissioner, Office of Clinical Policy and Programs, Office of Clinical Policy, & Office of Good Clinical Practice. (2018). *Payment and reimbursement to research subjects*. https://www.fda.gov/regulatory-information/search-fda-guidance-documents/payment-and-reimbursement-research-subjects

University of Southern California. (2020a) *Research guides: Theoretical framework*. https://libguides.usc.edu/writingguide/theoreticalframework

University of Southern California. (2020b). *Research guides: Writing your problem statement*. https://libguides.usc.edu/writingguide/introduction/researchproblem

Vacca, R. T., & Vacca, J. A. L. (2005). *Content area reading: Literacy and learning across the curriculum* (8th ed.). Pearson/Allyn & Bacon.

Williamson, C. (2020). Withholding policies from patients restricts their autonomy. *British Medical Journal, 331*(7524), 1078–1080. https://doi.org/10.1136/bmj.331.7524.1078

4

DATA COLLECTION

In this chapter, we explore methods and approaches to collecting quantitative and qualitative data. All applied research projects require some sort of data collection. This chapter reviews all the components needed to collect quantitative and qualitative data for your capstone research project.

By the end of this chapter, you will be able to do the following:

- Identify primary and secondary data sources.
- List four primary data sources commonly used in evaluation studies.
- Describe four broad data collection categories.
- Define probability and nonprobability sampling.
- Describe four levels of quantitative measurement.
- Identify two methods for calculating reliability.
- Describe different approaches to establishing validity.
- Identify five types of measures used in quantitative evaluation studies.
- Conduct qualitative interviews using interpersonal elaboration skills.

▪ Sources of Data

Completing your capstone research project requires you to gather information or data on your target problem. There are two broad categories of data sources—secondary and primary. Secondary data are those that are collected by another entity or for another purpose. These are data that have already been collected and available for use in your capstone project. Primary data, on the other hand, are data that are collected specifically for your research. These are data that you gather to address your identified target problem.

SECONDARY DATA

The advantage of using secondary data is that they have already been collected so the need for a data collection time period and effort is eliminated. The savings in terms of time, money, and effort are substantial. The primary challenge in using secondary data is finding a data set that addresses the identified target problem. There are numerous

> **Reflection Questions**
> 1. What kinds of secondary data would be relevant to your program and its clients if it were available?
> 2. How might access to secondary data sets help your program and its clients?

national data sets as well as a variety of state and county data sets. Municipalities also collect various health, human service, and employment data. In addition, there are data sets collected by professional associations and organizations. Finding a data set that includes data on your variables of interest, your target population, and your target geographic area is the major obstacle to using secondary data for your program and/or service evaluation.

We recognize that finding secondary data for your capstone project will be challenging; nevertheless, we recommend that you always search for secondary data sets as part of your capstone project plan. Your search should include existing governmental data sets, professional associations, and organizations. Table 4.1 lists some of the secondary data sets that are accessible over the internet.

TABLE 4.1 SAMPLE OF AVAILABLE SECONDARY DATA SETS

NAME	URL	DESCRIPTION
ICPSR	https://www.icpsr.umich.edu/web/pages/index.html	ICPSR maintains a data archive of more than 250,000 files of research in the social and behavioral sciences. It hosts 21 specialized collections of data in education, aging, criminal justice, substance abuse, terrorism, and other fields.
CHR&R	https://www.countyhealthrankings.org	The CHR&R program provides data, evidence, guidance, and examples to build awareness of the multiple factors that influence health and support community leaders working to improve health and increase health equity. The rankings are unique in their ability to measure the health of nearly every county in all 50 states.
CDC—PSRs	https://www.cdc.gov/psr	The PSRs highlight—for all 50 states and the District of Columbia—the status of public health policies and practices designed to address the following important public health problems and concerns: alcohol-related harms, heart disease and stroke, nutrition, physical activity and obesity, food safety, HIV, prescription drug overdose, healthcare–associated infections, motor vehicle injuries, and teen pregnancy.

(continued)

TABLE 4.1 SAMPLE OF AVAILABLE SECONDARY DATA SETS (*continued*)

NAME	URL	DESCRIPTION
CDC—BRFSS	https://www.cdc.gov/brfss	The BRFSS is health-related telephone surveys that collect state data about U.S. residents regarding their health-related risk behaviors, chronic health conditions, and use of preventive services.
CDC—WONDER	https://wonder.cdc.gov	CDC WONDER manages nearly 20 collections of public-use data for U.S. births, deaths, cancer diagnoses, tuberculosis cases, vaccinations, environmental exposures, and population estimates, among many other topics. These data collections are available as online databases, which provide public access to ad-hoc queries, summary statistics, maps, charts, and data extracts. Most of the data are updated annually; some collections are updated monthly or weekly.
Community Commons	http://www.communitycommons.org	Community Commons is a collaborative initiative working to create healthy, equitable, and sustainable communities. The site has online databases on economy, education, environment, equity, food, health, housing, and transportation.
U.S. Census Data	https://data.census.gov/cedsci	data.Census.Gov is a platform to access data and digital content from the U.S. Census. The site contains census data, the American Community Survey, the American Housing Survey, economic indicators, foreign trade, governmental statistics, and housing data sets.

BRFSS, Behavioral Risk Factor Surveillance System; CDC, Centers for Disease Control and Prevention; CHR&R, County Health Rankings & Roadmap; ICPSR, Inter-university Consortium for Political and Social Research; PSRs, Prevention Status Reports.

PRIMARY DATA

When secondary data sources are not available for your evaluation research, then you will need to collect new primary data for your capstone project. There are a number of different methods for collecting primary data that are covered in other chapters in this book. This chapter focuses on the different sources for your data collection. Most applied research projects designed to evaluate social work programs and services, human service organizations, and community needs assessments collect primary data from human beings. The sources of data are different categories of people. Four common applied research data sources are clients, staff members, key informants, and community members.

Clients are a common data source for program and service evaluations. As recipients of the program or service, their perceptions about the utility and effectiveness of the services can provide important feedback for quality improvement. Clients are also often the preferred source for outcome information on the intervention and/or program. Many program outcomes are specified in terms of client change on identified targets and measures.

Another excellent source of primary data for applied research studies is employees of the organization or agency. This includes direct service personnel, support staff, as well as supervisory and administrative staff. Direct service staff involved in the delivery of agency programs and services have firsthand knowledge of what is working well and what needs improvement. They also have unique perspectives on the functioning of the agency, staff morale, and the extent to which the organizational culture supports their work in delivering client services. Agency supervisory staff and administrators are also potential data sources for applied research studies. Depending upon the focus of your evaluation, the perspectives of agency supervisors and administrators can provide valuable insights into your research questions.

Another potential data source is what are often referred to as "key informants." Key informants are people who are knowledgeable about the social issue or problem you are studying. They are experts who have firsthand knowledge about your research topic. Studies that collect data from key informants typically recruit a wide range of key informants, including professionals, organizational leaders, community leaders, and/or political leaders. Key informants with their particular knowledge and expertise can provide insight on the nature of problems and provide recommendations for potential solutions. If key informants are used in your capstone research project, it is important to make sure that all the different groups are represented. Start by identifying the different groups that are knowledgeable about your research topic and then identify potential participants within each group. This will help ensure that you obtain a range of perspectives on the social issue or problem that you are investigating. The U.S. Agency for International Development (AID) Center for Development Information and Evaluation (1996) identified the following five situations where key informants are useful:

- When decision-making can be achieved through qualitative and descriptive information
- When it is important to gain an understanding of the perspectives, behavior, and motivations of customers and partners of an activity or project in order to explain the shortcomings and successes of an activity
- When generating recommendations is the key purpose
- In order to interpret quantitative data by interviewing key informants about the how and why of the quantitative findings
- In order to help frame the issues that are relevant before designing a quantitative study (pp. 1–2)

Another potential source of primary data is community members. Community members can describe their community, access community issues and needs, identify best practices, and/or provide evaluation feedback. Although community members do not have the specialized expertise on the target problem, they do have expertise on their community, its culture, and its various components and divisions. Kind in mind that the definition of "community member" varies by the purpose of your research. It might mean those who live in a geographic area or members of a subgroup of the population, such as former military personnel, people with disabilities, or people who are recent immigrants.

In addition to data collected from various stakeholders and community members, existing agency records and documents can also be a source of primary data. Agency records and documents have the advantage of addressing your target population and geographic area. The potential disadvantages are missing or incomplete information and the lack of information on your identified target variables.

Data Collection Methods

Primary data collection methods fall into four broad categories: surveys, focus groups, direct observation, and document reviews. "Surveys" are a common method for quantitative evaluation studies. Quantitative survey methods include personal interviews, telephone interviews, and mailed, emailed, or web-based questionnaires completed by the respondent. Each approach uses a structured interview schedule or questionnaire that collects data from individual participants. The advantages of using questionnaires are cost and time savings as well as the ability to reach a large number of participants within the same time frame. The disadvantages of questionnaires are lower response rates, missing data with respondents skipping items on the questionnaire, and having the opportunity to clarify any questions or concerns about the research and/or items on the questionnaire.

Interview schedules are completed by the researcher or research assistant by asking the participant for their responses to the various items on the form. Questionnaires are completed by the participants without the presence of the researcher or research assistant. The advantages of personal interviews are the ability to clarify any questions or concerns as well as helping ensure that all the items/questions are completed. The major disadvantage is that personal interviews require additional resources and take longer to complete the data collection process.

"Focus groups" and personal interviews are two common data collection methods used in qualitative-type evaluation studies. The researcher facilitating the focus group uses open-ended questioning and elaboration skills to obtain in-depth information on the topic under investigation. Focus-group participants are selected based on their knowledge of the problem as well as how representative they are of the study population group. Focus groups usually have between six and 15 similar persons who are led through a series of open-ended questions. The purpose is to arrive at consensus answers. Focus groups are very helpful in understanding the "Why" question. A major limitation is the lack of representativeness in the findings. Another limitation is the inability to provide descriptive data on the magnitude and scope of the issue being assessed (Poulin et al., 2020).

Personal interviews are often used to collect primary qualitative data from individual respondents. As with focus groups, the researcher uses open-ended questioning and elaboration skills to obtain in-depth information on the topic under investigation. The advantage of personal interviews is the ability to ask follow-up questions to obtain in-depth information on the person's feelings, experiences, and perceptions. Qualitative personal interviews are an excellent choice when the research questions seek to understand the why behind the respondent's answers. They allow for a more in-depth exploration of the topic being investigated. Similar to focus groups, the major disadvantage of qualitative personal interviews with a small number of participants is the inability to provide descriptive data on the magnitude and scope of the issue being assessed. A second disadvantage is the lack of anonymity, which can be a serious obstacle when sensitive subjects are the focus of the study.

Reflection Questions
1. What do you see as the advantage of using focus groups to conduct a program evaluation?
2. What do you see as the disadvantages?

"Direct observation" is another method often used to collect primary data. Observation is a data collection method where the researcher looks at the activities of the study participants in their typical environment. Direct observation requires some sort of systematic documentation of the participants' activities and/or behaviors. This can be done through videotaping, by compiling field notes, or completing behavioral checklists. Direct observation works well if the data being collected are behavioral and observable. It is difficult to observe how people are feeling and/or what they are thinking. An advantage of direct observation is that it can capture information that participants may not think to reveal or see as important during interviews and/or focus groups. A disadvantage is that it is limited to studying participants' behaviors and observable events.

"Document reviews" can also be used to collect primary data. As with direct observation, it requires some sort of systematic documentation of the record's content. This requires specification of the kinds of information being retrieved from the documents as well as some type of data collection instrument. An advantage of document reviews is their easy access and not having to schedule or arrange data collection with a number of different individuals. Data collection proceeds primarily on the researcher's schedule. Disadvantages include missing or incomplete documents as well as being limited to the types of information already contained in the documents. Often, information directly related to your study are not included in the documents being reviewed. In a way, the content of the documents often dictates the focus of the data collection rather than the study's purpose guiding the data collection.

Sampling

Most applied research studies use some sort of sampling to select participants for the evaluation. Sampling is used when the population being studied is too large, or it is not feasible to collect data from the entire population due to geographic distance, funding, or other factors. Sampling is a process of selecting participants from a target population.

The type of sampling you use depends upon the purpose of your study. There are two main types of samples—probability and nonprobability.

All probability samples use random sampling. Random sampling ensures that everyone on your population list has an equal chance (probability) of being selected for the study. The opposite holds for nonprobability sampling approaches. The study participants are selected based upon the researcher's sample selection capabilities and not on a fixed selection process.

PROBABILITY SAMPLES

Information on the different types of probability samples can be found in any basic social work research textbook. In this chapter, we are focusing on the two types of probability samples that are often used in program evaluations—simple random samples and systematic sampling.

"Simple random sampling" gives every single member of a population a random chance of being selected. Each individual in the population has the same probability of being chosen to be a part of a sample. If you have a relatively small population from which you are selecting a sample, from you can put all the names in a hat and pull out however many you want for your sample. A table of random numbers can also be used to select a simple random sample. Number your population, chose a random starting point on the table of random numbers and then all the following numbers in the table that are within the number range of your population list are selected until you reach your desired sample size.

"Systematic sampling" is a type of random sampling where every nth member from a population is selected into the sample. To conduct a systematic sample, you first need to determine the sampling interval. This is done by dividing the number in the population being sampled by your identified sample size. For example, if your population totaled 500 and you wanted a sample of 100, then your sampling interval would be 5 (500/100 = 5). You would then randomly select a starting point between 1 and 5 and then select every fifth person for your sample.

> **Reflection Questions**
> 1. How might you compile a list of former or current clients from which to draw a random sample?
> 2. How would you draw a probability sample of former or current clients?

The major advantage of probability sampling is that it gives you the best chance to create a sample that is representative of your study population. It eliminates the chance of bias entering into the selection process and increases the chances that you can generalize your study finding to the study population. The primary obstacle to using probability samples is being able to list and identify your study population. Often doing so is not feasible, given the nature of and resources available for applied research studies and program evaluations.

NONPROBABILITY SAMPLES

Information on the different types of nonprobability samples can be found in any basic social work research textbook. Three types of nonprobability sampling are covered in this chapter—convenience, purposive, and snowball. Nonprobability sampling is often used when there is limited information of the research topic and the goal of the study is to generate hypotheses for future research. Nonprobability samples are also used in qualitative and/or exploratory research as well as when budget and time constraints limit the use of probability sampling.

"Convenience sampling" is a sampling method that relies on data collection from population members who are conveniently available to participate in the study. The sample is selected at the convenience of the researcher. An example of convenience sampling is when a researcher evaluating a teen program visits the program and asks the teens in attendance that day to participate in the program evaluation. The main criteria for selection are a willingness to participate in the study and being at the program that day. The advantage of convenience sampling is that the cost and time required to obtain a study sample are small compared to using a probability sampling technique. This enables you to achieve the sample size you want in a relatively fast and inexpensive way. The major disadvantages are possible bias in the selection process and lack of representativeness.

"Purposive sampling" is when the sample is chosen only on the basis of the researcher's knowledge and judgment. The researcher carefully selects each individual for inclusion in the study sample. The selection is based upon the researcher's knowledge of the purpose of the study and the desired qualities of the study participants. The researcher in the teen program example might use purposive sampling to include only those teens who are consistent and frequent participants in the teen program. Teens who participate only occasionally would not be asked to participate in the program evaluation. The major advantage of purposive sampling is obtaining a sample of participants that fit the purpose and characteristics of the population being studied. The disadvantages are the same as those for convenience sampling.

"Snowball sampling" is used when it is difficult to identify potential participants or when the topic of investigation is very sensitive and not openly discussed. Snowball sampling uses existing sample members to identify and recruit other participants. The researcher uses existing study participant's networks to identify additional study participants. In the teen program example, the research might want a sample of teens who are homeless and living on the street. To do so, the researcher would begin with homeless teens who attend the teen program and then ask each to identify other homeless teens for participation in the study. The major advantage of snowball sampling is the ability to obtain a sample of hard-to-reach participants. The disadvantages are the same as with other nonprobability samples.

■ Quantitative Data Collection

LEVELS OF MEASUREMENT

In quantitative research, there are four levels of measurement—nominal, ordinal, interval, and ratio. Understanding the level of measurement of your variable is important because the level of measurement dictates the types of statistical methods that can be used to analyze your data. Level of measurement does not pertain to qualitative research studies that do not have quantitative data.

"Nominal" measures use numbers or letters to classify the data. The assigned number or letter values name the attribute. There is no ordering or ranking of the values. For example, a person's gender might be classified as (a) male, (b) female, or (c) transsexual. The values are just classifications or descriptions of the various categories.

"Ordinal" measures rank the order of the variable's attributes. There is an order from low to high among the values. The distance between the different values of an ordinal measure is not relevant or assumed to be equal. An example of an ordinal measure is the level of education with the following values: (a) less than high school, (b) some high school, (c) completed high school, (d) some college, (e) completed college, and (f) postcollege. The level of education is a ranking going from less than high school to postcollege. However, the interval between the values is not interpretable.

The "interval" level of measurement classifies, orders the values, and specifies that the distances between each interval on the scale are equal. Interval measures do not have an absolute value of zero. A person's age is an example of an interval-level measure. The interval difference between someone aged 1 and 2 years is equal to the interval distance between someone aged 30 and 31 years. Age also does not have a value of zero.

Reflection Questions
1. Why use the highest level of measurement available in your quantitative evaluation study?
2. What are the limitations of using only categorical level variables?

"Ratio"-level measures are the same as interval-level measures, except that they have an absolute value of zero. An example of a ratio-level measure would be the number of clients seen during the past 6 months. An absolute zero is possible, and the values are ordered with equal distances between intervals.

TYPES OF VARIABLES

In quantitative research studies, there are three major types of variables: independent, dependent, and control variables. These types of variables are not relevant in qualitative research studies.

"Independent" variables in applied research studies are the treatment variable or the variable that can be manipulated. "Dependent" variables are the outcome variables. They represent the outcome of the intervention. For example, in evaluating the teen program, an independent variable could be the weekly support group and a dependent variable could be increased self-esteem. "Control" variables are those that are held constant while examining the effect the independent variable has on the dependent. Entering a control variable into the statistical analysis allows the researcher to examine the effect that the independent variable has on the dependent variable while removing the influence that a third (control) variable has on the relationship. For example, in the teen program evaluation, the effect the support group has on self-esteem might be influenced by the participants' housing status. Thus, the influence of housing on the relationship between support group and self-esteem would be statistically removed.

MEASUREMENT GUIDELINES

Every effort should be made to use the best measures available. According to Berlin and Marsh (1993), four criteria are useful in judging the adequacy of different measures: relevance, sensitivity to change, reliability, and validity.

Relevance

"Relevance" refers to the extent the measure is directly related to the targeted outcomes. Is there a good fit between the measure and the expected changes? The relevance of any measure is a function of the identified target problem or the specific change objectives. Make sure the measure you choose matches what the client hopes to change.

Sensitivity

"Sensitivity to change" is the second criterion of a good measure. Not all measures are capable of capturing change. Some are more sensitive than others. It may be possible to use measures that have shown change in previous evaluations and have thus been proved useful. A measure's track record of detecting change is one of the best indicators of its sensitivity to change (Bloom et al., 2009). Often, however, information on a measure's sensitivity is not available; thus, it is not always possible to know in advance whether a measure will be sensitive to change. Berlin and Marsh (1993) suggest that global measures are usually less sensitive to change than measures directly related to specific behaviors targeted for change. Measures of behaviors that occur more frequently are more likely to be more sensitive than measures of behaviors that occur less frequently. High-frequency behaviors are more responsive to small changes, while low-frequency behaviors may respond only to major changes (Bloom et al., 2009).

Reliability

"Reliability" refers to the consistency of measurements. When measuring client change, you want to be reasonably confident that the differences among the first measurement and subsequent ones relate to changes in the client and not to problems with the measure. An instrument that can do this is said to be "reliable." "Every type of measure involves some kind of error, and the measure is reliable to the extent that the error is minimal" (Berlin & Marsh, 1993, p. 97). The two most common ways of testing the reliability of a measure are to assess its internal consistency and test–retest characteristics. "Internal consistency reliability" is the extent to which the individual items that make up a scale or index are correlated with one another. "Test–retest reliability" refers to the extent to which the same result is obtained when the same measure is administered to the same client at two different points in time. Both types of reliability are important. However, in evaluating client change, test–retest reliability is critical. To the extent possible, use measures that have been tested for reliability and have reliability coefficients of .80 or higher (Poulin, 2010). A commonly used statistic here is known as "Cronbach's alpha."

Validity

"Validity" refers to the extent to which an instrument measures what it is supposed to measure and not anything else (Royse et al., 2016). For example, if you are assessing a client's self-confidence, the instrument should measure self-confidence, not a related concept such as self-esteem. Because concepts in social work tend to be complex, no measure will be entirely valid, only more or less so (Royse et al., 2016).

There are various ways to determine the validity of an instrument. The least rigorous kind of validity is "face validity." Does the instrument appear to measure the concept? A measure is said to have face validity if knowledgeable persons agree that it measures what it is intended to measure (Poulin, 2010).

Another type of validity is "content validity." This method also relies on expert opinion. In this case, experts are asked to review the concept to see if the entire range of the concept is represented in the items included in the scale (Royse et al., 2016). For example, a scale designed to measure stress should have items that represent the different components of stress, such as feeling tense, feeling pressured, having difficulty sleeping, and being short tempered.

Neither content nor face validity empirically demonstrate a scale's validity. This can be done in a number of ways.

A scale's concurrent validity is demonstrated by comparing its results with another scale that has previously been determined (proven) to have validity when administered to the same group of subjects (Royse et al., 2016). If the two scales are highly correlated, at .80 or above, the new scale has demonstrated concurrent validity.

"Construct validity" refers to the extent to which an instrument actually measures the concept in question. Construct validity is established by demonstrating convergent validity and discriminant validity. A measure is said to have "convergent validity" if it is correlated in a predicted manner with other measures with which it theoretically should correlate (Bloom et al., 2009). For example, a measure of the strength of a helping relationship should correlate positively with measures of trust and openness. Those who are more trusting and open are more likely to develop strong, helping relationships with their social workers than those who are less trusting and open.

> **Reflection Questions**
> 1. Why is validity an important concept in applied research studies?
> 2. What are the implications of using measures in a program evaluation that have low reliability?

A measure's "discriminant validity" is demonstrated by a lack of correlation with measures with which it theoretically should not be correlated. This indicates that the measure can discriminate between concepts. For example, there is no theoretical basis for predicting how certain client problems will correlate with the development of a helping relationship with the social worker. Clients with high self-esteem are as likely to develop a strong helping relationship as those with low self-esteem. Similarly, a client's level of depression is not associated with the strength of the helping relationship (Poulin, 2010).

Construct validity is demonstrated when a measure is correlated with other measures with which it theoretically should be related (convergent validity) and not correlated with measures with which it theoretically should not be correlated (discriminant validity). When selecting measures to evaluate client change, look for some evidence of the validity of the measure. At the very least, the measure should have face validity. Empirical verification of the measure's validity is preferable.

TYPES OF MEASURES

There are a number of measurement methods appropriate for social work practice evaluations that are easy to construct and implement. The more frequently used measurement tools are:

- Client logs
- Behavioral observations
- Rating scales
- Standardized measures

Electronic copies of the scales and forms described in the subsequent sections can be found on the Springer Publishing Company's Student Toolbox webpages at http://springerpub.com/capstone

Participant Logs

Having clients prepare narrative accounts of their activities, thoughts, and feelings is an effective method of monitoring progress. "Participant logs" or journals can help clarify a person's experiences and circumstances that contribute to a problem situation. It enables participants to "track the antecedents and consequences, or the feelings and thoughts, surrounding the occurrence of a specific event" (Berlin & Marsh, 1993, p. 99). Logs allow a research participant to systematically take notes on the occurrence of a target problem and the events surrounding each occurrence. Doing so prevents distortions and misperceptions caused by faulty memory (Bloom et al., 2009).

Logs are easy to construct. Most are divided into columns, with the types of information the participant should record listed at the top of each column. The columns should record the incident or behavior, when it occurred, and how the client responded to it (Bloom et al., 2009). Information on circumstances just prior to and just after the problem event may also be included in logs.

Two decisions need to be made regarding the completion of logs. The first is when to record the information, and the second is what to record. Participants can record at preset time periods or immediately following the occurrence of the target event. Recording at preset time periods works if you have narrowed down the occurrence of a target event to a specific period, that is, if you know in advance approximately when the target problem is likely to occur. For example, a family might complain about sibling fights after school and during dinner. The log then might cover the time period of 3:00 p.m. to 7:00 p.m. in the evening. The person keeping the log would record all the sibling fights that occurred during this time period.

TABLE 4.2 SAMPLE CLIENT LOG

CLIENT LOG				
DATE & TIME	EVENT (THOUGHTS, FEELINGS, OR BEHAVIOR)	CIRCUMSTANCES BEFORE EVENT	CIRCUMSTANCES AFTER EVENT	REFLECTION ON EVENT

The second option is to use open-time categories. This method is sometimes referred to as "critical incident recording" (Bloom et al., 2009). With this type of log, the participant decides whether to record an event. They decide if the event is related to the problem or target and then record it as soon as possible after it occurs. This method works best when you need information about events that are likely to be spread out over the entire day.

In addition to specifying when the recording will take place, you also need to clarify in advance what will be recorded. By design, logs give the participant control over the content. Clients choose which of the many thoughts, feelings, and behaviors they experience daily to include and exclude. Information recorded on the log should be limited to what the person believes is important (Bloom et al., 2009). Thus, you need to be clear about what constitutes a recordable incident. Clarify the types of events that would be appropriate for inclusion in the log. Table 4.2 shows a sample log.

Behavioral Observations

"Behavioral observations" are direct observations of participant behavior (Jordan & Franklin, 2015). The frequency and duration of the specific behaviors can be observed and recorded (Bloom et al., 2009). Behavioral observation can provide detailed information on the occurrence of behaviors and the context of those behaviors. It represents one of the most reliable and valid methods of measuring participant change.

Typically, the first step in using behavioral observation is to operationally define the target behavior. An example would be specifying the types of disruptive behavior a child displays in the classroom, such as getting out of their seat or talking with classmates while the teacher is talking. The target problem must be clearly defined in behavioral terms and must be observable. Observation cannot be used to measure target problems that focus on feelings or thoughts. It is limited to measuring the frequency, duration, and context of behaviors.

The second step is to select the observer or observers. Often, the observers are significant others, family members, or other professionals who have access to the client's person-in-environment interactions. For example, a young child having a problem controlling their temper can be observed at home by a parent and at school by a teacher or teacher's aide.

The third step is to train the observers. Observers must know in advance exactly what behavior to look for and how to recognize the behavior when it occurs (Jordan & Franklin, 2015). In addition, they have to be trained to conduct the observations. You must decide whether to record all instances of the behavior or a sample. Continuous recording involves recording every occurrence of a target behavior every time it occurs (Bloom et al., 2009). A simple form can be created that includes at a minimum the date, time, location, and brief description of the behavior. The continuous recording approach requires the observer to be willing and available, and it works best when the target behavior does not occur with great frequency. Often, these conditions cannot be satisfied, and a sampling strategy is used (Poulin & Matis, 2020).

Time sampling is appropriate when events occur continuously or frequently. "Time sampling requires the selection of specific units of time, either intervals or discrete points, during which the occurrence or nonoccurrence of a specific behavior is recorded" (Berlin & Marsh, 1993, p. 107). The assumption is that the sample behavior would be the same if all occurrences of it were recorded (Haynes, 1978). There are two types of time sampling: interval and discrete. "Interval sampling" involves selecting a time period and dividing it into equal blocks of time. The observer records the occurrence or nonoccurrence of the behavior during each interval. The behavior is recorded once for each interval, regardless of how many times it occurs (Bloom et al., 2009).

Reflection Questions
1. How might you incorporate a client log into an evaluation of your program?
2. How could you incorporate behavioral observation?

"Discrete time sampling" involves selecting specific time periods and recording all instances of the target behavior that occur during the selected periods. The key issue in this type of recording is to select periods that are representative in terms of the target behavior. If the behaviors occur often and regularly, you would need fewer periods to obtain a representative sample of them (Bloom et al., 2009). If the behaviors occur during certain time periods, for example, during meals, then the selected periods must correspond to the behavioral patterns of the participant. Exhibit 4.1 is a sample behavioral observation form.

EXHIBIT 4.1

SAMPLE BEHAVIORAL OBSERVATION FORM

Client's Name _____ Recorder's Name _____

Target Behavior _____

Location _____

_____

Date and
Time _____ Description of Behavior and Context _____

_____

Rating Scales

"Individualized rating scales" are measures of client problems that are created by the researcher. These types of measures are also referred to as "self-anchored rating scales" (Jordan & Franklin, 2015). The major advantage of an individualized rating scale is that it measures the specific problem or concern that you want to measure. Thus, a rating scale is directly linked to the feeling, thought, or event that is being evaluated.

The low, middle, and high points of the scale are labeled with short, succinct terms. The labels (anchors) describe what the numbers represent (e.g., behaviors, thoughts, and feelings that the participant would experience at various points along the scale). It represents their perceptions and experiences.

Individualized rating scales usually have 5 to 10 points. Scales having more than 10 points are difficult for participants to score and are, therefore, not recommended (Bloom et al., 2009). For example, if a self-esteem scale had 1 to 100 points, it would be very difficult to determine the difference between ratings of 70 and 75. Scales with seven points are considered ideal (Jordan & Franklin, 2015). An example of an individualized rating scale is given in Exhibit 4.2.

Individualized rating scales are easy to construct. A wide range of characteristics of the target can be rated (Bloom et al., 2009). It is important for the target to be clearly articulated and for each rating scale to measure only one aspect or dimension of the target (Gingerich, 1979). Bloom et al. (2009) warn against using different dimensions at each end of the scale, such as "happy" at one end and "sad" at the other. People often experience contradictory feelings and can feel happy and sad at the same time. It is preferable to develop two measures, a sadness scale and a happiness scale, rather than one scale on which both dimensions are rated. They also recommend that the target and its measurement be worded positively, something the participants want to achieve and not just eliminate (Bloom et al., 2009). For example, if the problem is feelings of sadness, the goal might be to increase feelings of happiness, and the rating scale would measure the level of happiness.

The next step is to decide on the number of scale points and develop anchor descriptions for the two end points and possibly the middle point. Scales with seven or nine points are popular because they have a clear midpoint. The numbers on the scale represent gradations for the target problem from low to high. The higher the score, the more

EXHIBIT 4.2

SAMPLE INDIVIDUALIZED RATING SCALE

Comfort in social situations						
1	2	3	4	5	6	7
Terrified, overwhelmed, completely unable to engage in conversation with strangers		Somewhat anxious, yet able to respond when spoken to			Relaxed, confident, able to initiate conversations with strangers	

EXHIBIT 4.3

SAMPLE GENERAL RATING SCALES

Amount of anxiety						
1	2	3	4	5	6	7
Little or no anxiety		Moderate anxiety			Extreme anxiety	
Frequency of feeling lonely						
1	2	3	4	5	6	7
Never		Sometimes			All the time	

frequent, serious, important, or problematic the target problem. These anchor descriptions define the meaning of the numbers on the rating scale. Anchors should describe the behaviors, thoughts, or feelings the participant would experience along the continuum of the scale (Bloom et al., 2009).

An alternative to individually constructed anchors is general anchor descriptions. Rating scales with general anchors can be used for different target problems. For example, a general rating scale that measures feelings of connectedness could be used to measure a participant's relationships with each member of their family. The disadvantage of general anchors is that they are more ambiguous and less precise than individually tailored anchors (Coulton & Solomon, 1977). Exhibit 4.3 provides two general rating scales.

Individualized and general rating scales are excellent tools for measuring client progress and change on identified target problems. There is some evidence that the validity of single-item rating scales is comparable to that of standardized measures (Nugent, 1992). However, the internal consistency reliability of individualized rating scales cannot be established because they are single-item scales. Rating scales do, however, have a high level of applicability and are excellent tools for measuring target problems and assessing participant progress.

Standardized Measures

"Standardized measures" are instruments developed following empirical scale construction techniques with uniform administration and scoring procedures (Jordan & Franklin, 2015). Their reliability is known, and their validity has usually been empirically tested.

Standardized measures are available for a wide range of client behaviors, including marital satisfaction, self-esteem, anxiety, and family relations. Some standardized measures assess global behaviors, such as generalized contentment, while others assess specific behaviors and problems, such as fear, depression, or sexual satisfaction. Standardized measures are available in rapid assessment formats with up to 25 scale items, as well as in lengthy, comprehensive formats with hundreds of scale items. Rapid assessment instruments are easy to use and to incorporate into practice evaluation studies.

There are numerous sources of standardized measures. *Measures for Clinical Practice* by Corcoran and Fischer (2013) is an excellent two-volume collection of rapid assessment instruments. Volume 1 contains measures for use with couples, families, and children, and Volume 2 contains instruments for individual adults. The two-volume set contains more than 300 different brief assessment instruments, with supporting information on each instrument's purpose, scoring, reliability, and validity. Another great source of rapid assessment instruments is *Measures of Personality and Social Psychological Attitudes* (Robinson et al., 1991) that organizes the measures by clinical topic (e.g., self-esteem, depression, anxiety).

A useful list of commercially available measures can be found in *Clinical Assessment for Social Workers* by Jordan and Franklin (2015). The WALMYR Publishing Company is also an excellent source for commercially available measurement instruments designed specifically for use in social work practice. WALMYR sells a number of individual and family adjustment scales as well as comprehensive multidimensional assessment instruments. Many library databases also specialize in measures like this. You may have access through your library, and many are free.

Standardized measures, especially the rapid assessment variety, are well suited for use in applied research studies. If you can locate measures that closely correspond to the identified target problem, they offer several advantages, including having known reliability and validity, not requiring extensive training, and ease of administration and scoring (Corcoran & Fischer, 2013).

Qualitative Data Collection

Data collection is very different for qualitative studies. It is more of a process of getting the participants to tell their story using language. The data are the participants' narratives on the topic being studied. Obtaining the data is accomplished by asking open-ended questions and then getting the study participant to elaborate on their responses. Thus, data collection for qualitative evaluations is basically a process using interpersonal skills similar to a social work interview. The typical format for qualitative studies is semistructured personal interviews. The researcher develops a set of topics/questions related to the study purpose and conducts a personal interview with the study participants. The following reviews basic interviewing skills used to help study participants tell their stories and provide in-depth responses to the interview questions.

OPEN-ENDED QUESTIONS

There are basically two types of questions: those with predefined responses and those without predefined responses. The former is usually referred to as "closed-ended questions." They do not encourage a detailed and elaborate response and generally

Reflection Questions
1. What three open-ended questions would you include in a qualitative evaluation of your program?
2. Are you more inclined to do a quantitative or a qualitative program evaluation? Why?

should be avoided. An example of a closed-ended question is, "Do you get along well with the other kids at school?" An appropriate response would be either "yes" or "no." This is the only answer called for. Not much information is obtained from this type of question (Poulin, 2010).

Alternatively, one should ask open-ended questions that elicit more information from the study participant. For example, the researcher could ask, "How do you get along with the other kids at school?" This cannot be answered with just a yes or no response. The participant has to formulate a more detailed or elaborate response to answer the question. Although the questions are similar, the open-ended one encourages elaboration, whereas the closed-ended one does not.

Open-ended questions are a simple and easy way to get study participants to tell their stories. They give participants opportunities to tell their stories in more depth than do closed-ended questions (Kadushin & Kadushin, 2013).

MINIMAL PROMPTS

As the term implies, "minimal prompts" are brief nonverbal or verbal indications of encouragement. "Nonverbal" minimal prompts include nodding the head, using facial expressions, or employing gestures that convey receptivity, interest, and commitment to understanding (Hepworth et al., 2017). These nonverbal prompts can be very effective in encouraging elaboration. They communicate in an attentive and nonintrusive way that you would like the participant to tell you more and that you are interested in hearing their story.

"Verbal" minimal prompts are brief utterances such as "Mm-mmm" or "Ah-ha" or other short phrases such as "Tell me more" or "I see." As with the nonverbal prompts, the verbal ones encourage the participant to go on without interrupting or asking a series of questions.

Another type of minimal prompt is an "accent response" in which the worker repeats a client's word or short phrase in the form of a question. The word or phrase selected should be the core component of the client's message. For example, if the participant says, "I just hate all the kids at school," the researcher might say "Hate?" or "The kids?" to prompt them to give more information about their feelings about the kids at school. Accent responses are easy to use, do not interrupt the flow of communication, and are very effective in getting participants to explore their feelings and concerns in depth (Poulin, 2010).

SEEKING CONCRETENESS

It is common for people to express their feelings and describe their experiences in vague, general terms. Hepworth et al. (2017) point out that communicating one's feelings and experiences requires specificity. They call the process "seeking concreteness"; others refer to it as "clarification" (Cormier & Cormier, 1991) or moving from the general to the specific (Shulman, 2009).

Often, people begin their stories in general terms because they have never put their feelings and experiences into words. They need help in exploring their feelings and experiences. Asking for specifics helps participants articulate their stories.

Seeking concreteness is easy to do. The key is to recognize and respond to vague and overly general comments. For example, a community member might say, "The neighborhood is falling apart. It is just not the same anymore." This is a fairly vague statement. At this point, one does not know what is causing the frustration. The researcher could seek more concrete information by asking an open-ended follow-up question, such as, "How has it changed?", or by "What do you mean by falling apart?" Both responses invite the participant to elaborate on their concerns (Poulin, 2010).

SUMMARIZING

"Summarizing" is a basic interviewing skill that is often used to highlight key points in a conversation with a client. When used this way, summarizing can help the participant and researcher make the transition to a different topic. Summarizing, however, can also be used as an elaboration technique. This entails making connections between relevant aspects of a participant's story (Hepworth et al., 2017). Summarizing can help participants explore in-depth feelings and experiences that they might not recognize as being connected.

Summarizing is a more difficult skill to use than the other elaborating skills discussed earlier. It is a filtering and feedback process. It requires the ability to identify the key components of the story, pull them together, and repeat them back to the client in a combination statement–question form. The statement–question form prevents the researcher from taking the position of knowing or presuming to know that the different points are connected for the participant.

EXPLORING SILENCES

Shulman (2009) calls this skill "reaching into silences" and describes it as attempting to explore the meaning of the silence. The challenge with silences is that it is hard to know exactly what the participant is saying (Shulman, 2009). They might be processing a thought, struggling with powerful emotions, feeling bored, or any number of things. People are often uncomfortable with silence and rush in to fill it up. Doing so ensures that the meaning of the silence will be lost as the researcher moves on to something else. The silence needs to be actively explored. A clue to its meaning is the interviewer's own feelings (Shulman, 2009). Understanding one's own feelings at a particular moment helps one to make an educated guess about the meaning of the participant's silence. Shulman's phrase "reach inside of silences" suggests that you should actively explore the meaning of the silence.

The first strategy for dealing with silence is containment. Give the individual some time, and stay with the silence. A simple probing question, such as, "You are quiet right now. What's going on?," is often sufficient to get the person to open up. You have acknowledged the silence and encouraged them to elaborate. If your feelings suggest that the participant is feeling *(hurt),* then you could ask an open-ended question, such as, "Are you struggling with the *(hurt)* you feel?" Even if you are off base, there is little harm done. The person can correct the misperception. Either way, the silence has been acknowledged and its meaning explored. Rather than feeling uncomfortable during periods of silence, view them as opportunities to better understand your participant and their story (Poulin, 2010).

FOCUSED LISTENING

"Focused listening" (Shulman, 2009) or "active listening" (Chang & Scott, 1999) is the process of concentrating on a specific part of the interviewee's message. The researcher tries to identify the primary themes in their story and be sensitive to clues they may give regarding the underlying feeling content of the message. The researcher also tries to understand what the message means to the person (Chang & Scott, 1999). What are they really saying, and what meaning does it have for them?

Focused listening requires the interviewer to tune in to the meaning behind the participant's words. This involves listening to the words, nonverbal communication, and affect as well as what is not being said. Listening and understanding the interviewee's message is the first component of empathy. The second component is communicating your understanding back to the person. Doing so encourages further elaboration (Poulin, 2010).

REFLECTIVE EMPATHY

Conveying empathy and understanding is vital to the interview process. Participants need to feel understood. Those who feel that they are not understood are unlikely to share personal thoughts and feelings. Why risk vulnerability with someone who does not understand you? The ability to respond empathetically is a critical interviewing skill, particularly when one has to overcome mistrust and reluctance.

In its simplest form, empathic responding is "reflecting" back a person's message. At this level, the empathic response accurately captures the factual content and feelings expressed by the individual. The response communicates an equivalent message. Reflective empathy is more effective if you paraphrase the participant's words rather than just "parrot back" the same words.

The use of empathetic responding is vital to the development of trust and open communication. We recommend responding empathetically whenever your interviewee is dealing with or expressing affective content. If there is an emotional component in the message, either on the surface or below it, an empathic response is needed (Poulin, 2010).

PRACTICE EXERCISES

1. Identify potential data sources for an evaluation of a program or service provided by your field placement agency. For each data source, list likely challenges you would encounter in using the data source for your capstone project.
2. Develop probability and nonprobability sampling plans for one of the data sources identified earlier. Identify any potential obstacles you would encounter in implementing your sampling plans.
3. Identify an independent, dependent, and at least two control variables for an evaluation of a program or service provided by your field placement agency. Specify how each variable will be measured and indicate the level of measurement for each variable.

TECHNOLOGY EXERCISES

1. Using the internet, research a secondary data source that has information relevant to a program or service provided by your field placement agency. List the variables in the data set that could be used in an evaluation of the agency program or service.
2. Research and identify a standardized measure that could be used as the dependent variable for an evaluation of the agency program or service identified earlier. Describe the reliability and validity of the standardized measure as well as its appropriateness for the evaluation.

REFERENCES

Berlin, S., & Marsh, J. (1993). *Informing practice decisions*. Macmillan.

Bloom, M., Fischer, J., & Orme, J. (2009). *Evaluating practice: Guidelines for the accountable professional* (6th ed.). Pearson.

Chang, V. N., & Scott, S. T. (1999). *Basic interviewing skills: A workbook for practitioners*. Nelson-Hall.

Corcoran, K., & Fischer, J. (2013). *Measures for clinical practice: A sourcebook* (Vols. 1 and 2, 5th ed.). Oxford University Press.

Cormier, W., & Cormier, S. (1991). *Interviewing strategies for helpers* (3rd ed.). Brooks/Cole.

Coulton, C. J., & Solomon, P. L. (1977). Measuring outcomes of intervention. *Social Work Research and Abstracts, 13*, 3–9. https://doi.org/10.1093/swra/13.4.3

Gingerich, W. (1979). Procedure for evaluating clinical practice. *Health and Social Work, 4*, 104–130. https://doi.org/10.1093/hsw/4.2.104

Haynes, S. N. (1978). *Principles of behavioral assessment*. Gardner.

Hepworth, D. H., Rooney, R., Rooney, G. D., & Strom-Gottfried, K. (2017). *Direct social work practice: Theory and skills* (10th ed.). Cengage Learning.

Jordan, C., & Franklin, C. (2015). *Clinical assessment for social workers: Quantitative and qualitative methods* (4th ed.). Oxford University Press.

Kadushin, A., & Kadushin, G. (2013). *The social work interview* (5th ed.). Columbia University Press.

Nugent, W. R. (1992). Psychometric characteristics of self-anchored scales in clinical application. *Journal of Social Service Research, 3*, 137–152. https://doi.org/10.1300/J079v15n03_08

Poulin, J. (2010). *Strengths-based generalist practice: A collaborative approach* (3rd ed.). Cengage Learning.

Poulin, J., Kauffman, S., & Barnett, M. (2020). Mezzosystems assessment: Organizations and communities. In J. Poulin & S. Matis (Eds.), *Social work practice: A competency based approach* (pp. 281–316). Springer Publishing Company.

Poulin, J., & Matis, S. (2020). *Social work practice: A competency based approach*. Springer Publishing Company.

Robinson, J. P., Shaver, P., & Wrightsman, L. S. (1991). *Measures of personality and social psychological attitudes*. Academic Press.

Royse, D., Thyer, B. A., & Padgett, D. K. (2016). *Program evaluation: An introduction to an evidence-based approach* (6th ed.). Cengage Learning.

Shulman, L. (2009). *The skills of helping individuals, families, groups and organizations* (6th ed.). Cengage Learning.

U.S. Agency for International Development Center for Development Information and Evaluation. (1996). *Performance monitoring & evaluation TIPS: Conducting key informant interviews*. Author. http://pdf.usaid.gov/pdf_docs/PNABS541.pdf

II

APPLIED RESEARCH DESIGNS

5

PROGRAM EVALUATIONS: POLICIES, PROCESS, AND OUTCOME ASSESSMENTS

This chapter discusses the evaluation of existing policies and programs. This begins a definitional distinction between policies, programs, and services. Then, the discussion of their similarities and differences follows. The unique concerns of policy analysis, program evaluation, and the types of program evaluation are provided. In addition, the methodologies, strengths, and weaknesses for each kind of an evaluation are examined.

By the end of this chapter, you will be able to do the following:

- Identify the difference between the policy, the program, and the service.
- Identify the purposes and common components of each research target.
- Learn to read and write logic models and goals and objectives.
- Describe the difference between formative and summative program evaluations.
- Describe and apply the methods of evaluation.
- Describe the limits of each method.

■ Evaluation of Programs and Policies

The evaluation of programs and policies allows the researcher to understand the choices and consequences or worth, merit, or significance of such programs and policies (Scriven, 1998) as well as uanswer critical questions about what a society views as important. It can also provide critical understanding about what kind of problem approaches work, do not work, and why.

Policy or program evaluations provide opportunities for sophisticated research. There are literally thousands of social service organizations in the United States, and each of these organizations often run multiple programs. Policies as well make for a good target. Governments create not only policy but also agencies and organizations.

POLICIES, PROGRAMS, AND SERVICES DEFINED

"Policies" refer to intentional statements of purpose or rules and guidelines that govern or define how an organization operates (Centers for Disease Control and Prevention [CDC], 2015). Governments, whether federal, state, or local, and all organizations have policies. These entities create and follow rules. These rules can be large and all encompassing, or they can be very limited in focus. For example, some organizations have extensive policies around trauma-informed services. Many other agencies have no policies around such things.

Policies can come from governmental action, legislative action, executive orders, judicial decisions, or administrative choices as a response to a problem. They can also come from non-governmental sources (University of Kansas, 2015a, 2015b). This is actually similar to non-governmental organizations as well. Think about your own agency. Its rules were established when the organization was founded, or through changes by boards of directors or the administration over time.

> **Reflection Questions**
> 1. What policy issues are important to you? Why?
> 2. Pick any policy of interest. Think about *why* that approach is used to address the social problem. What other alternatives might be appropriate and effective? Why?

"Programs" are typically the structures that carry out policy. They are discreet activities, services, or sets of services, typically focused on implementing a specific goal or goals established by a policy. Often, they have a specific funding source. They may also have specific or unique administrative staff and dedicated service providers. Broadly defined, they are any set of organized activities supported by a set of resources to achieve a specific and intended result (Scriven, 1998). Programs may include things such as direct service interventions, community mobilization efforts, research initiatives, advocacy work, and training programs and other kinds of service intentions (CDC, 2012).

"Services" are the discrete actions or activities created by programs to carry out the intentions of the program. Many of the activities that you actually do in your field placement, for example, are service implementations. Services can also exist as a service sets. This is common. It means that although many social service agencies provide at least one service, to implement at least one program, created by at least one social policy, there are often many crosscutting possibilities.

> **Reflection Questions**
> 1. In your field placement, identify one policy, one program, and one service that is offered. What, if anything, does each need to more effectively serve your clients?
> 2. Talk to staff in the agency. Why did the agency choose to implement the program and service identified earlier? What factors affected the decision?

Purposes

Evaluation research can serve many purposes (Patton, 1987), including:

- *To describe* the policy, program, or service. The most common of such research is describing what the policy, program, or services actually do. Also very common is describing and keeping a record of the implementation of the policy, program, or service. Such research will give you a record of "what happened"

- *To monitor* the implementation of policy, program, or service, so that you can identify problems, give feedback to the implementing organization, and apply "fixes" if need be
- *To understand or identify* the reason or the reasons why a policy, program, or service was chosen
- *To understand or identify* the reason or the reasons a policy, program, or service was or was not successful
- *To determine whether the project met its purposes or objectives* (in program evaluations, this is called an "outcome evaluation") and is probably the most common type
- *To identify longer term consequences* (often called "impact evaluations")
- *To determine the cost-effectiveness and cost–benefit analyses and meta-analyses* (which integrate outcomes from multiple studies to determine an overall judgment or summary conclusion about a particular research or evaluation question)
- *To mobilize or empower* by understanding and informing others what a policy or program does or does not do
- *A mixture of these*

COMMONALITIES AND DIFFERENCES OF RESEARCHING POLICY, PROGRAMS, AND SERVICES

The purposes identified suggest that evaluation research attempts to describe, understand, and improve policies and programs. Some aspects of research are similar. For example, the service population of each may be formally defined in advance of your research. Further, the methodologies are generally similar. Yet, important differences between policy and program analysis have been identified as well. The CDC (2012) lists these differences as follows:

- The target of policy analysis is a larger system, while programs typically target organizations of specific programs.
- The degree of control and "boundaries" are more complex with policy analysis.
- Comparison groups may be more difficult to establish with policy.
- The scale and scope of data collection may be greater with policy.
- Policy data sources may be more complex.
- The type and number of persons involved may vary.

Policy Evaluation

The intention of analyzing policy may be multidimensional, but one definition captures the process. Policy evaluation applies evaluation principles and methods to examine the content, implementation, or impact of a policy. Evaluation is the activity through which we develop an understanding of the merit, worth, and utility of a policy (CDC, 2012; Scriven, 1998). For a research project such as what you are developing, this opens many possibilities.

Indeed, the different possible purposes of analysis mean that your research allows for different kinds of questions that may be studied. The World Health Organization identified a comprehensive discussion of the topic and, presents a broad range of questions as broad as, or as narrow as, the following:

- What were the intentions or purposes of the policy?
- What happened to bring about the policy? This could include the context, the events, and supportive or limiting factors.
- Who supported and who opposed the policy? What individuals, organizations, or other interests have a role supporting or opposing the policy? Why?
- What was the initial intention of the policy? Why that intention instead of something else?
- What are the descriptive elements of the policy? Whom is it supposed to serve? What is it supposed to provide? How was it provided? How was it paid for?
- Does the policy have clear expectations or goals? What are those expectations?
- Does the policy meet those expectations or goals?
- What are the impacts beyond the expectations or goals of the policy?
- Is the policy an efficient way to achieve those goals or expectations?
- What other alternatives exist?
- Is the policy adequately funded?
- Is the implementation of the policy well conducted?
- In addition, for any or all of the above questions, why or why not?
- What may be done to improve the policy? Who supports or opposes changes to the policy? (Gilson et al., 2018)

Conceptually, these questions can be asked in many ways through different lenses or frameworks. These different frameworks use different types of questions, different assumptions, and different data sources. Sometimes, the study is prospective (e.g., a cost–benefit analysis), and sometimes, it examines what is and why (Patton et al., 2016).

■ **Reflection Questions**
1. What do you think are the most important questions about a policy that should be asked? Why?
2. What makes a policy analysis feasible to do? What kinds of things might make it difficult? Why?

What makes for good analysis? In part, the answer comes again from the CDC (2012). At a minimum, they see the criteria of utility, feasibility, propriety, and accuracy as important. However, there are many different kinds of questions.

POLICY ANALYSIS FRAMEWORKS

With such a rich list of possible questions, the issue for you is what type of analysis should you do? As an overarching theme, the different questions fall into one of two "bundles." The first bundle addresses policy outputs (what the policy does or results in doing), and the second addresses more complex questions of how and/or why. For our purposes, we can list four major framework types, but within each type are many variations: descriptive analysis, historical and legislative analysis, values and concept analysis, and outcome analysis. We discuss the first three in some depth in this chapter and save the fourth for our discussion on program evaluation.

Description Frameworks

Different frameworks bring different underlying assumptions to the research. However, almost all analysis frameworks, both retrospective and prospective (Patton et al., 2016), require at least some descriptive information. For some projects, just the descriptive information may be adequate. Of course, different policy domains might require different kinds of descriptive information. Yet, there are some important similarities that cross many content domains. There are some generic types of information that are always important. These may be thought of as the who, the what, and the how of a policy. As a useful framework, Terrell (2012) suggests that a good description should examine the policy's:

- Social Allocations—who gets what the policy provides?
- Social Provision—what benefit does the policy provide?
- Delivery—how are benefits provided?
- Finance—how are benefits paid for?

The CDC (2019) takes this another step and breaks down questions into Framing Questions and a series of criteria questions focusing on political, operational, budgetary, and economic impact areas of assessment.

For the most part, these questions can be answered through the formal and legal documentation on the policy. Laws, executive orders, and judicial opinions might contain much of this descriptive information. Rarely, however, does the entity that creates the policy provide all of the rules necessary to carry it out. This means that the regulatory body that writes the minutiae related to the law contains important details. A good evaluation that attempts to address such an analysis should identify either the documents that will be used to conduct the analysis or a methodology for identifying these documents. Making this a little easier is the fact that most governmental entities keep extensive records of what they produce. Much of this information is provided to the public. Many states and the federal government regularly provide libraries with copies of documents that may be of use.

Historical and Legislative Analyses

Description is sometimes adequate, but often just one component of more complex analyses. One additional possibility is historical analysis and/or legislative history. The focus here is *how* the policy came about. Two similar questions may guide your work. First, you can ask, "Why is this policy at this time?" Many social problems have long histories, yet only at certain times do we address the problem. This analysis examines the context and actions that brought about the policy action.

A good historical analysis will ask what issues drove the events to make a policy necessary or desirable? It may also question what social forces, groups, interests, or individuals came together at a particular moment in time to bring about a policy.

The legislative history examines these questions but may also include more details related to the deliberations within the policymaking entity. Understanding who and how the policy problem moves through the process can tell a lot about power and its application. Thus, a good legislative history will look at things such as who supported the law, who opposed it, who marshaled it, and for what purposes.

Your evaluation should spell out these questions, again with the data sources that you use. You may also use the personal records and correspondence of the important participants. Many important historical and political leaders keep such documents. Sometimes, libraries will keep this material in their archives. As earlier, identifying those individuals and organizations and the potential sources of such information will be useful for your research.

Values and Concept Analysis

A deeper form of analysis attempts to get at *why* a given policy alternative was selected. Policies reflect values and important social beliefs. An analysis of these ideas can tell you very much about that society. In some ways, this analysis can be the most academically useful. Indeed, values are embedded in any examination of social choice (Tong, 1986).

Terrell (2012) provides a model. This model begins with the descriptive analysis but adds a further set of questions. The model assumes that a set of values predominate in our culture. These values serve as both goals of policy and operational characteristics. Specifically, Terrell identifies these values as freedom, equality, equity, and adequacy. Thus, the purpose of such a policy analysis is to examine the degree to which these values are supported and operationalized by the policy.

Other values-based analyses may bring other assumptions. Some may look at how ideology, patriarchy, or power and oppression are manifested by a policy. Such models may look at how the policy reinforces social beliefs or how social constructions are important to the policy.

A good analysis using this framework may contain both qualitative and quantitative content. Qualitatively, the policy is assessed for evidence of the application of values or ideology in and through the policy. There are no absolute rules that determine the criteria. You will want to examine the criteria established in the literature.

Adequacy, however, may have objective criteria in pre- and postquantification of identified outcome variables. For example, you can compare levels of need or service over time. A perfect example of this is found with the Affordable Care Act (ACA). The percentage of Americans without health insurance fell from 17.8% in 2011 to 10.0% in 2016. It has risen slowly again since 2016 (Tolbert et al., 2019). These differences suggest a policy that is working.

Outcome and Effectiveness Analysis

The previous example of the ACA moves us into research into policy outcome and effectiveness. Description tells us what the policy intends. The values and concept analysis seek to understand *why* a given policy was selected. Outcome and effectiveness studies, however, hope to determine whether policies address the problem. The methods used here generally involve identifying data sets with variables that match the policy's desired outcomes. Thus, your research should seek to identify both those goals and those data sets. As the methodology used for outcome and effectiveness studies is very similar to that of summative program evaluation, we pick up the discussion of how to do such a study in the subsequent section.

Program Evaluation

CONTEXT

Programs are ubiquitous. To give some context, there are 1.6 million nonprofit organizations in the United States (Independent Sector, 2020). There are also thousands of federal, state, and local governmental organizations that operate programs. Many of these may be of interest for your research.

TYPES OF PROGRAM EVALUATION

Of all program evaluations, we focus only on two types. The first type is what is known as a "formative evaluation" which looks at the implementation of the program. The second type is what is known as a "summative evaluation" and there are two types of summative evaluation. The first type is an "outcome" evaluation, which most commonly looks at the degree to which the program met its objectives. The other is called an "impact" evaluation, which hopes to examine the effects beyond the goals and objectives of the program. Each of these types have qualitative, quantitative, or mixed-method possibilities. We examine each type in the subsequent section.

Formative Evaluations

Formative evaluations look at the implementation of a program. These are useful for providing descriptions of what the program does. They are also used to observe the program in real time for the purposes of monitoring and improving the program. The most common type of formative evaluation is a "process" evaluation. Process evaluations can be qualitative, quantitative, or mixed method. They can also be quite broad and look at many program characteristics, or quite narrow and focused. Your research should be very clear about these characteristics. To understand this better, we break this discussion down into purposes, methods, and utilization.

PURPOSES

The most common purposes for formative evaluation are to track the implementation of the program and make recommendations for program improvement. Formative evaluations, however, can be retrospective, to help determine why something worked, or why it did not work.

This brings up an issue that you must address in your capstone project. At what point do you begin your data collection, and how does that timing mesh with academic deadlines? Ideally, you can observe a program over an extended period and gather rich detail. Unfortunately, academic deadlines may force you to narrow your examination, or to examine the problem retrospectively. Events that happened before you begin to observe a program may leave important details out of your examination.

A second consideration is what aspect of the program you choose to examine. Process evaluations can look at any one of a number of components of a program. There are micro, mezzo, and macro variables that may be relevant to your evaluation. Your literature, theory, or interest may be your guide. The following is a nonexhaustive list of possibilities:

- *General program characteristics.* Many of the same questions that are used in policy analysis are applicable here. What are the goals? Are the goals of the program clear? Are there competing goals? How are the goals reconciled? Is the program adequately funded? Who controls the funds?
- *Organizational characteristics.* Programs are implemented by organizations. Understanding the various aspects of that organization may shed light on why the program acts as it does. You may have questions about staff characteristics, levels, training, or demographics. Administration is another area for study. Are administrators sufficiently committed, competent, educated, and focused? Organizational procedures and rules are also targets for study. What about client needs? Is the program offered at times and in ways that will ensure success, or is it located and offered at times and in ways that make positive outcomes less likely? Finally, is the program adequately described and marketed? Do clients know about the program?
- *Client characteristics.* Are there characteristics that make some clients more successful? This can include things as broad as family support, transportation, access to childcare, and even client motivation.
- *General climate.* The context, community, and environment of the program is also a fruitful target for investigation. What might be going on in the larger world that is important to examine?

METHODOLOGIES

You can examine processes through qualitative, quantitative, or mixed-method research. From experience, most well-done processes evaluations will build on both quantitative and qualitative approaches—mixed methods. Some possibilities are listed here for you to describe the general approach of the methodology, as well as its strengths and weaknesses for formative research.

Reflection Questions
1. What variables do you think might be most important for explaining a program's success or failure? Why?
2. Think of a program that you know. What outside factors should be looked at to help improve the program?

Qualitative Methodologies for Formative Evaluations

A common part of evaluation is description, which often builds upon qualitative observation. There are two methods in particular that you might find useful: document reviews and focus groups.

- *Document reviews.* Written records contain a wealth of information that can be useful to you. From the source policy, through administrative materials, and down to case records with individual clients is found quite significant information about the program and what has happened. Three concerns that you will address in your research are (a) a determination of the population of documents that you will use, (b) what variables to examine, and (c) how you will access these sources. Those concerns all inform one another. One further possibility as a useful document source is simply the local newspapers from the local community. Larger macro or systemic variables, (in other words, the general climate), can sometimes best be determined by such examination.

Now there are limitations to this approach. Like any research project, you can choose the wrong data set, records can be inadequate or falsified, and the analytic approach you choose may not be sensitive enough to the kinds of variables that influence the program. Further, document reviews by their very nature are retrospective. Finally, document reviews may be limited in their ability to capture sentiment and affect. This suggests a second methodology that might be useful, the focus group.

- *Focus groups.* Focus groups are targeted, directed conversations. They are quite effective, if done repeatedly, at capturing trends and changes over time. Such an approach has its own methodological issues. First, you must identify the questions and variables you seek to examine. Fortunately however, some degree of flexibility is possible by the fact that focus group direction can be altered depending upon the answers that are provided.

In addition to the questions and variables, determining who will participate should also be addressed. Not everyone looks at problems the same way. Different groups of people know different things about the program, and different groups of people may have different attitudes about what they know. This means that you want to carefully consider which individuals will be included for which questions. Try and match your questions with the persons who can best address them. Administrators may know administrative issues quite well, but they may know very little about how the line staff operates. Similarly, clients may know nothing about how a program was established, but may know a great deal about how well the services work. At the same time, different client, staff, or administrators may have different perspectives on the same issue. Thus, you want to design your focus group with two very important sample considerations. First, you want to direct questions to people who know about those questions, and second, you want to ensure that the people who participate are reasonably typical of the groups they are representing.

The first of these issues is probably best addressed by holding multiple focus groups. You may ask some of the same questions to each group, but you may also ask questions about which that group likely knows more. The second problem of different perspectives in the same group may be addressed by effective sample selection. Focus groups try to find typical participants.

Focus groups capture the data quickly. You can also ask people about how they feel, or what they understand. The major limitation of focus groups is that you always risk the possibility of poorly designed questions, groupthink as people answer the questions, or misinterpretation in your analysis. Finally, there may be financial costs involved.

Quantitative Methodologies for Formative Evaluations

Quantitative approaches also have all of the advantages and disadvantages of quantitative research in general. There are two methodologies that may be useful for you: secondary analysis and/or some form of survey. Secondary analysis is discussed in the following paragraph. The problem of the survey is also examined.

Surveys are just sets of organized questions. The strength of this approach is that it can be used to yield large amounts of data quickly and obtain generalizable data and/or very specific data about specialized program characteristics. As with all surveys, the concerns are what questions are asked of which individuals. The first concern, what questions, is best considered by thinking again about your variables. Surveys can be designed in such a way as to be quite broad in topic, or quite specific. There are a few types of questions, however, that are quite common as components of surveys in this kind of research. For example, satisfaction surveys can assess the general level of feeling about services provided. Many agencies use such surveys on a regular basis. They can be distributed once or a few times a year, or even every time a client uses a service. In particular, satisfaction surveys can be designed to yield very specific information about every interaction or every communication with the organization. Now, such ongoing data collection may not be appropriate for the kind of research that you are writing for a capstone project. More likely, you hope to capture a discreet amount of information in a discreet time.

Surveys can also focus on any given component of a program. You may, for example, ask questions about leadership, supervision, or the level of training alone. Building upon the literature in any of these areas can be highly useful to you. Such data can also be useful to the organization so that it better understands what its strengths and weaknesses are.

Now it is important to remember as a quantitative method, most of the questions that you ask will have predetermined and limited categories in which persons can respond. It is quite common for these categories to be structured along some kind of continuum scale, with Likert or Likert-type scales providing the response options. However, many such quantitative surveys also contain a few open-ended questions to gather more detailed information that can be used to help explain or expand quantitative answers.

The types of questions alone, however, are only one part of the quantitative descriptive information needed for your evaluation research. In some ways, what is more confounding is to whom you will provide the surveys. Again, surveys can be widely distributed, randomly distributed, or targeted to a small and specific group. It may or may not be practical to ask all your questions of everyone who is affected. It may be more beneficial for you to create a sample that fits the criteria you establish. As you know, samples can be either randomly or nonrandomly generated. If you create a sample nonrandomly, either through some purposive selection or by self-selection of participants, you will want to specify that very clearly in your proposal along with your reasons for drawing that particular sample.

You also need to think about and specify whether data will be self-report or gathered by in-person approaches, such as interviews, internet, smartphone, or telephone. Self-reports may be appropriate if your sample is large, spread out, literate, and are technologically connected. Both self-report and in-person approaches have strengths and weaknesses. There is no perfect method, so what is most important for you is a good rationale and justification for the approach that you choose. This rationale and justification will be included as part of your write-up, as will the limitations of the approach you choose.

Mixed Methodologies for Formative Evaluations

Depending upon the questions that you want answered by your formative evaluation, you may also choose to mix the previous methods as part of your overall approach. Mixed methods are one common way to address program complexity. A problem of course is how to interpret data from multiple different sources. What is important is to develop a rationale and justification for the approach and then stick to the approach that you choose at the point of analysis and write-up.

■ Summative Evaluations

Summative evaluations look at outcomes. They seek to report what resulted from the program. Summative evaluations provide retrospective results and achievement. Yet even so, there are many examples of summative evaluation—indeed perhaps some of the best—where the evaluator has been a part of the evaluation from the very beginning. As with formative evaluations, there are different types and purposes. The two most common types are *outcome* and *impact* evaluations. There are also cost-effectiveness and cost–benefit analyses and meta-analyses (which integrate outcomes from multiple studies to determine an overall judgment). As most of the materials associated with policy analysis are appropriate for impact analysis, we only briefly discuss it here before we look at outcome evaluations.

"Impact evaluations" focus on the long-range results of the program or project and changes or improvements as a result (e.g., long-term maintenance of desired behavior, reduced absenteeism from work, reduced morbidity and mortality). Such evaluations generally move beyond the stated objectives of the program and often focus on long-term results or changes. In this way, they are similar to some types of policy analysis. Good studies may, however, be costly and involve extended commitment. In addition, the findings may be difficult to directly relate to the effects of a program. Other (external) influences on the target audience occur at the same time the program effects are occurring. Thus, impact evaluations are rarely appropriate for time-limited capstone research projects.

PURPOSES

"Outcome evaluations" may include descriptive elements, but the primary purpose is to examine the program's defined objectives. Thus, outcome evaluations are more narrowly focused than other types of evaluation. Programs exist for specific purposes. Ideally, these purposes are stated at the point of their creation. Such targeting and specificity in the program world are presented as the program's goals and (more measurably) objectives. Before we look at the evaluation of a program's goals and objectives, we look at what program goals and objectives are, and how they are constructed. Your own proposal may be required to include them. We also will look at a graphic representation of a proposal, known as a "logic model."

GOALS AND OBJECTIVES

Programs are often based upon the design articulated in a proposal. Someone somewhere wrote a proposal for the program that you hope to evaluate. The focus of the program—the targets of what the program ultimately hopes to achieve—are most clearly stated in a section called the "Goals and Objectives."

Goals and objectives are specific statements of intent. Clear goals and objectives make the obligations and activities of the project very specific. They provide a "skeleton" for all of the detail of a program. Upon the skeleton is found content about how the services will be delivered, who will deliver them, under what conditions, and how money will be spent. All of these elements are typically in specific sections of a proposal and generally written as a narrative.

The goals and objectives, however, are not written as a narrative. Instead, they are given as a list with some very specific kinds of information: what the program hopes to achieve, for whom, by when, how often, and how. In other words, when the project is completed and all the money is spent, the program intends to complete all of the objectives as written.

Goals and objectives do different things. Goals are the broad, end states the program hopes to achieve or at least contributes to achieving. Because they are the desired end states, goals need not be 100% specific and measurable. What? Well think of it this way. Most social problems are multidimensional. Rarely does any intervention address all of the needs associated with a problem. Most will address one, two, or at most a few of the dimensions of these problems.

How can you demonstrate measurable achievement? The answer is by breaking apart the goal into smaller units that are measurable and do-able. These, when stated, are the program's objectives. They are measurable statements, concrete, and attainable by the program. They are derived from the goals. There are two types of objectives that articulate slightly different things—*outcome objectives* and *process objectives*.

- *Outcome objectives*. Outcome objectives are *indicators* of goal attainment. They may measure either "the degree" to which the goal will be met or some dimension, element, or part of the goal. For example, think about a program that addresses the problem of environmental racism in a community. A program may have as its goal the reduction of environmental racism. However, environmental racism is a multidimensional concept. The issues of housing, the location of environmental threats, the problem of the concentration of poverty, the problem of racism in general, and the perspective of politicians and business leaders in the community are all associated with it. Any one of the components could become the target of the program and, by its reduction, demonstrate a reduction in community environmental racism. Thus, the goal could be reducing environmental racism, but the objectives could be to increase housing in areas of lower environmental risk, increasing employment, educating the community about racism, and increasing knowledge of the problem in the political and business community. If well designed, by making changes in those factors you provide indicators or evidence that the problem of environmental racism has been reduced. Therefore, the outcome objectives are measurable changes in the dimensions of a problem.

- *Process objectives.* Process objectives, on the other hand, are concrete and measurable statements of the processes, services, or interventions that will lead to objective attainment (and therefore goal attainment). Using the same example as earlier, providing training programs for business and political leaders could be an effective intervention. Providing loans for people to build homes in areas of lower environmental risk can be effective activities or efforts used to meet the outcome objectives.

Look at another example—one with a research focus. Suppose a program in Southern California is seeking funding to examine the consequences on quality of life caused by climate change. After the examination of the literature, the research question is: What are the effects of climate change on coastal indigenous communities? From this, the organization develops two proposal goals. First: "To understand the effects of climate change on indigenous communities on the Southern Pacific Coast." Second: "To determine the social service needs of indigenous communities on the Southern Pacific Coast." Excellent, but quite broad. Why? Well there are many different indigenous communities on the Gulf Coast. There are also a huge number of potential types of climate change manifestations, possible effects and, therefore, possible needs.

From these goals, the following process objectives are developed. The whole Goals and Objectives section of your program evaluation might now look like the example provided in Box 5.1.

BOX 5.1

GOALS AND OBJECTIVES FOR CLIMATE CHANGE RESEARCH

Goal 1: To understand the effects of climate change on indigenous communities on the Southern Pacific Coast

    Objective 1.1: To survey 100 members of the Chumash nation to determine how climate change is impacting their livelihood by May 2022

    Objective 1.2: To create a report describing the survey findings by July 2022.

Goal 2: To determine the social service needs of indigenous communities on the Southern Pacific Coast

    Objective 2.1: To establish a one-stop shop for service needs among members of the Chumash nation who have been affected by climate change by January 2023.

    Objective 2.2: To develop a sustainability plan for the one-stop shop by December 2022.

CONSIDERATIONS FOR WRITING GOOD GOALS AND OBJECTIVES

There are generally accepted rules for writing good goals and objectives. As you will see, these rules are incredibly important for the evaluation. First, if you look at Figure 5.1, you see that they are written as a list, and the goals have objectives associated with them. Second, all evaluations must have *at least* one goal. Consider having more than one goal if:

- the problem has several dimensions that the program hopes to address (e.g., community economic opportunity includes *jobs, employers, resident skill levels*, so maybe a different goal for each);
- the problem has several different client groups with different intervention needs (e.g., parents, kids, employers); and
- the project has several components (e.g., treatment, prevention, education).

Third, every goal must have at least one objective. Fourth, the objectives must be very specific. To write good objectives, many people suggest using an acronym **SMART** (CDC, 2017). SMART stands for:

- **S**pecific. The objective achieves a specific result (do not be general) and is connected to your described problem.
- **M**easurable. The objective must be measurable. You must be able to determine whether the objective is achieved (include quantities of change whenever possible—although yes/no is also measurable).
- **A**ttainable. The objective is within capabilities of achievement (not unrealistic—reducing poverty by 100% is pretty unlikely).
- **R**ewarding. Achievement that it is satisfying.
- **T**imed. It will occur in an established time. The objective has a deadline within the grant proposal period (can be addressed by putting a date into the objective).

SUMMATIVE EVALUATION METHODOLOGIES

With the previous conversation in mind, it should become clear why having well-written objectives is nearly essential for a good summative evaluation. The central function of the summative evaluation is to ask if the program met its objectives—this is an outcome evaluation. Without measurable, time-limited objectives, how can you say if the program met the desired targets or not?

Now, as with formative evaluations, you can examine outcomes from the standpoint of qualitative, quantitative, or mixed-method research. From experience, if most objectives are written correctly, some form of quantitative approach is the most useful. However, explaining why a program met its objectives or did not, often demands both quantitative and qualitative approaches—mixed methods. The following are some possibilities for

$$A_1 - B - A_2$$

Where: A_1 = baseline or pretest measure of dependent variable
A_2 = outcome or posttest measure of dependent variable
B = agency effort/time, and is a surrogate measure for the independent variable

FIGURE 5.1 Quasi-experimental designs.

you to describe the general approach of the methodology, as well as its strengths and weaknesses for summative research. We start with quantitative approaches.

Analytical Assumptions for Summative Evaluations

Almost by necessity, a quantitative design is part of an outcome evaluation. Think about the logic for a second. An objective is a statement of change. The program wants to move from a condition where the objective has not been met to a condition where the objective has hopefully been attained. This change from one condition to another condition is, on the surface, a straightforward application of a quasi-experimental design. A quasi-experimental design requires at least two measures of what you hope to change (your dependent variable). This is demonstrated in Figure 5.1.

In its simplest form, every objective seeks to change or bring about something. The "something" is the dependent variable. Think about a few examples. An objective that seeks to reduce tobacco consumption by 40% seeks to change the level of tobacco consumption. An objective that seeks to reduce community violence by 100 violent incidences seeks to reduce violent incidents. An objective that seeks to increase literacy levels by 25% seeks to change literacy. Even purely yes/no answers apply. In an example earlier, the objective was to write a report on climate change. The condition to change is from no-written report to a written report.

Reflection Questions
1. Think about your education. What are some examples of dependent variables?
2. Think about your education. What are some examples of important independent variables?
3. What are some examples of objectives that could be written including the dependent variables listed earlier?

To demonstrate that the objective has been met requires a comparison from the first to the final measure of the dependent variable. Now, here is one slight difference from a traditional experiment. Sometimes, in fact often, the independent variable is not specified in the objective. Therefore, the measure of the independent variable is what we would call a "surrogate," an indicator of time and effort on the part of the agency.

So every evaluation of every objective must at its minimum have two measures of the dependent variable. The first measures the baseline or pretest condition—how much of the dependent variable existed before the program began. The second or final measure is a measure of how much of the dependent variable existed at the conclusion of the requisite time. Presumably, the one thing that made a difference between the first and the second measures of the dependent variable is the effort of the organization and the associated time needed.

Of course, complexity can easily convert quasi-experimental designs to one requiring control groups, placebo groups, and a variety of intervening variables. For example, if you want to demonstrate that in fact it was the agency that brought about change and not just dumb luck, the use of some types of control group might be necessary.

Quantitative Methodologies for Summative Evaluations

Several data sources and methods may help you assess objective attainment. Secondary analysis, surveys, and pretesting/posttesting are among the most common.

Surveys

Likely, the single quantitative methodology that will be most useful for you is some form of survey. The strength of this approach is that it can be used to yield large amounts of data quickly and obtain generalizable data and/or very specific data about very specialized program characteristics.

As with all surveys, the concerns become what questions are asked of which individuals. The first question—what questions—are best considered by thinking again about the variables you are interested in examining as defined by the objectives. If each objective contains information that may be captured by a question or set of questions, the survey is a perfect tool.

Now it is important to remember as a quantitative method, most of the questions that you ask will have predetermined and limited categories in which persons can respond. It is quite common for these categories to be structured along some kind of continuum scale, with Likert or Likert-type scales providing the response options. However, many such quantitative surveys also contain a few open-ended questions to gather more detailed information that can be used to help explain or expand quantitative answers.

The types of questions alone, however, are only one part of the quantitative descriptive information needed for your evaluation. In some ways, what is more confounding is to whom you will provide the surveys. Again, the objective should define who the target is. For large service populations, it may be more beneficial for you to create a sample that fits the criteria you establish. As you know, samples can be either randomly or nonrandomly generated. If you create a sample nonrandomly, either through some purposive selection or by self-selection of participants, you will want to specify that very clearly in your capstone paper along with your reasons for drawing that particular sample.

You also need to think about and specify whether data will be self-report or gathered by in-person approaches, such as interviews, internet, smartphone, or telephone. Self-reports may be appropriate if your sample is large, spread out, literate, and are technologically connected. Both self-report and in-person approaches have strengths and weaknesses. There is no perfect method, so what is most important for you is a good rationale and justification for the approach that you choose. This rationale and justification will be included as part of your write-up, as will the limitations of the approach you choose.

Pretesting and Posttesting

As we have discussed, a design that is useful for assessing objective attainment includes measurement of your dependent variable at two or more points of time. Some objectives seek to demonstrate that what has changed is something reflected particularly in the knowledge, attitudes, or behaviors of agency participants. Knowledge and attitudes can easily be caught by the use of some form of test. You likely have experienced this directly in your academic career. Perhaps you have taken a test at the beginning of a class and then again later on or at the end of the class. This is a clear example of a pretest and posttest.

Often, programs seek to enhance participant understanding or knowledge. For participants who are literate and otherwise capable, some form of testing can capture those changes. For example, your agency might have as an objective to improve knowledge of safe sex practices by 30%. If you wanted to assess this behaviorally, you might ask the participant to keep a log, and every time they have a sexual encounter with another person, they note that in their log. This, however, is both intrusive and addresses the behavior rather than the knowledge. A series of questions about safe sex practices, perhaps true-or-false questions, can easily be administered at the beginning of your program participation and then at the end. Many programs with safe sex or substance use objectives use such questions.

Overall, testing is a reasonable approach for capturing knowledge or attitude changes over time. It may not, however, be the best approach capturing behavioral change. When people respond about behavior, a problem of honesty may affect how they answer their questions. The approach also depends again on a person's literacy and cognitive abilities.

Available Data Sets (Secondary Analysis)

To some degree, all objectives are measured pre and post something. That, of course, is again the definition of objective outcome evaluation. What is variable are the data sets that you use to examine a pre- post change. For a great many objectives, the data sets that you use may be something that someone else collects or has collected. Just as there are agency records that may help with formative examinations, there are also many existing data sources that can be used for secondary analysis in an outcome evaluation. As discussed throughout this text, records are kept in a variety of forms by a variety of record-keeping organizations. For many objectives, these data are invaluable. For most objectives, one or two sources will be very useful.

First, many social service agencies collect data at intake, through service provision phase, and at termination. If these data are adequately aligned with what the objective hopes to see change, and if the data have a high degree of integrity, these records may be very useful. The problem here is that agency records are often incomplete or inappropriately linked to the objective being evaluated to be useful. Nevertheless, almost all agencies have at least some records that are appropriate for some kinds of objectives. Some examples follow:

- For objectives that are simple counts of services, records as unsophisticated as sign-in sheets or tracking logs may be helpful. Consider an objective that states, "The program will provide a minimum of 10 HRS of counseling to a minimum of 100 clients." Even the simple sign-in sheets may be adequate for measuring the degree to which the objective was met.
- For objectives that hope to show specific changes in client goals, staff records in the form of goal-attainment ratings may be useful. Consider an objective that states, "The program participants will demonstrate 70% improvement in goal completion each year." Assuming staff maintain accurate goal attainment records, this objective can easily be examined.
- For objectives that hope to show behavioral changes, records can be kept either by staff in situations where the behavior is observable, or, if the behavior is something that likely occurs outside observable treatment, the client can be

trained to capture the appropriate information. For example, consider an objective that states, "The program participants will reduce aggressive acts toward other participants by 20% each month during groups." In this case, staff members can be trained to capture the information.

A second source of data sets is the kind of information that may be captured by outside organizations and agencies. A great many governmental as well as nongovernmental organizations regularly collect information about a variety of social problems. Of course, the most well known as such data sets are from the U.S. Census. In addition to the decennial census, the census bureau undertakes a large number of studies each year about a variety of topics. Everything from demographics to poverty and housing are collected through mechanisms such as annual community surveys. Such surveys may well provide comparative data for variables you are interested in examining. Another example is crime. The Federal Bureau of Investigation (FBI) aggregates data from literally every single police department in the United States into a system called the "uniform crime reporting system" (UCRS). Also, the U.S. Bureau of Labor Statistics collects employment as well as unemployment records. In addition, a variety of health indicators is collected by state and federal agencies.

Of course as with all available data, you have to ascertain whether the data set exists and if variables in those data sets match your needs in a time period and are geographically appropriate to what you are evaluating. Further, data integrity, although generally good, is sometimes affected by political factors. Data may be incomplete or of questionable accuracy.

Qualitative/Mixed Methodologies

Qualitative data are less commonly used for objective attainment measurement. There are exceptions, but generally quantitative methods are more appropriate. On the other hand, mixed methods are most clearly called for as supportive of summative findings. Indeed, the very best evaluations typically do both. Formative evaluations often use qualitative data sources to describe activities and processes or to identify important variables. Summative evaluations, on the other hand, focus very narrowly on the objectives themselves. Thus, including both qualitative and quantitative content can allow you to describe, assess, and explain a program and why it does or does not work.

There is no right or wrong way to do this. Most of the evaluations that the authors of this chapter have undertaken have used a combination of document analysis and focus groups to provide description and context, while quantitative data sets have been used to directly assess objective attainment. This may or may not be appropriate for your capstone research project. Still, more information often will give you better answers, and the degree to which you can get such answers, the better off you may be.

PRACTICE ACTIVITIES

1. Write down a list of problem areas that you might find interesting to research. In a column next to it, try to identify a policy, program, and service that you could examine for your research study. Then in the third column, think about the issues you would need to overcome to conduct that research.

2. Using the same list of items from the list just mentioned, see if you can find at least one journal article that has investigated the policy, program, or service.
3. Ask your field instructor if the agency regularly evaluates its programs. Ask which programs it evaluates and ask what the purposes of those evaluations are.

TECHNOLOGY EXERCISES

1. Go to your library's website and look up their online databases. Without actually conducting a full search, see how many examples of a policy analysis you can find. Then, see how many examples of program evaluations you can find.
2. Now, think about the social problem that you might be interested in examining. Identify the population that might be affected by that problem. Examine the internet site Fedstats.gov and search for that problem in the population of interest. What data sets do you find that might be useful to you? Write those down for later use.

REFERENCES

Centers for Disease Control and Prevention. (2012). *Program evaluation for public health programs: A self-study guide.* https://www.cdc.gov/eval/guide/introduction/index.htm#ftn4

Centers for Disease Control and Prevention. (2015). *Definition of policy.* https://www.cdc.gov/policy/analysis/process/definition.html

Centers for Disease Control and Prevention. (2017). *Writing SMART objectives.* https://www.cdc.gov/dhdsp/evaluation_resources/guides/writing-smart-objectives.htm

Centers for Disease Control and Prevention. (2019). *Policy analysis key questions.* https://www.cdc.gov/policy/analysis/process/docs/table1.pdf

Gilson, L., Orgill, M., & Schroff, Z. (2018). *A health policy analysis reader.* World Health Organization. https://www.who.int/alliance-hpsr/resources/publications/Alliance-HPA-Reader-web.pdf

Independent Sector. (2020). *Charitable sector.* https://independentsector.org/about/the-charitable-sector

Patton, C., Sawicki, D., & Clark, J. (2016). *Basic methods of policy analysis and planning* (3rd ed.). Routledge.

Patton, M. Q. (1987). *Qualitative research evaluation methods.* Sage.

Scriven, M. (1998). Minimalist theory of evaluation: The least theory that practice requires. *American Journal of Evaluation, 19,* 57–70. https://doi.org/10.1177/109821409801900105

Terrell, S. R. (2012). Mixed-methods research methodologies. *The Qualitative Report, 17*(1), 254–280. https://nsuworks.nova.edu/tqr/vol17/iss1/14

Tolbert, J., Orgera, K., Singer, N., & Domico, A. (2019). *Key facts about the uninsured population.* https://www.kff.org/uninsured/issue-brief/key-facts-about-the-uninsured-population

Tong, R. (1986). *Ethics in policy analysis.* Prentice Hall.

University of Kansas. (2015a). *Changing policies: An overview.* The Community Toolbox. https://ctb.ku.edu/en/table-of-contents/implement/changing-policies/overview/main

University of Kansas. (2015b). Developing logic models. The Community Toolbox. https://ctb.ku.edu/en/table-of-contents/overview/models-for-community-health-and-development/logic-model-development/main

6

NEEDS ASSESSMENTS

This chapter discusses the process for conducting needs assessments. This begins with a definition of "need" followed by the description of the purposes of needs assessment. Then, a discussion of the different methodologies available for use is presented. To better understand the use of needs assessment, the discussion of the differences between organizational and community needs assessment is included.

By the end of this chapter, you will be able to do the following:

- Define need.
- Describe the purposes and common components of different types of needs assessment.
- Learn to read and write logic models and goals and objectives.
- Describe the different methodologies available for needs assessment.
- Understand some of the limitations of needs assessments.

Needs Assessment

It would not be an overstatement to say that needs assessment is part of every activity undertaken by social workers. The central theme in any intervention at any level depends upon some determination of need. Further, the more accurate and complete the understanding of the need, the more likely the intervention will be appropriate and successful. Purposes identified for needs assessments include the following:

- To learn more about group or community
- To get an honest and objective description of needs
- To become aware of possible unknown needs
- To document needs, for funding and advocacy
- To align services with needs
- To get group and community support
- To get more people actually involved in the subsequent action itself (University of Kansas, 2015a)

Because needs assessment is so fundamental to social work practice, it provides opportunities for social work research. If you intend to use a needs assessment as part of your capstone project, you will be making a contribution that may last well beyond your field placement. As individual, family, or small group assessments fall more properly into other practice domains, this chapter focuses on organizations and communities.

■ Needs Defined

The term "needs" is used in speech constantly. Just a few examples from your own life demonstrate the ubiquity of the term. For example, you need food, housing, water, and air. Without these needs being met, you will likely become sick and potentially die. There are some things that are necessary for survival. It is also the case, however, that you use the term "need" for things that might make your life easier. An electric washing machine or a telephone or smartphone are such items. Cars, telephones, electricity, and even indoor plumbing are all technologies that have changed people's lives in dramatic ways. Similarly, computers, cell phones, smartphones, and the internet are important, but none of these items are necessary for life.

Could we survive without them? It could be argued that in a modern economy, communication and transportation are critical components of an infrastructure. There is little doubt that without all of those things, finding and keeping an employment situation would be much more difficult. However, the operative concept here is "more difficult," *not* impossible.

Now, a somewhat different example: Assume you have a perfectly serviceable, working automobile that gets reasonable gas mileage. Why trade it in for a different one? Similarly, are the features in smartphone version 2.0 really that much worse than those in version 2.1? If not, why do so many people upgrade their smartphones every couple of years? What about clothes? Is a pair of sneakers that cost US$90.00 that much better than a pair that cost US$30.00? Perhaps if you were a basketball player and the fraction of a second of extra bounce you got might make it worth it to you. Finally, how often when shopping have you seen pants or a dress or a shirt that you said you must have, or indeed you said you need? Do you really?

What this discussion has pointed out is a couple of important things about need. First, need has different levels of true importance. There are some things that we need for our survival. There are some things that we need to make our lives easier. Some things have become more important as time has passed. In addition, there are some things that we really do not need but instead want.

If you are studying need, you will want to consider different perceptions. Need is to at least some degree and sometimes very definitely socially constructed. While some needs are constant and essential to life, other things are less critical and subject to change. Not having them will not necessarily kill a person—at least in the short run. Yet having an adequate amount or sample of such a thing is important.

As a quick refresher, what "social construction" means here is that many objective phenomena in our lives have variable definitions, importance, priorities, or meanings. In other words, there is a subjectivity that overlays the objective character. This mix of the subjective and objective has implications for both measuring and prioritizing needs. The simplest definition of a need is that it is an object, process, or phenomenon that affects a person's, organization's, community's, or nation's quality of life. Maslow's hierarchy of needs (Hopper, 2020) provides a list of such things. In his list, there are biological, safety, security, psychological, and higher order types. Putting aside his argument about hierarchy for a moment, it is clear that all of these are important, but social meaning can subjectively influence all. Further, different groups may prioritize needs differently. Finally, the distinction needs to be made between a need and a want. A "want" is a desire for something, but that something may or may not be critical to quality of life.

> **Reflection Questions**
> 1. How can you determine the difference between a need and a want? In your own life? In your client's life?
> 2. When we talk about need having both an objective reality and a subjective meaning, do you think they can be separated for the purposes of a research study?

DETERMINING AND ANALYZING NEED

In a good assessment, understanding the importance of the social construction and the difference between needs and wants is critical. This effects even how need is measured. There are four ways of demonstrating that a need exists:

- *Normative analysis.* A need may be shown to exist by comparing the level of possible need to a known predetermined (normative) level. If a person falls below that established level, an argument can be made that a need exists. The best example here is something like calories. A human must have 1,500 to 2,500 calories a day, and if a person falls below that level for a sustained period, they will suffer.
- *Comparative analysis.* A need may be shown to exist by comparing two or more groups, and if one of the groups has less (or more) of something, an argument can be made that a need exists. A good example here might be high school graduation rates. If one school or community graduates a lower percentage of students than another, the argument can be made that a need exists.
- *Expressed analysis.* A need can be shown to exist simply by asking people what they need. This method does not use a comparison group, but instead assumes that people will freely express their concerns. An example here might be asking members of an organization what they need. To some degree, this is a way of measuring wants. People are telling you what they want.
- *Services utilization analysis.* A service utilization analysis is a little bit different than the previous in that assumptions about what services are needed are built into the assessment. Here, the comparison is made between the levels of services, or the types of services, and what is actually being used.

For three of the four types of analysis, some kind of comparison group or concept exists. In the case of a normative need, you compare the level of need that you find to some existing standard. There are not very many examples of true existing norms. Most of these are biological: Food, water, housing, clean air, and exposure to dangerous substances may be about all the true normative examples that we have. Now, as stated, many other things that have become increasingly important for modern life might almost meet the definition. It is also the case that the society in which a person lives creates some normative expectations. For example, students are required to go to school until age 16. Thus, you could argue that comparing a percentage of students who dropped out before age 16 reflects the normative need in a given community.

A comparative analysis also requires something to which the need level you find can be compared. Most often, this comparative group is a different geographic unit. For example, if you are assessing the need in a given neighborhood, you could compare that need level to perhaps the larger city, state, or nation. A good illustration of this might be something like the number of food stores within a 1-mile radius. A demographically, culturally, and regionally similar environment may also be used, but it gets "trickier." Comparing police response times in a community that is much wealthier, affluent, and less dense to a very poor community is useful. It is more useful, however, to compare it to communities that in most respects are the same. Why? The closer the communities are to each other in size and demographics, the stronger the argument will be that a need exists.

Service utilization analysis also compares the needs of an organization or community, but in one respect, the comparison is quite different. Here, you are comparing the type or availability of a service to an assumed level of need. In some respects, this is an analysis of an analysis. Comparing what is used or available to a need implies that the need has already been assessed.

Reflection Questions
1. What are some examples of "normative needs"?
2. Are normative needs less/more important than wants? Why?

An expressed need analysis does not, however, necessarily require a comparison. Actually, the individuals expressing the need have already made a comparison between their expectations and reality. You could also argue that by listing all of the wants as expressed, you are comparing one level of want to another.

Understanding how participants socially construct their world may be useful to interpret perceived needs and wants. "Wants" are reflections of the thoughts and priorities of the people you ask. You could ask the same question, "What does your organization need most?" to 10 different organizations, and you would find 10 different lists. Moreover, each item on each list could mean something a little bit different. Thus, who responds to an assessment will shape their answers. Social status, income, education, gender, race and/or ethnicity, sexual orientations, and occupation all may affect the responses provided in the assessment. You can see such effects in contemporary discussions about police violence, race relations, and climate change. Political affiliation and ideology—strong factors in social construction—influence social priorities large and small. The intensity of concern is also affected.

In summary, needs have an objective reality, which are shaped by demographics and beliefs. Who is asked about the need must be taken into account, and this will be very important for your capstone project. A second critical consideration is that the articulation of the need requires either some kind of comparison or explicit expression. If you choose to demonstrate the need through the comparison approach, your project should be very clear on what the comparison provides and the source of the comparative data.

TYPES OF STUDIES TO EXAMINE SEVERITY

With an understanding that needs can be demonstrated or analyzed in different ways, there are different ways by which you can capture the data. This is not the same as the methodologies, which we examine later in this chapter. This, rather, refers to some generic types of studies and how to interpret the data.

To help clarify this, think about the difference between simply counting the level of the need versus putting it in some kind of context. For example, if you use a study that said that one state had 1,500 coronavirus cases while another state had 500 cases, it certainly would appear that 1,500 is more serious than 500. Of course, on one level, that is true. Now consider that the first example of 1,500 came from a state with 6 million residents, while the 500 came from a state with 1 million residents. If you compare the percentage by population, you see that the state with 500 cases may have a much more serious problem.

Prevalence and Incidence

The most basic type of study begins with the simple count of how widespread the problem(s) is or are. These are "prevalence" studies, in that they attempt to ascertain how many examples of the problem exist. There are lots of examples of this type. For example, how widespread is hunger? How many persons experience lead poisoning? How common is vicarious trauma among workers in an organization?

Such studies hope to provide at a minimum counts of how widespread the problems might be among persons assessed. Currently, we are in the midst of the coronavirus pandemic. To be able to determine the effect and consequences of the pandemic, we need to know how many people are affected. Research findings can, however, be made more meaningful by using some type of comparison group. Further, it can be even more useful by creating a percentage or rate. The percentage is simply how great the need is per 100 in the overall population. It is calculated by dividing the number of affected persons by the population, and then multiplying the result by 100.

For many types of needs, that is an adequate statistic. For other problems, however, particularly for larger populations, the more common statistic is a rate. The rate is the percentage-like calculation based upon a larger number of people. Typically, the larger number is 1,000, or 100,000, or 1 million. In the United States, such rates are used for many purposes.

A second type of study examines "incidence." While prevalence studies examine how widespread the problem might be at a given point in time, incidence examines the spread of the problem. Incidence studies are interested in knowing how rapidly or slowly the problem is increasing or decreasing. When you hear about the rate of a problem going up or going down, you are hearing the results of incidence research.

> **Reflection Questions**
> 1. When is knowing the incidence of a problem more important than its prevalence? When is prevalence more important?
> 2. For a problem like crime, what issues might be confronted if attempting to assess its incidence and prevalence?

In essence, incidence studies demonstrate data trends over time. These trends, such as the rates discussed earlier, are often in standard units, such as 14 or 30 days. Typically, to show prevalence data, you need to collect data at multiple points and time.

NEED VARIABLE SELECTION AND MEASUREMENT

One final theme should be discussed related to measurement. Variables measuring need may have a standard definition, while others leave the interpretation to participants. A great many need measures, particularly those that affect communities, have very standardized definitions and ways of measurement. If you choose to examine data comparatively, it makes sense to collect those data using the standard measurements. For example, poverty and unemployment have specific meanings under federal definitions.

Other variables may have differing definitions, and it is important to understand what you are measuring and how it can be useful to you for comparison purposes. At the level of the organization in particular, there are a great many concepts and variables that have differing measures. This might mean that comparisons are difficult. There is no standard measure for, say, leadership or effective administration or even efficient service delivery. This provides both a problem and an opportunity for you.

Finally, there are a great many situations where your needs assessment will measure participant wants or interpretations. In these cases, understanding the appropriate approaches for collapsing data is both necessary and necessarily to be defined in your capstone paper. Asking a question such as "What needs to change to make this a better place to work?" will yield a large variety of responses. Asking an open-ended question of 500 people can easily yield 700 different answers. Knowing how to collapse those, (at a minimum using some kind of content analysis), is necessary.

Organizational Needs Assessment

Organizations serve a critical role in the efficient distribution of goods and services. As social workers, we are educated by organizations; we serve clients and organizations; we refer clients to other organizations; and many of us relax through organizations. For our purposes, "organizations" are groups of two or more persons who have some collective identity and shared goals. Organizations typically have informational/legal components (auspice, mission/goals, rules and policies, bylaws, and strategic plans), structural components (the parts of the organization), procedural components (communication, information, and authority), technology, and the organizational environment. Doing needs assessment of an organization may well examine the aspects of those components.

Understanding the definitional characteristics just listed, there are really two kinds of organizational needs assessments. Needs assessments can examine the organization itself through "capacity assessments." Needs assessments can also examine what the organization does in the larger world, and we call those "service assessments." Both types are important if organizations hope to achieve their goals efficiently.

CAPACITY ASSESSMENTS

"Capacity assessments" examine the internal workings of an organization. What capacity assessments seek to determine are issues that affect the ability of the internal workings to achieve the goals of the organization.

Questions and Variables

Because organizations are complex entities, determining the variables you hope to examine is a critical first step. Capacity assessments can examine the organization broadly, hoping to learn about all the various aspects, or narrowly. Broad assessments make sense if there are few clues about areas of concern and the organization. Some organizational theories, such as ecological, systems, or trauma theory, also suggest that the entire organization be assessed. Narrow assessment focusing on one or more variables makes sense if the organization is aware of the weakness, or if the researcher is coming from the theory that provides guidance.

Both approaches are legitimate. The broad assessment makes sense if the organization knows it has problems but is not sure where. The narrow assessment makes sense if some previous analysis has highlighted an area for examination, or again if the researcher is guided by a theory that suggests where to look. There may also be overlap. Recently, the role of trauma in an organization has become better understood. Trauma may affect the whole organization; thus, broad analysis is appropriate.

There is no perfect single framework. Nevertheless, whether broad or narrow, a good capacity assessment should begin with questions that allow a thorough description of the organization. Exhibit 6.1 contains some examples of capacity assessments used by the authors of this text.

EXHIBIT 6.1

CAPACITY ASSESSMENT QUESTIONS

Part I. Overall organizational description:
- What is the name of the organization?
- What are the mission and vision of the organization?
- What are the goals and objectives of the organization?
- What is the organization's legal auspice?
- Does the organization have a strategic plan? What are the organization's program goals for the future?

Part II. A description of existing structure and services of the organization:
- What is the history of the organization?
- What client population or populations does the organization serve?
- What services or programs does the organization provide?
- What is the administrative structure of the organization? (Provide an organizational chart.)
- How many staff members work at the organization?
- How are the programs funded?

(continued)

Part III. A description of the organization's relationship to its environment:
- What niche does the organization or program fill in the community (what needs does the agency address)?
- Are there other organizations in the area that also provide these same services? (Note—be brief here!)
- What is the demographic composition (number or percentage by age, race, income, gender) of the clients at the organization?
- What is the demographic composition (number or percentage by age, race, income, gender) of the staff at the organization?
- With which collaborating organizations or agencies does the organization work to provide services?

Part IV. An analysis of the organization's ability to optimally function and adapt to change. For each question, examine and discuss the informational/legal components (auspice, mission/goals, rules and policies, bylaws, and strategic plans), structural components (the parts of the organization), procedural components (communication, information, and authority), technology, and the organizational environment.
- How well does the agency serve the identified goals and objectives? *Does* the agency *actually* meet its mission?
- What are the primary strengths of the organization?
- What are the current challenges facing the organization?

This assessment begins with description. Narrow assessments, on the other hand, can focus on any one of those questions as the basis of the analysis. One example of a narrow focus might be on leadership. Leadership has received a great deal of attention in recent years, both in academic and professional communities. There are varieties of useful and empirically validated leadership inventories that can be useful. Similarly, management effectiveness, budgeting efficiency, and employee satisfaction all have useful and often validated instruments that may be appropriate for your purposes. Likewise, any number of open-ended questions about the themes can be extremely useful.

SERVICE ASSESSMENTS

"Service assessments" examine the service provision within an organization. There are two kinds of questions that service assessments may address. First, are the services provided appropriate to the demand? Second, what do consumers feel about the services? Both attempt to create a better service match between the client/community and the organization. The primary difference between the two is really just a degree of opinion upon which the decision is based.

One particular method that is very useful for this type of analysis is called "geographic information system mapping" or GIS mapping. Using GIS maps, it is possible to match the locations of clients and service providers. Although such data are usually used in aggregate,

> **Reflection Questions**
> 1. If you were conducting a capacity assessment for your field placement, how difficult would it be to find the information described in Figure 6.1?
> 2. Why are opinions, such as satisfaction, important to examine when assessing an organization?

meaning larger population groupings such as neighborhoods with service providers, the information can be used by specific agencies to identify from where their clients are coming (Pennsylvania Spatial Data Access, 2015). Analyzing data this way can tell the agency quite a bit about the needs that their clients may have.

Questions and Variables

Service assessments that seek to assess the relationship between services provided and services needed begin largely with the assumption that the *kinds* of services needed are in fact being provided. The question becomes: Are *enough* of the services being provided? To a degree, this is largely just a matter of count. Typically, this involves actual counts of provided services in comparison with estimates of need in the catchment area.

Although agency-level data are hopefully available and accurate, they may not be. Further, many social problems are extremely difficult to measure accurately. The source of these data is an ongoing issue as well, which is discussed in detail in the section "Community Needs Assessment." Further, it is hoped that your agency's definition of the need used for internal counts matches the definition used externally. This is, however, not always the case.

Questions related to client opinions about needs may be somewhat easier to obtain. Mechanisms based upon open-ended questions, such as "What is the most important problem?" "How satisfied are you with the service?" and "Would you believe you need to get better?," can all be measured in ways that give the client latitude. These types of assessments are generally reasonably easy. What might be difficult is again the interpretation of the data.

METHODS

The methodology you choose to collect your data is heavily driven by your research purpose and question. Both quantitative and qualitative methods may be appropriate. There are strengths and weaknesses of each approach for various kinds of questions. Before we dive into methods deeply, however, the problem of your sample is appropriate to discuss. This applies to both qualitative and quantitative methods.

Among mathematically perfect worlds, a representative sample drawn from a complete population using random approaches is most desirable. Yet deciding who is in and who is out of the population is difficult. Consider even who is an employee. Employees come and go. So do clients. Thus, the types of answers they would give could vary greatly.

Second, not all employees or all clients are fully aware of many of the organizational issues of interest. It is theoretically possible to create different populations of each based upon their knowledge characteristics. However, for a small organization, this would not make sense. You could easily end up with populations of one, two, or a handful. This makes many kinds of analysis unworkable.

Organizational research is one area where purposive sampling of some type is useful and often preferred. Both qualitative and quantitative methods can use small purposely created samples. So may the key informant sample. "Key informants" are individuals with specialized knowledge, often at a deep level. Similarly, you may wish to make a distinction between short- and long-term clients. They have different knowledge and different relationships with the organization. Many well-done research projects have used key informants. Of course, you lose the capacity to generalize, but you now have reasonably typical responses in your analysis. As with most of the methodological issues addressed in this text, most options are acceptable as long as they are clearly identified and justified.

Secondary Analysis

For many questions of need, secondary data and analysis of existing data are both desirable and reasonably simple. Agency records, both qualitative and quantitative, may contain large amounts of usable data. Qualitative data in the form of agency reports, legal documents, and other descriptive information can take you a long way to developing a rich description of the agency, its goals and purposes, and how it is organized. Similarly, for most issues of service provision, agencies can provide extensive records. These can include everything from case notes to sign-in sheets and even billing data. In many cases, quick transitions from spreadsheet to data analysis software are possible.

Of similar importance are the vast data sets that exist in the larger world. Many of the social problems we are interested in examining have entire organizations that are dedicated to doing little else but collecting relevant data. Crime, poverty, education, many health variables, many environmental variables, and occupational data at many geographic levels are quite easy to locate. However, two issues must be considered. First, if the data that you are accessing are used for comparative purposes, you must be certain that you have an appropriate justification for the comparison. If your organization is embedded in a larger geographic unit generally, you have a good justification. If you are looking to compare your data to a similar community, however, you need to be very careful about the criteria you use for comparison.

Surveys and Interviews

Surveys and interviews are indispensable for needs assessment research, most particularly, if you are interested in getting descriptive data, data about experiences, and data about opinions. Surveys and interviews assessing satisfaction or unmet needs are often essential. The central issue here, however, is whom to ask. Throughout an organization will be found a variety of opinions about any number of things. Different opinions are good. However, different opinions that come from sources that are dramatically unlike one another can be a problem. Differences need to be taken into account during the analysis and interpretation of the data. Hopefully, you can survey or interview enough people with the same characteristics so that you can obtain reasonably consistent results.

Focus Groups

Focus groups are quite effective at capturing group perceptions and attitudes. It may be a very useful tool for you to include as part of your agency study. Focus groups allow a great deal of flexibility as questions can flow from previous responses. As it is not just a discussion but also an organized conversation, the focus leader can move in a variety of ways based upon data that have been provided. You should provide an outline for base questions, but where those questions go after that, and the depth and follow-up, is the responsibility of the leader.

The biggest issues that have to be confronted for the focus group are whom to involve and what questions to ask. Questions generally should be guided by some existing data or theory. In addition, participants should be reasonably representative and typical of the groups desired. Of course, problems of groupthink in pure deception are always possible. That is why two or more groups with different participants may be desirable. Further, to capture trends, focus groups ought to be repeated on a regular basis if possible.

Community Needs Assessment

We spend all of our lives in and around communities. Communities are important to our lives in many ways, and working with communities is important for our profession (Reisch, 2017). Research on communities is a critical skill for social workers (University of Kansas, 2015c; University of Southern California, 2020). Depending upon the community in question, communities can serve as the matrix of our economy, provide safety and security, affect the quality of our education and socialization, act as an important integrative force, and provide mutual support. Although there are many similarities between organizations and communities (e.g., both are groups), there are some important differences as well. Organizations certainly do many of the things that communities do, perhaps all of them, but in a very real way the community is the source of those processes. Organizations, on the other hand, mediate between the community and us and may enhance what the community provides.

There are at least two major types of communities: communities of place or geography and communities of interest or affiliation (Hardcastle et al., 2011; Millington, 2010). Both types have borders or boundaries, membership, some commonality among participants, and some level of policies and rules to guide behavior. Although there is overlap in how this manifests in our country (Wilson, 2013), the major difference is that with a community of place, you can physically point to the boundary. Communities of interest or affiliation have borders that are more generally conceptual. A quick example should serve to make this clear. The university community can be defined geographically based upon the property that it owns, or it can be defined conceptually by participation in university-sponsored activities. Membership, the characteristic that is important for a needs assessment in either definition of community, can be established, although the approach might differ. In the geographic definition, attending, residing, or working at the university may be the demonstrable variable for identification. For the definition of community as interest group, this might expand to include people who give money to the university, people who attend sports events or cultural events, or even people who regularly read university newsletters.

There are obvious strengths and weaknesses with either definition. Presence in a place may be highly disconnected from most relevant elements of a person's life. Think about individuals who live in suburban or rural areas but commute to work and use services in nearby urban areas. Such persons may have little interaction with the geographic world to which they are most directly connected. Perhaps the most important mediating factor for both types is the degree of psychological connection or identity.

The main point here is not that one community is more or less important than the other, but rather a very clear definition of the community you are examining is a critical component of an effective and accurate assessment (University of Kansas, 2015b).

Many of the issues identified under organizational assessment apply to community needs assessment as well. Thus, this discussion provides some review of the earlier content but will focus on some of the special issues that differentiate organizations and communities.

BOUNDARIES AND MEMBERSHIP

As discussed earlier, a critical early step in a community needs assessment understands exactly what "the community" means. For the purposes of a proposal, this centers on the problem of boundaries and membership. In some cases, particularly for communities of interest or affiliation, the easiest determining factor is some form of member list. Of course, not all communities of interest have such lists, and how to construct one is discussed shortly. Further, not all membership lists are accurate. As such, you may choose to use a list, but with some additional inclusion or exclusion criteria.

> **Reflection Questions**
> 1. Try to identify one community of place and one community of interest of which you are a part. For each, identify issues of boundaries and membership.
> 2. Why might it be important to examine the opinions of persons who have left communities? What kind of information might they provide?

There are also some kinds of studies that could benefit from examining persons who have left the community. For example, were their reasons something simple such as they could not afford to be a member, or something more complex that speaks to the functioning of that community? Such information can tell you important things about the community.

On the other hand, it is much more typical for a community not to have a complete membership list. The challenge here for you is how to construct the most complete and appropriate list for your purposes. For communities of place, sometimes a surrogate indicator can be the basis for identification. In the past, addresses have commonly been used. It is possible to obtain a complete list of all of the addresses in an area from the post office. Likewise, phone numbers can be used. With the rise of the cell phone, however, the connection between physical location and a phone number is weakening.

In all these cases, however, the definition of membership, and your population, must be linked to the surrogate indicator, not persons. Thus, it may be that your formal population and your study population are not exactly the same. This is common and not a serious problem, but a problem nevertheless.

You can also begin with any existing population list and add or remove membership as data are found. Sometimes, this can be done by obtaining lists from multiple sources and then trying to create a master list. You may also use some form of modified snowball sampling, where you take any existing list and ask members to refer you to other members.

A further and quite common method are surveys involving door-to-door interviews that can provide the population. In a sense, the address serves as the surrogate, but through this form of surveying, which is sometimes called "canvasing," the address identifier is supplemented by asking how many persons reside at each address.

Another approach is to focus on the knowledge that specific individuals may provide. This, as discussed earlier, is called "key informant sampling." Rather than creating a population and drawing a sample to which you can generalize the data, here you want to obtain data from specialized individuals. Often, this involves again obtaining at least a partial list of persons with expertise and then a modification through snowball efforts as data collection continues.

One very useful benefit of such data collection is that it gives you multiple perspectives on a similar issue. For example, suppose you are interested in determining the extent and causes of poor race relations in a community. There are very likely groups that see the problem differently. Police, business people, residents, youth, persons in the religious community, and incarcerated persons may all have differing opinions. This is somewhat like the old story of a number of blind persons trying to describe an elephant. Each person who touched a different part of the elephant understood the elephant differently. Only when all the perspectives were put together was an accurate picture created.

Of course, even smaller samples can be useful. Most well-done qualitative research is completed with numbers well under 25. A few focus groups, or a few very rich in-depth interviews, may be adequate your purposes.

QUESTIONS AND VARIABLES

In most cases, community needs assessments focus on three types of data: opinions, knowledge, and observed behaviors or skills. Of course, your research question drives the variables that you include, but understanding the richness of the community generally requires an understanding of what people objectively experience and how they feel about that experience.

As with organizational research, community needs research can be widely or narrowly focused. Broad assessments make sense if there are few clues about areas of concern to the community. Likewise, narrow and more focused assessments are appropriate when specific topic areas are of greater concern to the community or if the researcher is guided by the theory or model of what is important to consider. Broad assessments can focus on general issues of concern across a variety of important community themes. These themes are closely linked to the purpose of a community, as discussed earlier. These areas include community economics, safety and security concerns, government, social relations, general integration, social services, health services, and similar topics. Narrow assessments can focus on any one of those issues or even part of one of those issues.

Both approaches are useful and legitimate. The broad assessment makes sense if the community knows it has problems but is not sure about severity or priority. Again, like organizations, narrow assessments are most useful if some previous analysis has highlighted an area for examination, or if the researcher is guided by a theory that suggests where to look. There may also be overlap.

Whichever approach you choose, the variables that you include in your study are critically important. As many community issues have standardized assessment characteristics, and as governments study many community issues at all levels, it is very useful to try to find measures that matched those in these other studies. Local, state, and federal governments regularly measure poverty, crime, economic development, housing, food, and many health indicators. While some of these measures are not perfect, and many of them speak not at all to satisfaction with the services associated with them, they still are useful. At a minimum, this usefulness comes from the fact that they often provide comparison data. As we have discussed, stronger arguments about unmet needs are made when comparisons are available. The fact that governments routinely collect much of this information provides such comparisons, both in time and in incidence and severity.

What is not provided by much governmental activity is again opinions about community problems. There are few consistent data about satisfaction or priorities. One of the most serious problems in any community practice, and community needs assessments as part of community practice, is that many decisions about needs and services are made with little community input. Sometimes, these decisions are correct and appropriate. However, at other times, they are highly inappropriate. A good example of this issue surrounds the problem of community crime. Many communities experience crime, but understand the problem very differently than law enforcement or governmental officials do. It is not uncommon for communities to understand that crime is a function of poverty and social incohesion. On the other hand, law enforcement typically sees the problem of crime as a problem of punishment and criminal justice. At its worst, these differences strongly contribute to the antagonism that exists between many disenfranchised communities and law enforcement.

GENERAL ISSUES OF DATA COLLECTION

One of the most serious problems in any community practice, and community needs assessments as part of community practice, is that many decisions about needs and services are made with little community input. Community research is actually one way to enhance participation of the community in community life.

A second issue that may or may not be more widespread in community research than other types of research is the problem of outsider trust. Almost by definition, when you do a needs assessment, you are coming into a community that very often is distressed. It is very possible that you are not the first researcher. Indeed, many urban areas and particularly those that are close to universities, have often been studied by multiple researchers over the years. Sometimes, the researcher makes promises to the community that are not kept. Perhaps worse is that over time a perception will grow that the communities have been used. The researcher is coming, taking data, and leaving with very little contribution to the improvement of that community.

This leads to the single most important suggestion in this chapter related to community needs assessments. The very best research when it comes to communities involves those communities. There are multiple ways that community members can become involved, from identification of initial problem areas to question development, data collection, interpretation, and dissemination. The authors of this text regularly create research advisory groups. Such groups work hand-in-hand with the researchers to make the research as useful and competent as possible. This practice benefits both the researcher and the community being researched.

■ Methods

Almost any method of data collection can be used for some type of community needs assessment. As noted before, the methodology you choose to collect your data is heavily driven by the purpose and research questions of your capstone project. Both quantitative and qualitative methods may be useful. Some of the strengths and weaknesses of each approach for the various kinds of questions are now discussed.

First, it is important to remember that purposive sampling is both useful and often appropriate for community needs research. Random samples are difficult to obtain and may miss some importance of the group's perceptions. If, however, one can be obtained, the capacity to generalize findings is further benefited by the possibility of comparison to existing data sets.

The inability to create a true generalizable sample is not, however, a problem. There are many times when the specialized knowledge of some smaller part of the community is very useful. What is important for many research projects is to make sure that data obtained are reasonably typical for the group being examined. One very common problem in small sample research is the possibility of providing too much importance to unique answers. In any group, some people will be more or less satisfied, angry, or fearful than the majority. Minority opinions may be very valuable if they are reasonably common. Making major decisions based upon uncommon answers is, however, an error. What you hope for are either very clear trends from a single data set or a triangulation of results pointing in the same direction from various data sets. How this is done is unique to each analytical approach it takes. Here we want just to provide this warning: Do not overappreciate or underappreciate individual data points.

SECONDARY ANALYSIS

Secondary analysis is both very commonly used and quite valuable in the community of research. As we have suggested, a very large number of very useful data sets are created regularly as part of normal governmental functioning. For many areas and questions of need, such data are useful for both primary analysis and comparative purposes.

The World Wide Web, however, has made finding data sets much easier. Using one quick example, Fedstats.gov holds a wonderful repository of data collected primarily but not exclusively by the U.S. Census. Now, these data may be geographically limited in ways that are not beneficial to you. If your community research is focusing on, say, the neighborhood that does not have an official legal name, finding an exact match and data set may be difficult. Many researchers depend upon zip codes for geographic location. Zip codes, however, often cross community boundaries. In addition, zip codes are of very little benefit if the neighborhood is one of interest rather than place.

What may be called for in the case of nongovernmentally collected data is to see if such data have been collected by a reputable nongovernmental organization. Many polling organizations regularly capture data, at least at the national level, about many attitudes and opinions. Assuming you are using the same measures as provided by these data sets, you might have useful comparative data available to you. Similarly, for many issues of service provision in the community, agencies can provide extensive records. As discussed under organizations earlier often quick transitions from spreadsheet to data analysis software are possible. Once you settle on your research purpose and questions, one of the first additional areas that you will want to investigate is possible sources of data and records.

SURVEYS AND INTERVIEWS

Surveys and interviews are of course indispensable for community needs assessment research. These surveys can be structured and targeted to capture exactly the right data from exactly the right source. Further, they have the advantage of capturing data from persons at a distance. Many communities of interest are spread out quite widely. Capturing data from these sources is essential to your research and much easier thanks to technology.

Of course, all of the typical issues of survey research apply. Issues of inclusion and exclusion, appropriate design, in-person interviews versus self-report, and cost must be considered.

One unique characteristic of much community research to consider is the use of community members to collect the data. There is a very rich history of such data collection procedures in this country. Members of the community have the advantage of knowing the terrain, sometimes the people being interviewed, and hopefully with appropriate levels of trust and communication skills appropriate to the community. This can be quite beneficial to the research and has the additional value of credibility in the eyes of community members.

From you and your community standpoint, this is mostly a win–win proposition. However, there are two major issues to consider. First, significant time must go into the training of those who are collecting data. Training of course is always important for people who interview data, but probably more so if you are using persons who are unfamiliar with the methods of science. This is probably going to take some time on your part, but recognize that you are empowering and educating members of the community. That is a plus.

The second issue is one that almost all research confronts and that is the problem of honesty among participants. This problem might be magnified if the people who are asking them very sensitive questions are their neighbors. Many of the issues examined in community needs assessment are quite sensitive. They might be asking about sex, substance abuse, violence, and neighbor relationships. For anyone, these raise ethical red flags. So ask yourself if you would feel comfortable telling someone you know, or who could know people whom you know, your answers to sensitive questions. Therefore, you certainly want to consider the ethics of such a process. Often, there is no right answer, but lots of potentially wrong ones.

FOCUS GROUPS

As with organizational research, focus groups can be an effective tool for community assessments. They can capture large amounts of data quickly and can capture trend data if used over time. The biggest issues for which focus groups have to be confronted are whom to involve and what questions to ask. Questions generally should be guided by some existing data or theory. In addition, participants should be reasonably representative and typical of the groups desired. Of course, problems of groupthink in pure deception are always possible. That is why a different group with different participants may be desirable. Further, to capture trends, focus groups ought to be repeated on a regular basis if appropriate.

MIXED METHODS

It is hard to envision a community needs assessment that does not have some degree of mixed methods. The use of secondary data analysis, survey research, focus groups, and even some community observations can be extremely beneficial for creating a full picture.

One such approach to mixed methods is the merging of data from the sources identified previously with the geolocation of clients. Software for mapping and many existing data sets that are pre-Geo–identified allow for some very complex analyses. And the merging of data of many types both visually and statistically can tell important stories about communities.

As a final thought, the most important consideration in any effective community needs assessment again is community involvement. No community needs assessment will succeed, and any practice benefits achieved, if the community is left out of the process. It is strongly suggested that some form of community involvement, such as a citizen advisory group, be integrated into your capstone research. This is both for your benefit and the community's. There are of course limits. You want to make sure that the community gets something in return for its effort, be it data or more. However, you certainly want to consider its needs as well as your own.

PRACTICE ACTIVITIES

1. Write down a list of community problem areas that you might find interest in researching. In a column next to it, try to identify a method that you could examine for your research study. Then in a third column, think of the issues you would need to overcome to conduct that research.
2. Using the same list of items, see if you can find at least one journal article that has investigated the problem area.
3. Finally, identify a community of which you are a member of. How would you define membership and community boundaries? What might be left out that is important?

TECHNOLOGY EXERCISE

Think about the social problem that you might be interested in examining. Identify the population that might be affected by that problem. Examine the internet site Fedstats.gov and search for that problem among the population of interest. What data sets do you find that might be useful to you? Write those down for later use.

REFERENCES

Hardcastle, D. A., Powers, P. R., & Wenocur, S. (2011). *Community practice: Theories and skills for social workers* (pp. 94–129). Oxford University Press. http://resources.css.edu/library/docs/cp4.pdf

Hopper, E. (2020). *Maslow's hierarchy of needs.* ThoughtCo. https://www.thoughtco.com/maslows-hierarchy-of-needs-4582571

Millington, R. (2010). *Different types of communities.* Feverbee. https://www.feverbee.com/different-types-of-communities

Pennsylvania Spatial Data Access. (2015). *GIS basics tutorial.* http://www.pasda.psu.edu/tutorials/gisbasics.html

Reisch, M. (2017). Why macro practice matters. *Human Service Organizations: Management, Leadership & Governance, 41*(1), 6–9. https://doi.org/10.1080/23303131.2016.1179537

University of Kansas. (2015a). *Conducting needs assessment surveys.* The Community Toolbox. https://ctb.ku.edu/en/table-of-contents/assessment/assessing-community-needs-and-resources/conducting-needs-assessment-surveys/main

University of Kansas. (2015b). *Defining and analyzing the problem.* The Community Toolbox. http://ctb.ku.edu/en/table-of-contents/analyze/analyze-community-problems-and-solutions/define-analyze-problem/main

University of Kansas. (2015c). *Strategies for community change and improvement: An overview.* The Community Toolbox. http://ctb.ku.edu/en/table-of-contents/assessment/promotion-strategies/overview/main

University of Southern California. (2020). *The social work toolbox: 10 skills every social worker needs.* http://msw.usc.edu/mswusc-blog/10-skills-every-social-worker-needs

Wilson, R. (2013). Another way to explain who we are: The 15 types of communities that make up America. *Washington Post,* November 12. http://www.washingtonpost.com/blogs/govbeat/wp/2013/11/12/another-way-to-explain-who-we-are-the-15-types-of-communities-that-make-up-america

7

QUALITATIVE CONCEPTS, APPROACHES, AND PROCESSES

This chapter provides you with a basic understanding of qualitative research and equips you with sufficient information to understand how qualitative research is undertaken. Different types of qualitative research are highlighted. Examples include case studies, grounded theory studies, and phenomenological studies. This chapter also provides an introduction to qualitative data analysis by reviewing three different approaches to it: interpretive approaches, the social anthropologic approach, and the collaborative social research approach. Three qualitative data methodologies are described: content analysis, thematic analysis, and narrative analysis.

By the end of this chapter, you will be able to do the following:

- Understand what qualitative descriptive studies are.
- List the eight characteristics of qualitative research and researchers.
- Describe various qualitative research designs including case studies, grounded theory, and phenomenological studies.
- Explain three general approaches to qualitative data analysis (i.e., interpretive, social anthropologic, and collaborative social research).
- Describe qualitative data analysis methods including content analysis, thematic analysis, and narrative analysis.

Qualitative Descriptive Studies

Qualitative research genres have become increasingly important modes of inquiry for the social sciences and applied fields such as education, nursing, community development, management, and social work. Long dominated by research techniques borrowed from the experimental sciences, the social sciences now offer a wide array of alternative research methods. If you are interested in conducting qualitative research for your capstone project, you can explore social phenomena in a variety of ways including case studies, group discourse analysis, narrative analysis, or by conducting needs assessments and program evaluations (Marshall & Rossman, 2015).

Qualitative researchers are often fascinated with the complexity of social interactions expressed in daily life and with the meanings individuals themselves attribute to such interactions. This scientific curiosity leads qualitative researchers into natural settings. Accordingly, qualitative research is pragmatic, interpretive, and grounded in the actual lived experiences of people. Rossman and Rallis (2011) propose eight characteristics of qualitative research and researchers.

Qualitative research:

1. is naturalistic;
2. draws on numerous methods that respect the humanity of study participants;
3. is emergent and evolving; and
4. is interpretive.

Qualitative researchers:

5. view social worlds as holistic and harmonious;
6. engage in systematic reflection regarding their own roles in the research they conduct;
7. are aware of and sensitive to their personal biographies and how their experiences shape the study; and
8. rely on complex reasoning that moves back and forth from deduction and induction.

Qualitative research, in essence, is a broad approach to the study of social phenomena. The various genres of qualitative inquiry (e.g., phenomenological, ethnographic, grounded theory, narrative, action, and case studies) draw on multiple methodologies and are naturalistic and interpretive (Marshall & Rossman, 2015). The remainder of this chapter provides you with information about each of these qualitative research approaches.

QUALITATIVE RESEARCH APPROACHES

As someone interested in conducting qualitative research, you have a number of different approaches from which to choose in developing your capstone project (Leedy & Ormrod, 2001; McMillan & Wergin, 2002; Mohajan, 2018). In general, most qualitative research is nonexperimental, meaning that it does not search for cause-and-effect relationships (Cottrell & McKenzie, 2005). Instead, as a research paradigm, qualitative research aims to provide depth of understanding. It uses words rather than statistics to describe meaning, to discover, and to better understand phenomena. Although research questions are used, and the answers to those questions are explored in great detail, it is less concerned with sample size than quantitative research methods. Qualitative research applies inductive reasoning and seeks uniqueness over generalization. As a qualitative researcher, you are engaged in part of the investigative process (Cottrell & McKenzie, 2005).

Qualitative research can be difficult to clearly define. It has no distinctive paradigm or theory across the different research designs (Denzin & Lincoln, 2011). It is sometimes defined by its source of information, such as an activity situated in a way that locates the research observer in the world of the observed. It has been described as studying things in their natural settings, in order to make sense of phenomena in terms of the meanings people attach to them (Denzin & Lincoln, 2000). Qualitative research has also been defined as an examination process of understanding based on specific methodologic traditions of inquiry that explore human problems, where the researcher constructs a complex, holistic picture of a phenomenon, analyzes words, reports detailed views of participants, and conducts their research in a natural setting (Creswell, 1998).

A wide array of qualitative research genres exists and there are many excellent books to serve as guides to their approaches and assumptions. However, despite this variety, there are some common considerations and procedures for its conduct and for specific ways of thinking that most qualitative researchers espouse (Rossman & Rallis, 2011). Common ways of thinking may include viewing social worlds as holistic and interconnected, placing a high value on people's daily subjective experiences, and promoting positive change. Procedurally, transparency is vital in qualitative research. Due to the fact that sample sizes are typically small, sometimes just a single case, qualitative researchers need to document every step of the research process. In consideration of those who may read their research report, documentation should include information about why they chose a particular approach; with whom they collaborated; how they gained permission to conduct their study; how they chose their sample, collected their data, coded and interpreted their data; and any limitations their study may have.

The Case Study Approach

A "case study" is a general term for the exploration of an individual, group, or phenomenon (Sturman, 1997). It is "an exploration of a bounded system or a case (or multiple cases) over time through detailed, in-depth data collection involving multiple sources of information" (Creswell, 1998, p. 61). A bounded system is one that is bound by time and space, for example, a parenting skills program for teen parents at a particular location and for a defined period of time (Cottrell & McKenzie, 2005). Thus, a case study can be understood as a comprehensive description of an individual case and its analysis.

Most often a case study is defined by what is being studied (e.g., individual, family, intervention; Stake, 1995) rather than as a research method (Creswell, 2009). Case studies are the favored qualitative method when the "why" or "how" questions being asked are limited in number and are linked to specific events and their interrelationships, when a holistic understanding of a situation is necessary, when the researcher has little or no control over events, and when there is a present-day focus within a real-life context. Case studies rely on historical and document analysis, interviewing, and, frequently, some form of observational data collection. There is a rich tradition of organizational research, community studies, and program evaluations that provide evidence for the emblematic power of research that is focused on depth and detail regarding the investigation of a specific phenomenon. Case studies help to take readers into settings with a vividness and a level of detail not typically found in more analytic reporting methodologies (Marshall & Rossman, 1999).

Anthropologists and sociologists have traditionally used case studies. However, other disciplines such as social work and other social sciences have come to embrace this qualitative approach to understanding a problem as well. For example, Fraser, Michell, Beddoe and Jarldon (2016) used a multiple case study approach to explore the use of Feminist Memory Work (FMW) with working-class women who were pursing degrees in social science. In that study, women narrated and interpreted what helped and hindered their efforts to study at their university. Data collection methods included observation, review of written narratives (i.e., individual cases), and group-processing transcripts. Fraser et al. (2016) found that the most significant benefit to using FMW was the spontaneous growth in confidence and solidarity in the women participants. Through the writing of their personal stories, and then sharing them with the other women in the study, they discovered that they were not alone and were not to blame for the hardships they faced.

Rather than investigating the impact of a treatment or intervention in a single-subject case experiment, in a single-subject case study you would observe and record a subject's reaction to a naturally occurring event. Take, for example, the issue of problematic wandering behavior in cognitively impaired older adults. In a single-subject case experiment, the researcher would determine the impact of a specific intervention on the subject (i.e., an older adult). Using the case study approach, you would seek to understand *why* the older adult is doing (or not doing) a particular behavior (i.e., problematic wandering) and *how* that behavior is impacted by their environment (i.e., physical characteristics of the location, fellow older adults, caregivers, staff). You would record not merely the behavior of the older adult within the environment (e.g., an assisted living facility), but would attempt to understand *why* the behavior occurs and *what* factors may influence the behavior.

A gerontology practice example of a case study research might involve studying a single cognitively impaired client with a history of problematic wandering behavior. If you were to conduct a case study of this client for your capstone research project, you would seek to fully understand all of the factors that affect your client's wandering behavior. One way to begin such an investigation would be to conduct a literature review on previously identified psychosocial factors that may influence wandering behavior and then review your client's files and case notes for evidence of those psychosocial factors in their history. You would also want to review the literature on effective strategies for managing wandering behavior and then document which (if any) of those strategies (e.g., environmental modifications, planned activities, physical exercise, and attention to psychosocial history) are being used by the field placement agency (Goldsmith et al., 1995).

There are two general formats of the case study approach: singular and multiple. When conducting a singular case study, meaning that you are examining only one case, there are a number of formats from which to choose. Some of the benefits of the single case study method are that it is not as time-consuming and/or expensive as multiple case studies, it allows the researcher to develop a deeper understanding of the case, and it enables the researcher to create a rich description of any phenomenon being studied.

A few of the different types of singular qualitative case studies are as follows (Cottrell & McKenzie, 2005; Gustafsson, 2017; Thomas, 2011):

- Snapshot case study—The case being examined represents one particular period, such as an hour/day/week in the life of a person or group, progress notes about counseling or support group sessions, diaries, and so forth. In this type of case study, the analysis is aided by a time-bound combination of events. As the snapshot develops, the picture represents a unified whole based on the information gathered over a very limited time frame.
- Longitudinal case study—This is similar to a snapshot study, but instead of being significantly time limited, it is a study of a single individual or group case over a longer period of time.
- Instrumental case study—This is when the case itself is of secondary interest, with the primary purpose being to provide insight into an issue (e.g., the psychological impact of the COVID-19 pandemic).
- Multiple case study—This is when the results of a couple or more instrumental case studies are analyzed, compared, and contrasted.

The multiple case study approach has some significant benefits. For example, using the instrumental case study example, the more individual or group cases involved in the study, the more insight we can gain about the psychological impact of the COVID-19 pandemic. Multiple case studies allow for a wider analysis of a phenomenon, lead to a more comprehensive understanding of the issue under consideration, inform the process of formulating important research questions, and aid in the discovery and evolution of theory.

Case study data can be collected by reviewing records and documents, observations, interviews, audiovisual materials, and other artifacts. Regardless of the case study method you use, you will need to clearly describe the case you are investigating. You can accomplish this by providing a detailed narrative for the reader that integrates and summarizes crucial information. Not unlike other qualitative research approaches, case study research requires you to spend considerable time, be personally involved with activities of the case, and reflect and revise meanings of what is taking place (Stake, 1995).

Grounded Theory

Grounded theory, first introduced in the 1960s and having its origins in the field of sociology, involves using systemic inductive guidelines for collecting and analyzing data with the purpose of generating theory (Charmaz, 2000; Lune & Berg, 2018). The pioneering authors of grounded theory, Glasser and Strauss, believed that theories should not be created from nonobservational or experiential deduction, but should be grounded in field-derived data (Creswell, 1998; Glaser & Strauss, 1967). In their seminal book, *The Discovery of Grounded Theory: Strategies for Qualitative Research*, Glaser and Strauss (1967) laid the foundation for one of the most prominent and authoritative qualitative research methodologies used today (Vollstedt & Rezat, 2019).

In a research study based on grounded theory, the goal is to discover or generate a theory related to an identified phenomenon based on collected data. The term "grounded" emerged from the idea that any theory conceived from one's research is extrapolated from and rooted in the data collected. According to Glaser and Strauss (1967), grounded theory blends the strengths of both inductive and deductive reasoning in the process of discovering theory within social research data. Due to the fact that coding categories are identified through a careful and transparent examination of the data:

> *Laymen involved in the area to which the theory applies will usually be able to understand it, while sociologists who work in other areas will recognize an understandable theory linked with the data of a given area. (pp. 2–3)*

For those unfamiliar with the terms "deductive reasoning" and "inductive reasoning," here is a quick primer. *Deductive reasoning*, or deduction, begins with a general statement, or hypothesis, and explores all available possibilities that may lead to a specific and logical conclusion. The scientific method uses deductive reasoning to test hypotheses and theories. In deductive inference, researchers start with a *theory* and then based on that theory make a prediction of its projected ramifications (i.e., a *hypothesis*). For deductive reasoning to be sound, the hypothesis must be correct. There are usually a number of steps to deductive reasoning. First, there is a *premise*, then a second premise, and finally an *assumption*. For example, "All men are mortal. Travis is a man. Therefore, Travis is mortal." It is assumed that the premises "All men are mortal" and "Travis is mortal" are true. Therefore, the conclusion is logical and true. In deductive reasoning, if something is true of things in general, it is also true for all members of that domain (Bradford, 2017).

Inductive reasoning is the opposite of deductive reasoning. Inductive reasoning makes broad generalizations from data. In other words, you start with your collected data, then you draw conclusions from the patterns your data identify. This is also referred to as "inductive logic." Using inductive reasoning, researchers move from the specific to the general. A researcher makes many observations (i.e., collects data), makes a generalization, and then speculates an explanation or a theory. An example of inductive logic is, "The first marble I pulled from the bag is green. The second marble from the bag is green. A third marble from the bag is also green. Therefore, all the marbles in the bag are green."

Even if all of the premises are true in a statement, inductive reasoning allows for the speculated conclusion to be false. Here is an example: "Melinda is a grandmother. Melinda needs to wear corrective eyeglasses. Therefore, all grandmothers need to wear corrective eyeglasses." The conclusion does not follow logically from the statements. Inductive reasoning has its place in the scientific method. Social scientists use it to form hypotheses and theories. Deductive reasoning allows them to apply the theories to specific scenarios (Bradford, 2017). Now that you have been given an overview of both inductive and deductive reasoning, let us return to the topic of grounded theory.

The overall goal of grounded theory is to develop theory. With that in mind, grounded theory studies often research phenomena or topics that lack a solid theoretical foundation. Whether no theory exists for the identified phenomena or the existing theories surrounding the phenomena are insufficient in that they lack important concepts, the relationships among the concepts are not clarified enough, or the relevance of the concepts and their interconnections has not been validated for the population or the context under study, grounded theory aims to fill in such gaps in the literature. Due to its origins in the social sciences, grounded theory's main interest lies in investigating the origin, nature, methods, and limits of human knowledge in order to predict and explain behavior within social interaction (Vollstedt & Rezat, 2019).

Grounded theory is a methodology characterized by the continual and complementary processes of planning, data collection, data analysis, and theory development. Additionally, grounded theory provides a distinct set of systematic methods that support contemplation from the data in order to develop a theory that is grounded in the factual and/or observational data. The methods of grounded theory include various coding procedures based on the method of constant comparison. New cases are included, and new data are collected continuously for inclusion into the analysis based on their potential contribution to the further development and improvement of the evolving theory. This sampling method is known as "theoretical sampling" (Vollstedt & Rezat, 2019).

The process of collecting data in accordance with theoretical sampling, data analysis, and theory development is continued until new data no longer contribute significantly to the development of the theory. When that happens, a state of "theoretical saturation" has been achieved. The theory that is the product of this data saturation process is also referred to as "grounded theory." The quality of a particular grounded theory is not evaluated according to the standard criteria of test theory (i.e., reliability, validity, and objectivity), but rather in accordance with principles such as plausibility, credibility, and trustworthiness (Vollstedt & Rezat, 2019).

Any scientific endeavor begins with a research question implying the essence of what the researcher seeks to understand. The overall purpose of any grounded theory study is to find an answer to the research question presented by the researcher. The methodologies of a study are the tools used to find the best possible answer to the research question, so it should be the research question that determines the methodology, and not the other way around. For that reason, it is important to ascertain what kind of research questions are appropriate for a grounded theory study. The nature of the research question will influence the methodology and the choice of data collection methods (Vollstedt & Rezat, 2019). Strauss and Corbin (1990) underscore that grounded theory research questions should be oriented toward action and processes.

For example, sexual health educators might seek to develop grounded theory related to Black females' sexual development, sociocultural conditions, and sexual health outcomes. Beginning with field data collection, and then through careful synthesis and analysis of the data, a theory may emerge. As an illustration, Crooks et al. (2019) employed grounded theory to explain why Black females in the United States disproportionately suffer from sexually transmitted infections (STIs), including HIV. Grounded theory was used to systematically examine the complex social process of sexual development in Black females. Crooks et al. (2019) used theoretical sampling to identify and recruit participants who could help them achieve a richer understanding of interactions among categories, and to identify sociocultural conditions that could possibly explain those interactions.

Interview questions were developed by the research team and were pretested on a group of Black females who were representative of the university and community sample used in the study. Initial questions were open-ended (e.g., "What has it been like for you to have had an STD?"). After identifying stages of sexual development from the analysis of those early interviews, the researchers began asking their participants more focused questions. Examples included, "Some females have talked about being a girl, being grown, and being a woman in terms of their sexuality. Does this make sense to you?" and "Can you tell me about your sexuality at each phase?" Responses to those questions helped the research team further differentiate and identify social processes and various sociocultural conditions correlated with them (Crooks et al., 2019).

Data collection continued through audio-recorded interviews until theoretical saturation was reached, that is, the point where there were not any new category properties, dimensions, or conditions being identified (Strauss & Corbin, 1990). Their data suggest that Black women go through three developmental stages in becoming a Black sexual woman: Girl, Grown, and Woman. The researchers found significant overlap in the age ranges of the stages. Participants identified two common sociocultural conditions that influenced their progression from one stage to the next: stereotype messaging and protection (Crooks et al., 2019).

Common stereotypical messages influencing their sexual development included ones implying that Black females were sexual objects, that they were expected to behave like sexual objects, and media and cultural messaging centered on the importance of having a "good body." Common protective factors identified through their participant interviews included having a parental figure in whom they could confide about sexual matters and the close supervision of children during the "Girl" stage (particularly when around adults), and female mentorship characterized by a sharing of sexual health information and lessons gained from sexual experience (e.g., contraceptive use, pregnancy, STIs, intimate partner violence; Crooks et al., 2019).

As just illustrated using the example of the study about Black girl's/women's sexual development in a sexist and racist society, by using theoretical sampling to identify and recruit participants the research team were able to achieve a robust understanding of interactions among their coded categories, and clearly identified sociocultural conditions that helped explain those interactions.

The Phenomenological Approach

The origins of phenomenological research are rooted in the traditions of phenomenology (i.e., the study and description of phenomena) and hermeneutics (i.e., the science of interpretations), and especially the philosophical views of Martin Heidegger and Edmund Husserl (Heotis, 2020). Husserl proposed that the essence of a phenomenon could be best understood through an investigation and description surrounding the central components of human experience while suspending presumptions (Giorgi, 2007; Reiners, 2012). Heidegger's hermeneutic view expanded on Husserl's work by moving beyond mere description by prioritizing interpretation and finding meaning embedded in everyday contexts (Gill, 2014). As a result, a number of phenomenological research methodologies have been developed to examine and understand the subjective experience in relation to psychological or social phenomena. Exploring both perspectives and analyzing their differences can help select a suitable research design (Finlay, 2009;

Wilson, 2015). The two orientations available to phenomenological researchers are referred to as "descriptive" and "interpretive."

Descriptive-oriented phenomenological research methods support the idea that capturing a precise and vivid description regarding the perception of lived experiences can lead to a rich understanding of the essence of the phenomenon being studied. As such, research questions may center around what it is like for participants to experience a phenomenon (Wilson, 2015). Being that the primary intent is to capture an accurate description of a participant's experience, the researcher sets aside their own prior experiences, assumptions, and theories. Using phenomenological terminology, the researcher brackets their personal generalizations. Bracketing, or the act of suspending judgment about the natural world to focus on an analysis of experience, is particularly essential during the process of data collection and data analysis (Gill, 2014; Groenewald, 2004; Reiners, 2012).

In contrast, interpretive-oriented phenomenological research focuses on examining lived experiences, since meaning is embedded in experience. In other words, a person's experience of a phenomenon, and how meaning is formulated from it, can be understood through the process of interpretation. In this way, research questions may focus on how a particular phenomenon is experienced by a participant (Wilson, 2015). For the researcher, having an understanding of how one makes meaning of the experience, central components of the phenomenon can be identified, analyzed, interpreted, and explained. With this in mind, researchers cannot completely detach their own presumptions (Reiners, 2012) nor should they fool themselves into believing that it is fully possible to do so (Groenewald, 2004).

Phenomenological researchers do not consider human experience an unreliable source of data; instead they view it as the cornerstone of knowledge about human phenomena. Phenomenological research is based on two primary premises. The first is that human experiences are valid, rich, and rewarding sources of knowledge (Morrissey & Higgs, 2006). As communicated by Becker (1992), experience is the basis of human behavior and the source of all knowing.

Experience, what we are aware of at any point in time, is the foundation of our knowledge of ourselves, of other people, and the world in general. Without human experience there would be no human world. (p. 11)

The second premise of phenomenological research lies in the perspective that the everyday world is a valuable and productive source of knowledge, and that we can all learn a lot about ourselves and realize key insights into the nature of a situation or event by analyzing how it occurs in our daily lives (Becker, 1992). Supporting this notion, Schutz (1967) proposed that the focus of phenomenological research should be on the ways in which the "taken for granted" day-to-day realities of our world are produced and experienced by humans.

In essence, phenomenology is a way if exploring people's day-to-day lived experiences. When conducting a phenomenological study, your aim is to try to understand one or more individual's thoughts, perceptions and beliefs related to a particular event or situation. A phenomenological researcher examines subjective phenomenon (Creswell, 2009). For example, a thoughtful understanding of the meaningful aspects of having a conversation with a valued mentor, or the experiences of interacting with one's peers through online education classes, and the meaningful connections and closeness we experience through the involvement with support groups may be of value to professional social workers or to anyone interested or involved in the conversational relations of people's everyday life (Mohajan, 2018).

A phenomenological study by Morrissey and Higgs (2006) investigated adolescent female sexual experiences, sexual behavior, attitudes, and development. Twenty Australian-born Caucasian women between the ages of 18 and 30 were recruited and interviewed. Each participant was first asked an open-ended question: "Tell me about your experience of your first sexual intercourse" (Morrissey & Higgs, 2006, p. 166), followed by questions aimed at framing and focusing the interview conversation. Each interviewee's responses were summarized into individual case reports of their subjective experiences based on the following experiential domains: physical, emotional, educational, developmental, transitional, and influential.

Morrissey and Higgs's (2006) findings contributed to the field of knowledge in sexuality education and adolescent psychosexual development by providing an understanding of the experience of first sexual intercourse for females, including preparation, decision-making, affect, meaning, and influence. Such an understanding is important and relevant to sexuality researchers, sexual health educators, adolescent girls, parents, designers of education curricula, public health agencies, and policy makers.

> **Reflection Questions**
> 1. Are there sociocultural phenomena (e.g., racism, classism, homophobia, transphobia, domestic abuse, conflict, educational inequality) that you would like to explore? Why?
> 2. In relation to the COVID-19 pandemic, what phenomenological study topics would interest you the most (e.g., how does the COVID-19 pandemic impact adolescent mental health)?

Qualitative Data Analysis Approaches

Qualitative researchers have a number of procedural options to analyze their data. According to Miles and Huberman (1994) there are three major approaches to qualitative data analysis: interpretive approaches, social anthropologic approaches, and collaborative social research approaches. Before diving into an exploration of qualitative data analysis, it is important to think about the main purpose of social work research. Regardless of the type of research you conduct, whether it be quantitative or qualitative, social work research should seek primarily to address issues of social justice and systemic inequality or, at the least, should not contribute to the deficit-framed social constructions of marginalized populations by failing to acknowledge issues of prejudice, discrimination, and oppression (Labra et al., 2019). It is advisable to keep this in mind as you begin to analyze the data you have collected.

INTERPRETIVE APPROACHES

Interpretive approaches to qualitative research presume that the content humans produce, whether short stories, photographs, fine art, or interviews, is created for the purpose of communication. This approach to qualitative data analysis allows you to treat human activity and social action as text, so that human action can be viewed as a collection of symbols conveying layers of meaning (Lune & Berg, 2018). Observational data and interviews, then, can be transcribed into analyzable text. How you interpret such a text depends in part on your theoretical orientation. For example, if you have a phenomenological inclination you may resist condensing or framing data by categorizing or sorting procedures. Instead, you will likely attempt to unearth or expose the essence of a narrative. Using this approach will provide you with a system for discovering a practical awareness of actions and meanings. If you are more inclined toward a general interpretation orientation using a subtype such as symbolic interactionists, systems theorists, or dramaturgists, you will likely want to organize and reduce the data you collect in order to discover patterns of human action, activity, and meaning. A focused and systematic analysis can identify such data as overt meanings, latent meanings, and intent.

SOCIAL ANTHROPOLOGICAL APPROACHES

This approach to qualitative data analysis is particularly useful if you are interested in examining the behaviors of everyday life, ceremonies and rituals, language and language use, and human relationships. Your analytic task, using this approach, is to identify and help to explain the ways people operate in a particular setting, how they come to understand things, account for their actions, and how they manage their lives on a day-to-day basis. Unlike the interpretive approach, social anthropologic approach examines the assortment of materials (data) gathered by the researcher. The goal is less about interpreting the "text" of one's transcribed field notes and interviews, and more about finding patterns that appear across numerous sources and materials. It is common for researchers using this approach to begin with a theoretical or conceptual framework and then immerse themselves into the field so that they can test or refine their conceptualization (Lune & Berg, 2018).

Researchers utilizing this approach have often conducted a variety of case study activities or field work, spending considerable time within a community, or with an assortment of individuals in the field. This process often requires you to analyze multiple sources of data such as observations, case notes, interviews, photographs, and other artifacts. It is up to you to determine what material to include or exclude, in what order to present corroborating materials, and what to report first and last. As a social work student, you may find this approach particularly fitting when using your field placement setting to conduct your research-based capstone project.

COLLABORATIVE SOCIAL RESEARCH APPROACHES

This approach works well if you work with your research subjects in a specific setting in order to achieve some kind of change or action (e.g., participation, reflection, empowerment, emancipation). When using the collaborative approach, you gather data with the help of your research subjects, viewed as "stakeholders," with the goal of addressing a situation in need of change or action. Stakeholders, in a social work context, are defined as an individual or group that has an interest in any decision or activity of a social service agency or organization and who may be affected by or have an effect on an effort. Stakeholders may include funders, employees, volunteers, interns, service providers, and people who utilize the services of an agency or organization (Rabinowitz, 2020).

In the collaborative social research approach, data are collected and then considered both as information necessary to understand a situation and as feedback in order to take appropriate action, resolve a problem, or satisfy a field experiment of some kind. The strategies applied in this approach may be similar to those of the interpretive and social anthropology approaches; however, the overall goal of the collaborative approach is to generate a shared perspective of the information compiled from materials collected through various sources (Lune & Berg, 2018).

> **Reflection Question**
> Of the three major approaches to qualitative data analysis (interpretive, social anthropologic, and collaborative social) which approach would you be most interested in using for your capstone research project and why?

CONTENT ANALYSIS

Content analysis is a widely applicable methodology used by many disciplines, such as political science, criminology, journalism, art, history, language studies, and library science (Bogden & Biklen, 2006). However, it is most extensively used in the academic and professional disciplines within the realm of social sciences (e.g., social work, psychology, sociology) and mass communications (Zhang & Wildemuth, 2009). Due to its objective and systematic approach in creating conclusive interpretations of available data, social workers often utilize content analysis to help explore and address a wide range of subjects and themes like social justice, income inequality, social movements, and gender inequalities, and issues connected to racial and ethnic discrimination can be explored and addressed (Prasad, 2008).

Qualitative content analysis has been defined as:

- "a research method for the subjective interpretation of the content of text data through the systematic classification process of coding and identifying themes or patterns" (Hsieh & Shannon, 2005, p. 1278);
- "an approach of empirical, methodological controlled analysis of texts within their context of communication, following content analytic rules and step by step models, without rash quantification" (Mayring, 2000, p. 2); and
- "any qualitative data reduction and sense-making effort that takes a volume of qualitative material and attempts to identify core consistencies and meanings" (Patton, 2002, p. 453).

In essence, these three definitions illustrate how qualitative content analysis endorses an integrated view of messages in relation to their specific contexts, one in which the sender, the message being sent, and the receiver of the message are all research objects to be studied. Qualitative content analysis goes beyond simply counting words or extracting objective content from messages to examine meanings, patterns, and themes that may be clear-cut or veiled within a particular message/text. It allows researchers to gain an objective understanding of social reality in a scientific manner (Weber, 1990; Zhang & Wildemuth, 2009).

The qualitative approach usually produces descriptions or classifications, along with statements from subjects that reflect how they view their social world (Zhang & Wildemuth, 2009). In this way, the unique perspectives of a study's subjects can be better understood by the researcher(s) as well as the readers of the study's results. Qualitative content analysis picks up on unique themes that illustrate the many ways that subjects assign meaning to a phenomenon, rather than simply reporting the statistical significance of the occurrence of distinct texts or concepts as quantitative content analysis does. Therefore, a primary goal of content analysis is to identify the multitude of attitudes, views, opinions, interests, and sentiments of individuals, homogeneous or diverse groups, communities, and organizations, so that replicable and valid context-informed inferences can be formulated (Mihailescu, 2019).

Potential Uses of Content Analysis

You may be wondering how content analysis can be used. As a research methodology, content analysis has many applications. As a tool to use in your capstone research project, you can use it to do the following:

- Determine the existence and frequency of concepts in a text (i.e., conceptual analysis) and then examine the relationships among those concepts (i.e., relational analysis).
- Describe behavioral and attitudinal responses to communications.
- Determine the emotional or psychological states of individuals or groups.
- Reveal cultural differences in a communication context.
- Identify patterns in the content of communications.
- Reveal the intentions, meanings, focus, or communication patterns of an individual, group, or social service agency.
- Pretest in order to improve a survey or an intervention prior to launch.
- Analyze focus group interviews and answers to open-ended questions to enrich quantitative data.

Formal Approaches to Content Analysis

Hsieh and Shannon (2005) describe three distinct approaches to conducting qualitative content analysis: *conventional*, *directed*, and *summative content analysis* (see Table 7.1). According to Hsieh and Shannon, these approaches differ based on the degree of emphasis given to indicative reasoning (i.e., a method of logical thinking where you form generalizations based on experiences, observations, and facts). When actually conducting qualitative research, you do not simply choose one approach and exclude the others; however, it is useful to think of these perspectives individually.

Conventional content analysis involves the process of inductively creating coding categories from the raw data. It is usually applicable when research literature is limited regarding the examined phenomenon. Such a process is what some methodologists refer to as a

TABLE 7.1 FORMAL CONTENT ANALYSIS TYPES

TYPE	PROCESS	PURPOSE
Conventional	Inductively create categories from raw data	Generate theories or theoretically grounded explanations
Directed	More organized approach incorporating analytic codes and categories obtained from existing explanations and theories in order to organize raw data	To help fill in the gaps in understanding for a phenomenon, when the existing research is incomplete
Summative	Counting and totaling existing words or phrases from raw data	To examine the usage of specific words and phrases to discover underlying meanings

SOURCE: Adapted from Hsieh, H. F., & Shannon, S. E. (2005). Three approaches to qualitative content analysis. *Qualitative Health Research, 15*(9), 1277–1288. https://doi.org/10.1177/1049732305276687

"grounded theoretical approach." The purpose of this approach is to generate theories or theoretically grounded explanations for the analyzed document's content. The code categories reflect the categories of meaning used by your study participants or in the context of your study environment (e.g., agency, organization, classroom). Utilizing this approach's perspective, you might collect data from participants in a specific social service agency and code for evidence pertaining to the issues that concern them, such as schedule flexibility, collegiality, cooperation, acceptance of diversity, discrimination, and unfair privileges.

Directed content analysis is a more organized approach that involves incorporating a greater amount of analytic codes and categories obtained from existing explanations and theories relevant to your research focus. You would use the directed approach to conduct a content analysis when the existing research about the phenomenon you would like to investigate is incomplete. The existing research on the phenomenon will assist you in developing additional research questions aimed at addressing the gaps in understanding about that phenomenon.

With directed analysis, you become immersed in the raw data, using previously identified themes and those that emerge from the data itself. The code categories you create will reflect the meanings and expectations that are fundamental to the theoretical framework that you have adopted in order to scrutinize your research project. Looking at the same social service agency setting, you might talk with study participants (both service providers and clients/consumers) about acceptance of diversity, but actually code the data for abuses of power, demonstrations of subservience, political maneuvering, religious-based condemnation, or other forms of bias or "covert" intent.

Summative content analysis begins by counting existing words or phrases from the raw data itself (the text). The main objective of this approach is to examine the usage of specific words and phrases, and not to necessarily understand the content's meaning. However, the overall goal of the summative method does involve attempting to discover the underlying meaning of your data through analysis and quantifying specific words. As the researcher, your exploration of the data includes latent meanings and themes that are apparent in the data. In the context of qualitative research, when something is considered as latent, it implies that it is not directly observable but rather inferred from other variables that can be and are observed.

Again, referring to the same social service agency setting previously mentioned, one might count instances of both accepting and discriminatory exchanges and encounters among service providers and clients/consumers in order to get a quick indication of whether the agency is overall a collegial place to be. Note that in such a case one would not ask research participants to list either negative or positive interactions. Doing so would measure only whether they feel that the setting is collegial or not. Instead, you might ask them to describe everything that happened since they arrived at work (if an agency volunteer/intern/staff/administrator) or during their last two appointments (if a client/consumer), after which you would code the narratives for both negative and positive events.

Given these different yet overlapping approaches to content analysis, you can see reappearing components regardless of the style of qualitative analysis you pursue. Adapted from Lune and Berg (2018), the following is a general set of qualitative analytic activities arranged in a typical sequential order:

1. Data are collected and converted into text in order to be "read" (e.g., field notes, progress notes, transcripts, image sequences, any other form of descriptive documentation).
2. Codes are developed analytically and/or inductively identified in the data and anchored to sets of notes or transcript pages.
3. Codes are reconstructed into categorical labels or themes.
4. Collected materials are sorted into these categories and/or themes, identifying similar phrases, patterns, relationships, and disparities or commonalities.
5. Sorted materials are investigated in order to isolate meaningful patterns and processes.
6. Identified patterns are contemplated in light of previous research and theories, and a small set of generalizations is concluded.

Although these six steps are often performed in a linear fashion, it is sometimes necessary to revisit earlier steps when new data are examined or when a colleague or fellow researcher provided their input. In addition, the six steps just outlined occur after you have already identified your research question(s) and sample(s) for analysis, set a reasonable time frame for your project, and began collecting your data (e.g., transcribed interviews, written responses to surveys with open-ended questions).

THEMATIC ANALYSIS

Learning how to conduct a thematic analysis can help you make sense of other, more specialized forms of analysis since it is relatively easy to learn (Braun & Clark, 2014). Much like content analysis, thematic analysis is used across a wide array of academic disciplines including psychology, medicine, health services, education, and social work (Braun et al., 2019; Cassol et al., 2018; Frith & Gleeson, 2004; Halverson et al.,

2014; Labra et al., 2019; Norris et al., 2017). "Thematic analysis" refers to an array of approaches aimed at identifying patterns across sets of qualitative data. Just as with content analysis, a "data set" refers to all materials accumulated within the scope of a given research study: written testimonials, verbal communications, transcribed interviews of participants, research questions, as well as all other relevant materials including annual research reports, newspaper articles, reports on the effectiveness of social work interventions, and so forth (Labra et al., 2019).

As an analytic method, thematic analysis is a useful entry point for learning how to conduct rigorous qualitative analysis (Braun & Clark, 2014). It offers researchers a great deal of theoretical flexibility in that it can produce a data-driven or a theory-driven set of findings, which can then address a wide range of research questions (Braun & Clark, 2006). Thematic analysis is a method where researchers sort and sift through the data set to identify similar phrases and/or relationships, enabling researchers to identify and organize relevant themes and subthemes that can be used as units of analysis, a common practice across many qualitative analytic approaches (Miles & Huberman, 1994).

Through the process of inquisitively rereading data sets, researchers become increasingly familiarized with the data and are able to better explore the meanings connected with the concepts that emerge from participant accounts (Lester et al., 2020). The practice of repeatedly reading data sets is a necessary component for the identification of significant themes in the collected materials. It is through the process of rereading data sets that the affective, cognitive, and symbolic dimensions of the collected data can be revealed (Labra et al., 2019). Thus, the central operation of thematic analysis is *thematization*, referring to the mental act or process of selecting particular topics as themes in discourse or words as themes in sentences (Collins Dictionary, 2020).

The Phases of Thematic Analysis

Thematic analysis involves six distinct phases (Braun & Clarke, 2014; Labra et al., 2019). It is important to note that the six phases presented in Figure 7.1 interact and overlap. Although generally a linear process, the six phases are not exclusively successive. Such characteristics signal that thematic analysis is not only flexible but also a rigorous method of data analysis. There are three distinct approaches that can be applied to thematic analysis: deductive (when themes are assigned prior to analysis), inductive (when themes emerge during the course of analysis), or, more commonly, a deductive–inductive combination. In addition to the well-known and practiced six-phase process of thematic analysis, Lester et al. (2020) introduced making the analytic process as transparent as possible as a seventh phase in the process. Although not as commonly cited, this phase is significant in order to ensure the validity of one's qualitative research process and analysis.

The Narrative Analysis Approach

Narrative analysis is an interdisciplinary approach that seeks to describe the meaning of experience for individuals, usually those who are socially marginalized, disenfranchised, discriminated against, or oppressed, in order to produce stories (narratives) about their lived experiences (Wilks, 2005). Autobiographies, biographies, and life histories as well

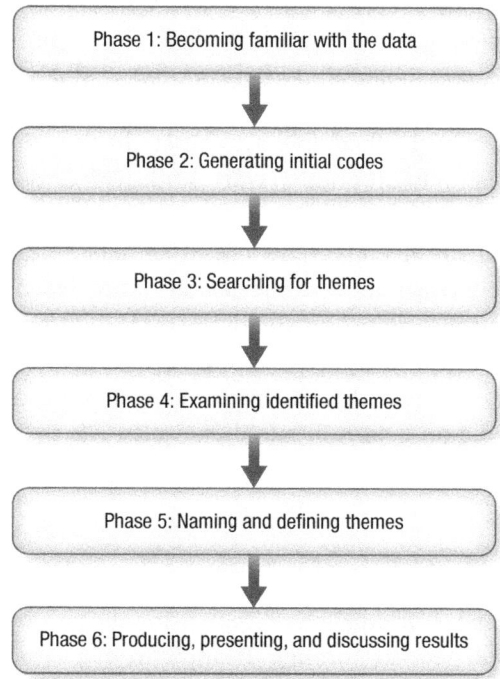

FIGURE 7.1 Six-phase thematic analysis process.

SOURCES: Braun, V., & Clarke, V. (2014). Thematic analysis. In A. C. Michalos (Ed.), *Encyclopaedia of quality of life and well-being research* (pp. 6626–6628). Springer; Labra, O., Castro, C., Wright, R., & Chamblas, I. (2019). Thematic analysis in social work: A case study. *IntechOpen*. https://doi.org/10.5772/intechopen.89464

as oral histories and personal narratives are all forms of narrative analysis. This method promotes the idea that a person or group's realities are shaped by the stories (their narratives) they themselves and others tell (Sahlstein-Parcell & Baker, 2017). All people engage in the construction of personal narratives, so storytelling is an integral part of better understanding peoples' lives.

As a researcher interested in narrative analysis, you explore and record the stories shared by participants. However, in order to gather the most authentic and truthful information possible, narrative analysis requires that you establish openness and trust between you and your participants (Marshall & Rossman, 2015). A primary tenet of any narrative inquiry is that it is conducted as a mutual and sincere collaboration between the researcher and those who agree to participate in the study. Over time, a caring relationship needs to develop before participants will be comfortable and feel safe enough to fully participate in telling their stories and reliving personal experiences, some of which may carry with them emotional burdens. This demands that you give full attention, actively listen, and give your participants full voice.

Narrative analysis values the symbols, signals, and expressions and feelings in language people use, validating how the narrator constructs meaning (Marshall & Rossman,

2015). Narrative analysis has been particularly valuable in developing critical and feminist theory, and when framed within such theoretical constructs, the overall purpose of narrative analysis will be emancipatory in nature (Bloom & Monro, 1995; Eisner, 1988; Lather, 1991; Riessman, 1993).

Narrative analysis can be applied to any written information, group dialogue, or in-depth interviews. It can rely on photographs, audio/video recordings, letters, journal records, autobiographical writing, email, text messages, twitter tweets, and other data (Mahmoud & Tehseen, 2020). If a researcher uses their field notes for a narrative analysis, they should always share those notes with the narrator(s) represented in those documents in order to adhere to the collaborative nature of the form of inquiry. Throughout the process of narrative analysis there is an open and honest recognition that the researcher is collaboratively constructing the reality of the narrator(s), and not simply recording and reporting. When reporting on a narrative analysis study, it is important to communicate to your readers every step of your methodology (Connelly and Clandinin, 1990).

PRACTICE ACTIVITIES

1. When approaching your qualitative study using the collaborative social research approach, you will be incorporating the input from a variety of "stakeholders" (i.e., your research subjects) in order to achieve some kind of positive change or action (e.g., participation, reflection, empowerment, emancipation). Think about your present or future social work internship placement site and make two lists: (a) list a potential area of positive change or action you would like to pursue (e.g., updated antidiscrimination policies; greater opportunity for agency clients to provide feedback for the services they receive) and (b) a list of the stakeholders (e.g., employees, volunteers, clients, family members of clients, supervisors) you would want to include in your study and why you want them included?
2. When conducting a narrative analysis, for example, of a case study, in order to gather the most authentic and truthful information possible, it is vital that you establish openness and trust between you and your participant(s). Write a list of five ways in which you will work to establish trust and openness with your participant(s).

TECHNOLOGY EXERCISE

Visit the website using the link that follows (or scan the QR Code). There you will find a list of case studies that focus on the issue of social isolation. Read one of the five case studies presented and answer the questions provided (e.g., What are some of the "lenses" that social workers can view this case? How might our treatment plans differ depending on which lens we use?).

Case Study Examples: https://grandchallengesforsocialwork.org/wp-content/uploads/2019/09/Eradicate-Social-Isolation-Faculty-Development-Institute-CSWE-2017.pdf

REFERENCES

Becker, C. (1992). *Living and relating: An introduction to phenomenology*. Sage.

Bloom, L. R., & Monro, P. (1995). Conflicts of selves: Non-unitary subjectivity in women administrators' life history narratives. In J. A. Hatch & R. Wisniewski (Eds.), *Life history and narrative* (pp. 99–112). Falmer.

Bogden, R., & Biklen, S. K. (2006). *Qualitative research for education: An introduction to theory and methods* (5th ed.). Pearson.

Bradford, A. (2017, July 25). *Deductive reasoning vs. inductive reasoning*. Live Science. https://www.livescience.com/21569-deduction-vs-induction.html

Braun, V., & Clarke, V. (2006). Using thematic analysis in psychology. *Qualitative Research in Psychology, 3*, 77–101. https://doi.org/10.1191/1478088706qp063oa

Braun, V., & Clarke, V. (2014). Thematic analysis. In A. C. Michalos (Ed.), *Encyclopaedia of quality of life and well-being research* (pp. 6626–6628). Springer Publishing Company.

Braun, V., Clarke, V., Hayfield, N., & Terry, G. (2019). Thematic analysis. In P. Liamputtong (Ed.), *Handbook of research methods in health social sciences* (pp. 843–860). Sage.

Cassol, H., Petre, B., Degrange, S., Martial, C., Charland-Verville, V., Lallier, F., Bragard, I., Guillaume, M., & Laureys, S. (2018). Qualitative thematic analysis of the phenomenology of near-death experiences. *PLoS One, 13*(2), e0193001. https://doi.org/10.1371/journal.pone.0193001

Charmaz, K. (2000). Grounded theory: Obstructionist and constructivist methods. In N. K. Denzin & Y. S. Lincoln (Eds.), *Handbook of qualitative research* (2nd ed., pp. 509–535). Sage.

Collins Dictionary. (2020). *Definition of "thematization."* https://www.collinsdictionary.com/dictionary/english/thematization

Connelly, F. M., & Clandinin, D. J. (1990). Stories of experience and narrative inquiry. *Educational Researcher, 19*, 2–4. https://doi.org/10.3102/0013189X019005002

Cottrell, R. R., & McKenzie, J. F. (2005). *Health promotion & education research methods: Using the five-chapter thesis/dissertation model*. Jones & Bartlett.

Creswell, J. W. (1998). *Qualitative inquiry and research design: Choosing among five traditions*. Sage.

Creswell, J. W. (2009). *Research design: Qualitative, quantitative and mixed methods approaches* (3rd ed.). Sage.

Crooks, N., King, B., Tluczek, A., & Sales, J. M. (2019). The process of becoming a sexual Black woman: A grounded theory study. *Perspectives on Sexual and Reproductive Health, 51*(4), 17–25. https://doi.org/10.1363/psrh.12085

Denzin, N. K., & Lincoln, Y. S. (2000). Introduction: The discipline and practice of qualitative research. In N. K. Denzin & Y. S. Lincoln (Eds.), *Handbook of qualitative research* (2nd ed.). Sage.

Denzin, N. K., & Lincoln, Y. S. (Eds.). (2011). *The SAGE handbook of qualitative research* (5th ed.). Sage. https://us.sagepub.com/en-us/nam/the-sage-handbook-of-qualitative-research/book242504

Eisner, E. W. (1988). The primacy of experience and the politics of method. *Educational Researcher, 20*, 15–20. https://doi.org/10.3102/0013189X017005015

Finlay, L. (2013). Exploring lived experience: Principles and practice of phenomenological research. *International Journal of Therapy and Rehabilitation, 16*(9), 1759–1779.

Fraser, H., Michell, D., Beddoe, L., & Jarldorn, M. (2016). Working-class women study social science degrees: remembering enablers and detractors. *Higher Education Research & Development, 35*(4), 684–697.

Frith, H., & Gleeson, K. (2004). Clothing and embodiment: Men managing body image and appearance. *Psychology of Men & Masculinities, 5*(1), 40–48. https://doi.org/10.1037/1524-9220.5.1.40

Gill, M. (2014). The possibilities of phenomenology for organizational research. *Organizational Research Methods, 17*, 118–137. https://doi.org/10.1177/1094428113518348

Giorgi, A. (2007). Concerning the phenomenological methods of Husserl and Heidegger and their application in psychology. *Collection du Cirp, 1,* 63–78. https://www.cirp.uqam.ca/documents%20pdf/Collection%20vol.%201/5.Giorgi.pdf

Glaser, G. G., & Strauss, A. (1967). *The discovery of grounded theory: Strategies for qualitative research.* Aldine.

Goldsmith, S. M., Hoeffer, B., & Rader, J. (1995). Problematic wandering behavior in the cognitively impaired elderly: A single-subject case study. *Journal of Psychological Nursing and Mental Health Services, 33*(2), 6–12. https://doi.org/10.3928/0279-3695-19950201-03

Groenewald, T. (2004). A phenomenological research design illustrated. *International Journal of Qualitative Methods, 3*(1), 42–55.

Gustafsson, J. (2017). Single case studies vs. multiple case studies: A comparative study. Student paper presented at the *Academy of Business, Engineering and Science.* Halmstad University, Halmstad, Sweden.

Halverson, L. R., Graham, C. R., Spring, K. J., Drysdale, J. S., & Henrie, C. R. (2014). A thematic analysis of the most highly cited scholarship in the first decade of blended learning research. *Internet and Higher Education, 20,* 20–34. https://doi.org/10.1016/j.iheduc.2013.09.004

Heotis, E. (2020). Phenomenological research methods: Extensions of Husserl and Heidegger. *International Journal of School and Cognitive Psychology, 7*(2), 1–3. https://www.researchgate.net/publication/344192530_Phenomenological_Research_Methods_Extensions_of_Husserl_and_Heidegger

Hsieh, H. F., & Shannon, S. E. (2005). Three approaches to qualitative content analysis. *Qualitative Health Research, 15*(9), 1277–1288. https://doi.org/10.1177/1049732305276687

Labra, O., Castro, C. Wright, R., & Chamblas, I. (2019). Thematic analysis in social work: A case study. *IntechOpen.* https://doi.org/10.5772/intechopen.89464

Lather, P. (1991). *Getting smart: Feminist research and pedagogy with/in the post modern.* Routledge & Kegan Paul.

Leedy, P. D., & Ormrod, J. E. (2001). *Practical research: Planning and design* (7th ed.). Prentice Hall.

Lester, J. N., Cho, Y., & Lochmiller, C. R. (2020). Learning to do qualitative data analysis: A starting point. *Human Resource Development Review, 19*(1), 94–106. https://doi.org/10.1177/1534484320903890

Lune, H., & Berg, B. L. (2018). *Qualitative research methods for the social sciences* (9th ed.). Pearson.

Mahmoud, A. B., & Tehseen, S. (2020). Narrative. In D. Hack-Polay, S. Hemelryk-Donald, A. B. Mahmoud, A. Ridyk, G. Bosworth, & R. Rahman (Eds.), *Migration as creative practice* (pp. 159–170). Emerald.

Marshall, C., & Rossman, G. B. (1999). *Designing qualitative research* (3rd ed.). Sage.

Marshall, C., & Rossman, G. B. (2015). *Designing qualitative research* (6th ed.). Sage.

Mayring, P. (2000). Qualitative content analysis. *Forum: Qualitative Social Research, 1*(2), Art. 20. https://www.qualitative-research.net/index.php/fqs/article/view/1089/2386

McMillan, J. H., & Wergin, J. F. (2002). *Understanding and evaluating educational research* (2nd ed.). Merrill/Prentice Hall.

Mihailescu, M. (2019). *Content analysis: A digital method.* Research Gate Open Access. https://www.researchgate.net/publication/333756046_Content_analysis

Miles, M. B., & Huberman, A. M. (1994). *An expanded sourcebook: Qualitative data analysis* (2nd ed.). Sage.

Mohajan, H. K. (2018). Qualitative research methodology in social sciences and related subjects. *Journal of Economic Development, Environment and People, 7*(1), 23–48. https://doi.org/10.26458/jedep.v7i1.571

Morrissey, G., & Higgs, J. (2006). Phenomenological research and adolescent female sexuality: Discoveries and applications. *The Qualitative Report, 11*(1), 161–181. https://nsuworks.nova.edu/tqr/vol11/iss1/9

Norris, J. M., White, D. E., Nowell, L., Mrklas, K., & Stelfox, H. T. (2017). How do stakeholders from multiple hierarchical levels of a large provincial health system define engagement? A qualitative study. *Implementation Science, 12*(1), 98. https://doi.org/10.1186/s13012-017-0625-5

Patton, M. Q. (2002). Qualitative research and evaluation methods. Sage.

Prasad, B. D. (2008). Content analysis. *Research Methods for Social Work, 5*, 1–20.

Rabinowitz, P. (2020). Section 8: Identifying and analyzing stakeholders and their interests. Chapter 7: Encouraging involvement in community work. In *Communications to promote interest and participation*. https://ctb.ku.edu/en/table-of-contents/participation/encouraging-involvement/identify-stakeholders/main

Reiners, G. M. (2012). Understanding the differences between Husserl's (descriptive) and Heidegger's (interpretive) phenomenological research. *Journal of Nursing & Care, 1*, 1–3. https://doi.org/10.4172/2167-1168.1000119

Riessman, C. (1993). *Narrative analysis*. Sage.

Rossman, G. B., & Rallis, S. F. (2011). *Learning in the field: An introduction to qualitative research* (3rd ed.). Sage.

Sahlstein-Parcell, E., & Baker, B. M. A. (2017). Narrative analysis. In M. Allen (Ed.), *The SAGE encyclopedia of communication research methods* (Vols. 1–4, pp. 1069–1072). Sage.

Schutz, A. (1967). *The phenomenology of the social world*. Northwestern University Press.

Stake, R. E. (1995). *The art of case study research*. Sage.

Strauss, A. L., & Corbin, J. M. (1990). *Basics of qualitative research* (vol. 15). Sage.

Sturman, A. (1997). Case study methods. In J. P. Keeves (Ed.), *Educational research, methodology and measurement: An international handbook* (2nd ed., pp. 61–66). Pergamon.

Thomas, G. (2011). A typology for the case study in social science following a review of definition, discourse and structure. *Qualitative Inquiry, 17*(6), 511–521. https://doi.org/10.1177/1077800411409884

Vollstedt, M., & Rezat, S. (2019). An introduction to grounded theory with a special focus on axial coding and the coding paradigm. In G. Kaiser and N. Presmeg (Eds.), *Compendium for early career researchers in mathematics education* (pp. 81–100). ICME-13 Monographs.

Weber, R. P. (1990). *Basic content analysis*. Sage.

Wilson, A. (2015). A guide to phenomenological research. *Nursing Standard, 29*(34), 38–44.

Wilks, T. (2005). Social work and narrative ethics. *British Journal of Social Work, 35*, 1249–1264. https://doi.org/10.1093/bjsw/bch242

Zhang, Y., & Wildemuth, B. M. (2009). Qualitative Analysis of Content. In B. M. Wildemuth (Ed.), *Applications of Social Research Methods to Questions in Information and Library Science, Library Unlimited*, pp. 1–12.

8

PRACTICE EFFECTIVENESS EVALUATIONS

In this chapter we explore how to conduct a practice evaluation. The chapter begins with a discussion of informal approaches to evaluating your social work practice followed by a discussion of formal practice evaluation using single-subject design (SSD) methodologies. The components of a SSD evaluation are reviewed as well as common designs. This is followed by a section on analyzing SSD data, a SSD case example, and a discussion of the ethics and social justice issues associated with SSD practice evaluations.

By the end of this chapter, you will be able to do the following:

- Describe two approaches to informal practice evaluation.
- Engage a client in a social work practice evaluation.
- Identify three common single-subject designs.
- Conduct SSD practice evaluations.
- Create a line graph with a celeration line.
- Visually and statistically analyze SSD data.
- Identify ethical issues associated with SSD practice evaluations.

Role of Evaluation in Social Work Practice

We have discussed that social workers are called upon by the National Association of Social Workers (NASW) *Code of Ethics* (2017) to engage in research in order to demonstrate commitment to the profession of social work. Social workers must engage in research-informed practice and practice-informed research (Council on Social Work Education [CSWE], 2015). Social workers must also integrate research information into their practice in order to be sure they are providing the best possible care for the clients they serve. Both are professional responsibilities.

The profession of social work has a long history of promoting systematic approaches to helping. Social work pioneer Mary Richmond in her early writings spoke to the need to support individuals on the basis of facts. As the profession has evolved over time, we have seen an influx of and the role of research to influence our practice. Research has helped us better understand the individuals, families, communities, and organizations with whom we work. Research has helped us better understand client development and growth. Research has also helped us regarding how we can intervene and support our clients (Poulin & Matis, 2020).

Social work research has evolved and will continue to evolve. We will make advancements in what we do now about client systems and how to best support them. In addition, as new conditions or concerns arise, we must use research to determine the best means of support. We caution our social work students to not consider your education done at the time of graduation. You must never stop learning. The knowledge of the profession is ongoing, and professional social workers must be continuous lifelong learners.

INFORMAL SOCIAL WORK PRACTICE EVALUATION

This section focuses on the practice effectiveness component of the evaluating practice competency. It addresses informal methods or approaches to determine the effectiveness of your social work practice with individuals, families, and groups.

SUPERVISION AND SELF-REFLECTION

One approach to evaluating the effectiveness of your social work practice with clients is through supervision. Social work supervision entails three components—administration, education, and support (Poulin & Matis, 2020). It is the educational component that can be used to evaluate your practice effectiveness.

An important part of the supervisory process is the willingness to share and be vulnerable. Sometimes we may not want to share certain things because they make us feel at risk. "Vulnerability" refers to a state of being open or exposed to criticism or judgment. It can be scary especially within the context of your supervisory relationship. Despite that, being vulnerable entails engaging in a process of self-reflection and being open to discussing your social work practice and practice effectiveness with your supervisor.

> **Reflection Questions**
> 1. How would you go about asking your client to participate in a practice evaluation? What would you say? How would you respond if your client says "no" to your request?
> 2. How open are you to feedback from your supervisor? What are your thoughts and feelings about having your work with clients evaluated?

Effective use of supervision to assess your social work practice effectiveness is dependent on the establishment of a trusting worker/supervisor relationship. The social worker must be able to trust the supervisor. Relationships cannot be built in the absence of trust. A certain degree of trust must be established for the worker to engage in the process of self-evaluation and the evaluation of their practice effectiveness.

Trust is essential for relationships to develop and grow between social workers and their supervisors. A strong relationship requires the absence of fear and suspicion and the presence of feelings of acceptance, support, and affirmation. Building trust with supervisors is an interactional process. Trust cannot be built in the absence of interpersonal interactions. It is built on a sequence of trusting and trustworthy interactions. The worker must act in a trusting manner and the supervisor must respond with trustworthy actions.

Within each interaction, three conditions are required for trust to develop. First, the worker must take a risk (make a choice) where the potential harmful consequences are outweighed by the potential benefits associated with the risk. Second, the worker must realize that the beneficial or harmful consequences associated with the risk depend on the supervisor's actions (response) as the helping professional. Third, the worker must experience the supervisor's actions as beneficial (Fong & Cox, 1983). All three conditions must be present for the interaction to contribute to the trust-building process.

The bond of trust is built over time, through a series of trusting actions (risks) and trustworthy responses (confirmations). Although it takes time for trust to be established, it can be destroyed through a single worker risk and supervisor disconfirmation (nontrustworthy) response (Fong & Cox, 1983).

The critical element in developing trust is risk. The supervisor is an active partner in the search for understanding and insights. This cannot happen if the worker is unable to take a risk by being open and honest about their social work practice with clients. Social workers have to be willing to share their thoughts, insights, feelings, and questions about their practice to be able to use the supervisory relationship to access their practice effectiveness. The primary task for the supervisor is to facilitate risk taking. The worker's task is to be self-reflective and to be willing to share information about their successes, mistakes, and ongoing challenges in order to assess client progress and make possible needed adjustments in their work together.

ONGOING CLIENT FEEDBACK

The social work value of competency discussed earlier implies that ethical social work practice involves an ongoing assessment of practice effectiveness throughout the helping relationship. This type of informal practice evaluation is based on the subjective responses of the clients. It is a joint and collaborative effort. Both the worker and the client have roles in this type of practice evaluation.

Ongoing informal evaluation is a relatively easy way for social workers to evaluate the effectiveness of their work with clients. In keeping with the principles of collaboration and empowerment, in which the client is the expert about their progress, subjective assessments play a prominent role in strengths-based social work practice and other practice models. Clients' subjective assessments of their situations are an important component of the helping process. The critical factor is whether the issues or concerns for which they are seeking help have, in their view, improved. It also helps the social worker and client identify what is working and what is not (Poulin & Matis, 2020).

Informal evaluation is an ongoing process. The client and worker begin by exploring the client's person-in-environment system and life experiences in order to identify concerns and factors that potentially affect them. During this and later stages, the social worker makes sure that their interpretations of the client's experiences are consistent with the client's perceptions. This approach to practice emphasizes listening to the client's story and understanding the client's perceptions of experiences. The worker needs to continually evaluate the extent to which their understanding of the client's experiences is consistent with the client's.

As work continues, informal evaluation techniques identical to the process just described play a role. The social worker has to make a conscious effort to ensure that there is agreement about the identified goals and specifics of the helping contract. The worker and client need to evaluate the client's commitment to the plan. Is it genuine? How strong is it? What can the social worker do to help the client maintain or strengthen their commitment to change?

The key to ongoing assessment of client progress and practice effectiveness is persistently and relentlessly following through on the intervention plan. It is checking in with the client between meetings. It is regularly monitoring progress and exploring why or why not progress is being made. In addition to providing feedback, seeking ongoing client feedback helps create expectations for success and for making the identified changes. It communicates that you care and that you are committed to helping your clients overcome the challenge they are facing.

Formal Practice Evaluation: Single-System Designs

This section focuses on a quantitative approach to evaluating micro social work practice effectiveness. It covers designing single-system evaluations and analyzing single-system data.

DESIGNING THE EVALUATION

Single-system designs hold great promise for social workers. The requirements for using them fit well with social work practice. Single-system designs require clear specification of the target problem, development of measurable goals, selection and implementation of an intervention, and continued monitoring of the client's progress on the identified target problem. All these requirements are consistent with the requirements of sound social work practice.

The first step in designing a SSD evaluation is to establish measurable goals and select outcome measures. The next step is to determine how you are going to implement the evaluation process. The term "evaluation design" is often used to describe how practitioners plan to evaluate progress and case outcomes (Bloom et al., 2009). One of the most widely used ways to evaluate practice effectiveness in social work is the single-system design (Miley et al., 2013).

Bloom et al. (2009) provide a comprehensive and detailed description of numerous types of single-system designs. However, the designs that are likely to be used as part of a social worker's ongoing practice are more limited. The single-system design selected depends primarily on what questions you are attempting to answer (Berlin & Marsh, 1993). Two questions appropriate for social work practice evaluations are: Is the intervention working? and Is the intervention causing the change?

More complex experimental designs provide information on the causal effect of the intervention. Did the client system improve because of the intervention? What aspects of the intervention are most important in causing the change? Answers to such questions contribute to social work knowledge. They help document the effectiveness of various interventions with different types of clients and target problems. However, answering questions about causality and implementing experiential-type designs are beyond the level of evaluation expected for most social work practitioners. They are better addressed through research than through ongoing social work practice with clients.

As noted earlier, social workers have a responsibility to promote the well-being of clients and provide services competently (NASW, 2017). This entails, in part, assessing the effectiveness of our interventions. Is the client making progress? Does the intervention appear to be working? Is the target problem improving, getting worse, or staying the same? This section focuses only on designs that provide information on client progress. Such designs best fit social work practice. They are easy to implement with client systems, and they provide important information on the effectiveness of the work.

> **Reflection Questions**
> 1. Among the clients with whom you have worked what are some of the target problems that would lend themselves to SSD evaluations?
> 2. What client target problems do you think would not lend themselves to SSD evaluations?

COMPONENTS OF SINGLE-SYSTEM DESIGNS

There are a number of single-system evaluation designs. Some components are common to all of them. The basic components of single-subject designs are as follows:

- Specifying the target problem
- Developing quantitative measures of the target problem
- Establishing baseline measures of the target problem before intervention
- Measuring the target problem repeatedly throughout the intervention
- Displaying the data on a graph
- Making comparisons across phases

Specifying the target problem, developing measures, and displaying data on graphs were discussed earlier.

Establishing a Baseline

The baseline is the measure of the target problem before the worker begins the intervention. Repeated measurements before the intervention are necessary to establish a baseline. The baseline allows you to compare the client's target problem before and after the intervention (Bloom et al., 2009).

There are two types of baselines—concurrent and retrospective. For a concurrent baseline, data are collected while other assessment activities are taking place. Repeated measures of the target problem are collected before you implement an intervention with the client system. For a retrospective baseline, the client reconstructs measures of the target problem from an earlier time period, using their memory. In many situations, delaying the intervention while a concurrent baseline is obtained is unacceptable. For example, it would be unethical to delay providing counseling services to people who experienced a traumatic event, such as a school shooting, in order to obtain baseline information on the victims' level of traumatic stress. In such cases, using a retrospective baseline is an acceptable alternative.

A common question is how many data points or measurements are needed for the baseline. The answer is that it depends. For meaningful comparisons to be made between the preintervention (baseline) and the intervention phases, the baseline has to be stable. That is, there has to be an observable pattern of measurement scores during the baseline period. A stable baseline is one that does not contain obvious cycles or wide fluctuations in the data (Bloom et al., 2009). Fluctuations are acceptable only if they occur with some regularity (Marlow, 2011). Thus, ideally, the baseline phase does not end until the baseline is stable. How long it takes is influenced, in part, by the amount of variation between the data points. The greater the variation (range of scores), the more data points needed to achieve stability. Conversely, if the variation between points on the baseline is relatively small (similar scores), fewer data points are needed to achieve stability (Poulin, 2010).

Using an unstable baseline is problematic. If the measures of the target problem fluctuate widely and no pattern exists, it is difficult to determine if change has occurred once the intervention starts (Bloom et al., 2009). In other words, it is unclear whether changes between the baseline and the intervention phases are due to usual fluctuations in the target problem or if change has actually taken place (Poulin & Matis, 2020).

> **Reflection Questions**
> 1. What do you see as the challenges in obtaining a baseline with your clients? How might you overcome those challenges?
> 2. If you asked your clients to complete a retrospective baseline, how confident would you be in their responses?

Making Comparisons

Assessing change requires making some sort of comparison. In traditional experimental evaluation designs, a treatment group is compared with a control group that does not receive treatment. In case evaluations using single-system designs, the client provides the basis for comparison. In essence, the client serves as their own control group. Is the client better after getting help than before? Without comparisons, it is impossible to assess change.

Work with clients can be divided into phases (Marlow, 2011). During the first few contacts, baseline data on the target problem may be collected; this is the assessment phase. The second phase is the next series of sessions, in which an intervention is implemented. If the first intervention did not achieve the desired results, a second intervention may be tried; this would be the third phrase.

Single-system evaluations use letters to label the different phases. Letter A is used to designate the baseline phase. The interventions are represented by subsequent letters: B for the first, C for the second, D for the third, and so on (Royse et al., 2016). A single-system design that consists of a baseline phase followed by an intervention is called an AB design. An evaluation that does not have a baseline and only one intervention is

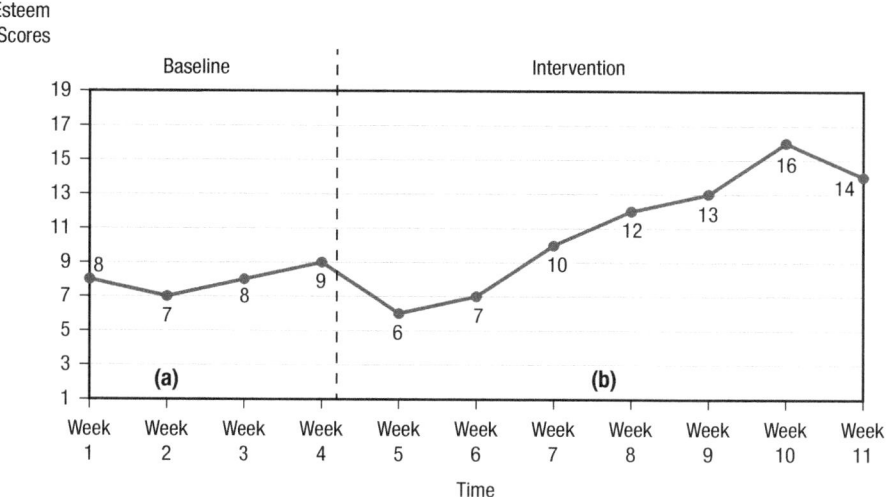

FIGURE 8.1 Sample AB design.

called a B design. An ABA design is one in which a baseline (A) phase is followed by an intervention (B) phase and a second baseline (A) period. The various phases of a single-subject design are usually labeled on the line graph and represented by dashed vertical lines. Figure 8.1 is a line graph of an AB design.

The AB design is the most frequently used single-system design in service settings (Marlow, 2011). In this design, repeated measurements of the target problem are taken during the baseline (A) and intervention (B) phases. Measures of the target problem are taken before the intervention is implemented and throughout the intervention. As with all single-system evaluations, the findings are analyzed by plotting the data points on a line graph.

The advantage of the AB design is its simplicity (Marlow, 2011). One must merely identify or develop an appropriate measurement of the target problem and then take repeated measurements during the baseline phase and the intervention phase. This design can easily be incorporated into social work practice. It is consistent with normal practice procedures in that an assessment data-gathering phase is followed by an intervention phase (Poulin, 2010). The design usually does not compromise or hinder the development of a helping relationship and the provision of service. It fits well into most practice models, and it provides evidence of whether the intervention is working or not.

The one area of potential difficulty with the AB design is obtaining a baseline. This is a problem with all single-system designs used to evaluate ongoing practice with client systems (Poulin, 2010). Delaying the intervention while baseline data are collected is problematic when the situation warrants immediate attention. Obtaining measures of the target problem over a prolonged period of time is often not feasible or desirable. In these situations, developing a retrospective baseline is the best. You and the client construct a baseline from the client's recollection of the target problem in the recent past. Although it is a compromise, a retrospective baseline provides a basis of comparison to answer the fundamental question: Is the intervention working?

The B design is the preferred option when it is necessary to intervene immediately, as in a crisis situation, without collecting baseline information or retrospective baseline information (Berlin & Marsh, 1993). It consists solely of an intervention (B) phase. Repeated measures of the target problem are taken throughout the intervention. This design is weaker than the AB design because preintervention comparison data are not available. It does, however, provide information on client progress, whether the target problem is improving, and whether the goals of the intervention have been achieved.

A third design that can be used to evaluate client progress is the ABC design. This design is an extension of the AB design. It entails the introduction of a second intervention (C) phase. If additional interventions are added beyond the second (C), they are labeled D, E, and so on. The ABC design is used when the first (B) intervention is modified or when the first intervention does not appear to be working. It does not provide information on which intervention caused change in the target problem nor does it allow for separation of the effects of the successive interventions. It does, however, provide information on client progress. Common single-system design options are summarized in Table 8.1.

ANALYZING SINGLE-SYSTEM DATA

Single-system design data are plotted on line graphs similar to those in Figure 8.1. Three types of significance can be used to judge change in the target problem: clinical, visual, and statistical. Clinical significance will be reviewed first followed by visual significance. The section concludes with a review of how to test the statistical significance of your intervention using linear regression analysis.

Clinical Significance

Clinical significance, also known as "practical significance," is based on the client and the social worker believing that there has been meaningful change in the problem (Bloom et al., 2009). Clinical significance is achieved when the specified goal of the intervention has been reached (Marlow, 2011). Determining clinical significance is generally a subjective process that requires discussion and negotiation among the involved parties. If everyone involved agrees that the target problem has been resolved, clinical significance has been achieved.

Determining clinical significance when a goal has not been fully achieved is more difficult: How much change is clinically meaningful? There are no criteria for establishing the clinical significance of partial change in the target problem. Client change can be considered clinically significant if those involved in the helping process agree that meaningful change has occurred (Poulin, 2010).

Visual Significance

Visual analysis is used for data that have been collected over time. It focuses on the trend and direction of the data. A trend occurs when data points move in a particular direction in a relatively steady manner. It can be a steadily increasing pattern, steady pattern of no change, or a steadily decreasing pattern. Data in which there are no discernible trends or patterns are considered unstable. Unstable data show wide fluctuations in the measurement of the target problem. The interpretation of unstable data is

TABLE 8.1 OTHER SINGLE-SYSTEM DESIGNS

DESIGN TYPE	DESCRIPTION OF DESIGN
B	Measurement occurs during the intervention phase. There is no baseline data collection phase. Example: A client enters an inpatient drug and alcohol rehabilitation program. Upon entry into the program, he immediately begins receiving medication to treat his physical symptoms of withdraw and begins individual cognitive-behavioral therapy with a social worker. Since the social worker did not have a period of baseline before starting her therapeutic work with this client, all of the data collected while providing the therapy would be considered the treatment phase (B).
ABA	There is a period of baseline data collection where no intervention is given. Following the baseline phase, the intervention is administered, and data are then collected. After a period of time, the intervention is withdrawn, and another period of baseline data collection occurs. It is noteworthy that treatment carryover effects can interfere with the second baseline in this type of design. Example: A child with behavioral outbursts begins behavioral health rehabilitation services (BHRS). During the intake process the treatment team collects data in the forms of observations, interviews, and scales in order to determine current needs and establish goals. This is the baseline phase (A). After collecting the baseline data, the team implements a behavioral modification plan that includes reinforcements and punishments in an attempt to increase positive behaviors and eliminate undesired behaviors. While the behavioral modification plan is being implemented, data are collected (B). Once the child has met his treatment goals, before discharging from services, the treatment team stops implementing the behavioral modification plan and tracks rates of behaviors. The phase while data are being collected after the intervention has been removed is a second baseline phase (A).
BAB	Measurement occurs during the intervention phase. The intervention is then withdrawn to collect baseline data. Following collection of baseline data, the intervention is reintroduced. Example: A woman with anxiety comes to a community mental health clinic for support. During her first session, the treatment begins with the social worker teaching her techniques to calm down, focus on her breath, and engage in mindfulness. The therapist asks the client to continue this intervention. Since there was no baseline period before the intervention was introduced, this case starts with the treatment phase (B). After several successful weeks using the intervention, the social worker stops the intervention and continues to collect data. Because there is no intervention being delivered, this is a baseline phase (A). The social worker eventually reintroduces the intervention and data are collected during the second treatment phase (B). (Poulin & Matis, 2020)

difficult. Little can be said beyond the fact that there is no pattern and the scores vary widely (Poulin, 2010).

The visual analysis of single-system data is based primarily on a comparison of the baseline and intervention phases. For meaningful comparisons to be made, the baseline data must be stable. If they are not, interpretation of the effect of the intervention is problematic. Interpretation is also difficult if the baseline data are moving steadily in a direction that would represent improvement on the target problem. For example, if a decrease in occurrence of the target problem represents client improvement and the baseline trend shows a steady decline on the measure, it would be difficult to attribute the improved scores to the effectiveness of the intervention because the data were already moving in the desired direction (Krishef, 1991).

Calculating a celeration line helps visually determine a trend in the data (Bloom et al., 2009). A celeration line connects the midpoints of the first and second halves of the baseline phase and extends into the intervention phase (Figure 8.2). The basic idea is that the trend established during the baseline phase is an estimate of what would happen if the baseline pattern were to continue and there was no intervention. The steps involved in calculating a celeration line are as follows:

1. Plot the baseline and intervention data on a line graph.
2. Divide the baseline section of the line graph in half, drawing a vertical line. If there are an even number of data points in the baseline, draw the line between the data points; if there are an odd number of points, draw the line through the midpoint number.
3. Divide each half into half by drawing dashed vertical lines on the chart.
4. Determine the mean score of the first half of the baseline by adding the scores in the half and dividing by the number of scores in the half. For baselines with an odd number of scores, omit the middle number.
5. Determine the mean score of the second half of the baseline by adding the scores in the half and dividing by the number of scores in the half. For baselines with an odd number of scores, omit the middle number.
6. Mark the dashed vertical line at the mean point for each half.
7. Draw a solid line connecting the two marks in the baseline and extend the line through the intervention phase (Poulin & Matis, 2020).

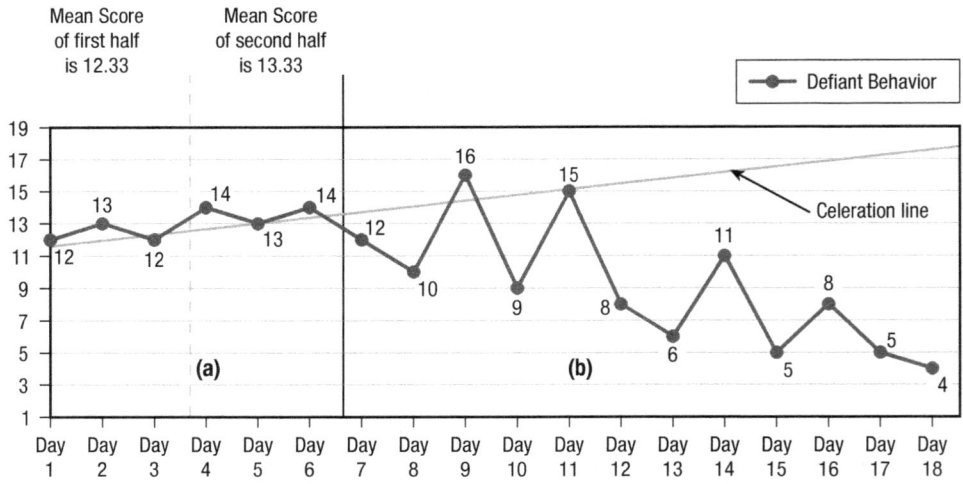

FIGURE 8.2 Line graph with celeration line.

Statistical Significance

There are a number of procedures that can be used to test the statistical significance of single-system design data. For a comprehensive discussion of the different approaches, see *Analyzing Single System Design Data* (Nugent, 2009). Interrupted time-series analysis (ITSA) is a widely accepted approach used by many disciplines to analyze single-system data (Hollander & Malinowski, 2016). The following provides an overview of how to conduct ITSA using ordinary linear regression. The regression analyses can be easily conducted using statistical analysis software such as Statistical Package for the Social Sciences (SPSS) or Statistical Analysis System (SAS).

ITSA is a way to determine if your time observations of a problem or condition change after you have implemented your intervention. Is there a statistically significant change in your outcome measure between the baseline (A) measures and postintervention (B) measures? The word "Interrupted" in the name refers to your intervention. The baseline (A) measures are interrupted by your intervention. Time-series refers to the fact that multiple points of time are used to measure your outcome variable during the baseline phase (A) and the postintervention (B) phase. ITSA requires a clear differentiation between the pre- and postintervention phases (Bernal et al., 2017). This is often difficult to achieve in social work practice but to the extent possible you will need a clear start date for your intervention after collecting your baseline data.

ITSA can be used to calculate the significance of changes in the levels between baseline (A) and postintervention measures as well as changes in the slope of the pre- and postintervention comparisons. Figure 8.3 illustrates the two types of changes that can be assessed using ITSA.

To test the significance of a change of level and slope using linear regression, your data set needs to have at least three independent variables and a dependent outcome variable. The dependent variable is a measure of your target outcome. We refer to this as your Y variable. The first independent is a time variable. Each time period you collect outcome data is

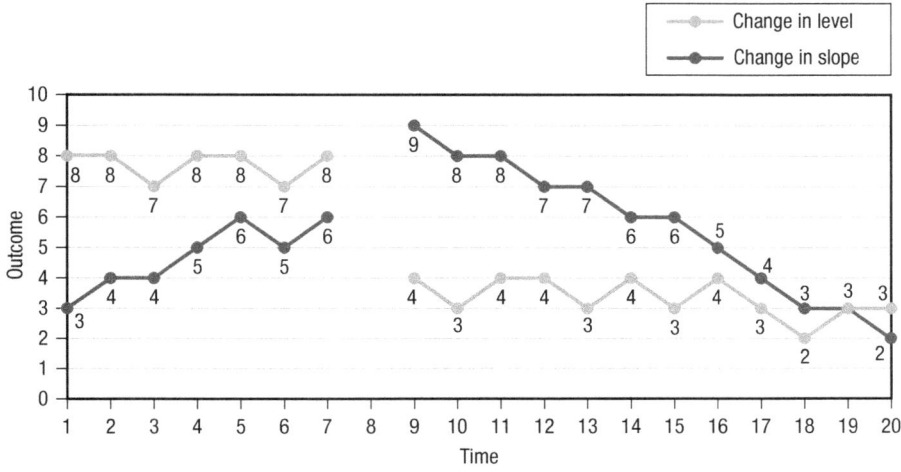

FIGURE 8.3 Change in level and change in slope.

assigned a number beginning with 1 and going up by 1 for each time period. For example, if you were collecting weekly, data week 1 would be coded 1, week 2 coded 2, and so forth, until you stop collecting data. We refer to this variable as your T variable. Your T variable is coded throughout the baseline and postintervention phases of your SSD evaluation. The second independent variable is a dummy intervention or treatment variable. We will refer to this variable as your X variable. For each time period during the baseline phase it is coded 0, and each postintervention time period it is coded 1. The third independent variable in your data set is your time after interruption (intervention) variable. We will refer to this variable as your XT variable. Table 8.2 shows a sample SSD data set that can be used for ITSA.

The regression formula for calculating the significance of a change in level is $y = \alpha + \beta_1 T + \beta_2 X + \beta_3 XT + \varepsilon$. After running your regression equation, the regression coefficient $\beta_1 T$ represents your time (T) variable, $\beta_2 X$ represents your intervention (X) variable, and $\beta_3 XT$ represents your time after intervention (XT) variable. The significance of the $\beta_2 X$ regression coefficient indicates if there is a significant change in the level of the outcome variable between baseline and treatment. The significance of the $\beta_3 XT$ regression coefficient indicates if there is a statistically significant change in the slope of your outcome variable between the baseline (A) and treatment (B) measurements.

Figure 8.4 is a line graph of SSD practice evaluation. The dependent variable or outcome measure is the number of daily disciplinary actions taken by staff with client one. The treatment variable is individual cognitive behavioral therapy provided by a social work counselor. Regression analysis was run to test the effectiveness of the treatment

TABLE 8.2 SAMPLE SSD DATA SET

TIME (T)	OUTCOME (Y)	INTERVENTION (X)	POST TIME (XT)
1	9	0	0
2	10	0	0
3	7	0	0
4	8	0	0
5	9	0	0
6	7	1	1
7	5	1	2
8	6	1	3
9	4	1	4
10	4	1	5
11	3	1	6
12	5	1	7
13	2	1	8
14	4	1	9

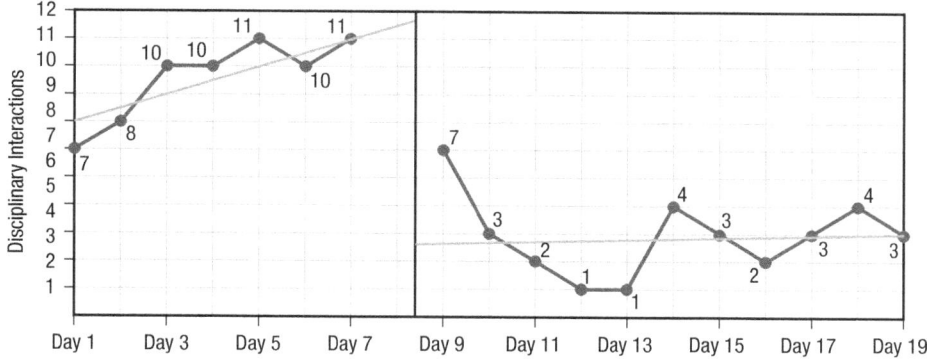

FIGURE 8.4 Daily disciplinary interactions—client one.

TABLE 8.3 REGRESSION ANALYSIS OUTPUT

	COEFFICIENTS[a]				
	UNSTANDARDIZED COEFFICIENTS		STANDARDIZED COEFFICIENTS		
MODEL	B	STD. ERROR	BETA	T	SIG.
1 (Constant)	6.409	1.407		4.555	.000
Time	.896	.365	1.416	2.456	.028
Intervention	−7.131	1.408	−.980	−5.065	.000
Post time	−.980	.402	−1.347	−2.439	.029

[a]Dependent variable: disciplinary actions.

in reducing the number of daily disciplinary actions. The regression analysis showed a significant change in both the level and slope of the outcome measure. The regression coefficient for the treatment variable (X) which estimates the change in level was −7.13 which is significant at the $p < .000$ level. As shown visually in the line graph, the level of the number of disciplinary actions dropped substantially between baseline and treatment. The regression coefficient for the time after intervention variable (XT), which estimates the change in slope of the treatment variable, was −0.98 which is significant at the $p < .03$ level. Thus, the visual change in the slope of the treatment variable is statistically significant. The output generated by the regression analysis is shown in Table 8.3.

■ Ethical and Social Justice Issues

There are a number of ethical issues that Simone (see Case 8.1) or anyone should address before undertaking SSD practice evaluations. Social workers have an ethical responsibility to provide competent services to their clients. This includes having the skills and

CASE 8.1   PRACTICE-INFORMED RESEARCH WITHIN A SUBSTANCE ABUSE TREATMENT CENTER

Simone is a social work intern at a substance abuse treatment center in an urban community. Simone is assigned to the 50-bed inpatient facility for teenagers. Her role in the facility is to provide mental health counseling individually and in groups to residents in the program. As a social work intern, Simone cofacilitates two patient groups and provides individual counseling to approximately 10 teenagers. She loves her placement and is continually looking for ways to improve her clinical skills and professional competencies.

One of Simone's clients (TY) is struggling with controlling his anger. She has been helping him try various coping strategies to deal with his anger management with limited success. Simone recently attended a social work conference where she learned about mindfulness techniques to help substance abuse clients cope with feelings, stress, triggers, cravings, and urges. Simone thought mindfulness skills might help TY better control his anger management issues. She had been practicing breathing exercises with TY but had not tried including a mindfulness component. Simone was excited about the possibility and hoped she would be allowed to do some sort of evaluation on the effectiveness of her new approach.

Simone's field instructor liked her idea and suggested that she do further research on mindfulness and that she develop an intervention/treatment plan for her to review. She emphasized the need to involve TY in creating the plan and that it include a detailed description of the mindfulness skills that would be used as well as how she would implement her intervention. The instructor also asked her to identify a measure that could be used to evaluate her treatment outcomes and develop an informed consent form for TY to sign. Together they decided that an AB design would be appropriate and that she should have a minimum of eight baseline measures before introducing her mindfulness intervention with TY. Exhibit 8.1 shows the practice evaluation consent form developed by Simone.

EXHIBIT 8.1

PRACTICE EVALUATION CONSENT

I, TY, freely give my consent to Simone M. to participate in an evaluation of our work together aimed at reducing my angry feelings and aggressive outbursts in my interactions with the staff and fellow consumers at the ABC Substance Abuse Treatment Facility. I understand the purpose of the practice evaluation and that my participation is voluntary.

I agree to complete the Short Anger Measure (SAM) daily for a period of 3 weeks and that I will participate in counseling sessions on Monday, Wednesday, and Friday mornings with Simone. I agree to do my assigned homework tasks between counseling sessions and that I will do my best to implement the anger management techniques that we review in our counseling sessions.

I understand that I may stop the practice evaluation at any time and that there will not be any negative consequences in doing so. I also understand that my withdrawing from the practice evaluation will not affect my treatment and participation in any of the program's services and/or activities.

Signature (TY) _____ Date _____

Signature (SM) _____ Date _____

Signature (Field Instructor) _____ Date _____

Simone and her field instructor decided on the Short Anger Measure (SAM) developed by Gerace and Day (2014) as the outcome measure for her evaluation. SAM is a 12-item self-report measure of angry feelings and aggressive impulses. Respondents are asked to answer on a 5-point Likert-type response scale from *never* to *very often* about various feelings during the past 24 hours. The scale scores range from 12 to 60. The higher the score, the higher the level of angry feelings. SAM was chosen for the evaluation because it is a brief measure that is easy to complete and can be used to measure change over time. It also has a fairly high reliability coefficient with a Cronbach's alpha of .91 and a test-retest reliability coefficient of .74.

TY agreed to complete the SAM measure every day for a 3-week period. Simone began her mindfulness intervention after collecting 8 days of baseline data. As shown in Figure 8.5, TY's baseline (A) was quite stable with scores consistently in the low to mid-50s. Simone was pleased with TY's progress during the treatment (B) phase. She felt that he was implementing mindfulness throughout his days and in his interactions with staff and peers at the facility. His angry feelings and aggressive impulses dropped during the treatment phase with SAM scores ranging from a high of 41 to a low of 14. The regression analysis revealed a significant treatment effect with a coefficient of −18.8, which was statistically significant at the $p < .001$ level. This indicated a statistically significant drop in TY's level of anger. Although the line graph showed a visual change in the slope of TY's baseline and treatment scores, the change was not statistically significant (−0.64, $p =$ n.s.).

Overall, Simone and her field instructor were very pleased with the results of introducing mindfulness in Simone's work with TY. His angry feelings and aggressive impulses had been reduced, and he was more receptive to making the changes needed to make progress on his recovery. Simone presented her findings to the clinical team at the facility and was asked to develop a continuing education presentation for the staff on incorporating mindfulness techniques into the program's counseling services. She was also asked to develop a workshop on conducting SSD evaluations.

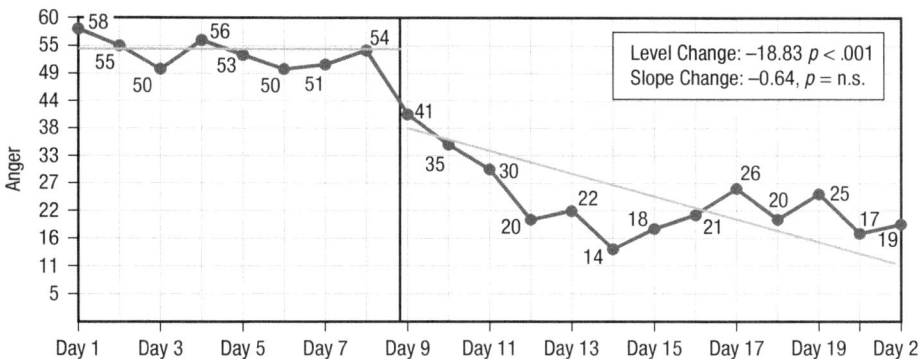

FIGURE 8.5 Feelings of anger—client TY.

expertise to provide social work services and the expertise to effectively conduct a practice evaluation. For Simone that would include the expertise to design and implement a mindfulness intervention as well as the expertise to design and conduct a single-subject design evaluation. Simone's expertise in providing the mindfulness intervention could be questioned. Attending a professional development workshop, doing supplemental readings, and researching and developing a comprehensive treatment plan are excellent beginning steps in terms of developing knowledge competency. Simone was lacking practice skills. Doing role-play sessions with her field instructor would have helped her develop her skills or at the very least allow her to practice implementing the intervention.

A second ethical consideration associated with practice evaluation concerns the level of involvement the client has in all aspects of developing the intervention and evaluation plans. This is where the ethics of practice evaluation differ from those associated with social science research (Holosko et al., 2009). The ethics of social work practice include involving the client in identification of target problems, treatment goals, and the helping process to the extent possible (Bloom & Orme, 1993). Client involvement in the helping process also applies to evaluating practice effectiveness. Although the case example indicated that Simone would obtain informed consent, information on the extent to which TY participated in developing the intervention and evaluation is unknown. Since the goal of practice evaluation is to assess potential client benefits and not generate generalizable findings (Holosko et al., 2009), following sound social work practice principles is critical. Collaborative strengths-based approaches are generally considered "best practice" in the delivery of social work services and in the development of the helping relationship (Poulin & Matis, 2020). Therefore, we argue that not involving clients as collaborative partners in the helping process or in the evaluation process is an ethical concern. Every possible effort to include clients in the process should be made. In retrospect, Simone's field instructor should have added that component to her instruction to develop an intervention and evaluation plan.

A third ethical issue relates to obtaining informed consent when there is power imbalance between the social worker–evaluator and the client. The worker-client relationship has a built-in power imbalance. By definition the social worker has more power than the client. The inherent power differential makes freely obtaining informed consent more complicated and potentially an ethical concern. Clients might agree to participate in the evaluation because they want to please their social worker. Or they may agree not because they want to but because they think they have to or there will be negative consequences if they refuse. It is the ethical responsibility of the social worker conducting the practice evaluation to do whatever possible to ensure their client freely consents to participate in the evaluation. One cannot ever truly know if consent is freely given, but the more the client is involved in specifying the intervention outcomes, treatment goals, helping process, and intervention approaches as well as the evaluation process, the more likely informed consent will be freely given.

> **Reflection Questions**
> 1. In thinking about a client with whom you might consider conducting a SSD evaluation, what do you see as potential social justice and rights issues?
> 2. How would you address the social justice and rights issues you just identified?

As part of Simone's informed consent, they also informed TY of his rights related to withdrawing from the practice evaluation. Participants who choose to begin participating in a research project or practice evaluation have the right to discontinue their involvement at any time. Social workers must be sure to share with participants in the informed consent that there will not be any negative consequences for withdrawing.

PRACTICE ACTIVITIES

1. Identify a client from your field placement. Design a SSD practice evaluation for your client that includes a specified target problem, a measure of the target problem, your proposed SSD design, length of your baseline and intervention phases, and a detailed description of your proposed intervention to address the target problem.
2. Create a fictitious SSD data set with an outcome variable (Y), a time variable (T), an intervention variable (X), and a time after intervention variable (XT). Create a line graph with a celeration line. Assess client change using visual analysis.
3. Create a practice evaluation consent form for the practice evaluation you designed in #1.

TECHNOLOGY EXERCISES

1. Enter the data set just created into a statistical software package. Conduct linear regression analysis to determine if there was a statistically significant change in the level and/or slope of the outcome measure between the baseline and treatment phases of the evaluation.
2. Add trend lines to the baseline (A) and treatment (B) components of your line graph just created. Add the regression coefficients and significant levels to the line graph.

REFERENCES

Berlin, S., & Marsh, J. (1993). *Informing practice decisions*. Macmillan.

Bernal, J. L., Cummins, S., & Gasparrini, A. (2017). Interrupted time series regression for the evaluation of public health interventions: A tutorial. *International Journal of Epidemiology*, 46, 348–355. https://doi.org/10.1093/ije/dyw098

Bloom, M., Fischer, J., & Orme, J. (2009). *Evaluating practice: Guidelines for the accountable professional* (6th ed.). Pearson.

Bloom, M., & Orme, J. (1993). Ethics and the single system design. *Journal of Social Service Research*, 18, 161–180. https://doi.org/10.1300/J079v18n01_09

Council on Social Work Education. (2015). *Educational policy and accreditation standards for baccalaureate and master's social work programs*. https://www.cswe.org/getattachment/Accreditation/Standards-and-Policies/2015-EPAS/2015EPASandGlossary.pdf.aspx

Fong, M. L., & Cox, B. G. (1983). Trust as an underlying dynamic in a counseling process: How clients test trust. *Personal and Guidance Journal*, 62, 163–166. https://doi.org/10.1111/j.2164-4918.1983.tb00176.x

Gerace, A., & Day, A. (2014). The short anger measure (SAM): Development of a measure to assess anger in forensic populations. *Journal of Forensic Nursing*, 10, 44–49. https://doi.org/10.1097/JFN.0000000000000010

Hollander, J., & Malinowski, O. (2016). The effectiveness of NLP: Interrupted time series analysis of single subject—Data for one session of NLP coaching. *Journal of Experiential Psychotherapy*, 19, 41–58. http://jep.ro/images/pdf/cuprins_reviste/76_art_5.pdf

Holosko, M. J., Thyer, B. A., & Danner, J. E. D. (2009). Ethical guidelines for designing and conducting evaluations of social work practice. *Journal of Evidence-Based Social Work, 6,* 348–360. https://doi.org/10.1080/15433710903126778

Krishef, C. H. (1991). *Fundamental approaches to single subject design and analysis.* Krieger Publishing Company.

Marlow, C. R. (2011). *Research methods for generalist social work* (5th ed.). Cengage Learning.

Miley, K., O'Melia, M., & DuBois, B. L. (2013). *Generalist social work practice: An empowering approach* (7th ed.). Pearson.

National Association of Social Workers. (2017). *Code of ethics.* https://www.socialworkers.org/About/Ethics/Code-of-Ethics/Code-of-Ethics-English

Nugent, W. (2009). *Analyzing single system design data.* Oxford University Press.

Poulin, J. (2010). *Strengths-based generalist practice: A collaborative approach* (3rd ed.). Cengage Learning.

Poulin, J., & Matis, S. (2020). *Social work practice: A competency based approach.* Springer Publishing Company.

Royse, D., Thyer, B. A., & Padgett, D. K. (2016). *Program evaluation: An introduction to an evidence-based approach* (6th ed.). Cengage Learning.

III

DATA COLLECTION AND ANALYSIS

9

QUANTITATIVE DATA ANALYSIS

This chapter discusses the processes of doing quantitative data analysis. It also examines the statistical tools that will be useful to you as you conduct your analysis.

By the end of the chapter, you will be able to do the following:

- Describe the purpose of qualitative data analysis.
- Understand how to measure your variables.
- Describe the terms "statistics," "data," and "data distributions."
- Describe the purposes and types of descriptive statistics.
- Describe the purposes and types of inferential statistics.
- Create a data analysis plan.

■ Quantitative Data Analysis

"Quantitative data analysis" refers to the use of numbers to analyze data (Asaduzzaman Fakir, 2016). A quantitative analysis enables statistical analysis and interpretation of large quantities of data by providing "quantitative or numeric description" (Creswell, 2009, p. 12) of observations. It has several characteristics that make it very useful, and indeed, it is one of the key analytical methods associated with science and positivism.

ADVANTAGES AND DISADVANTAGES OF QUANTITATIVE ANALYSIS

Quantitative analysis may summarize data into just a few numbers. For example, were I to ask you about the students at your college, if you had a great memory and the time, you could give me the name, age, race and/or ethnicity, and birthplace or residence of every student. However, is that realistic?

Instead, with quantitative tools, primarily statistics, you can summarize all of the observations into just a couple of sentences. Thus, it is efficient (Bryman, 2012). Secondly, it allows you to generalize and make inferences (May & Williams, 1998). A well-constructed sample allows you to make inferences about a population. You can also generalize. The rules of probability mathematics allow for this. These rules provide a third benefit. Rule agreement allows for replicability of research (Shank & Brown, 2007).

> **Reflection Questions**
> 1. How realistic do you think it is to take the researcher out of the research process? Why do you think that?
> 2. What are the disadvantages of taking the researcher out of the research process? What are the advantages?

Finally, it takes the researcher somewhat out of the research process. It attempts to make a clear distinction between the subjective and objective interpretation of reality.

These characteristics work well with the positivistic scientific paradigm. With rules, inference, generalizability, and greater objectivity, inferences can reach all the way to universal truths. That, however, is not a common result.

Quantitative methods also have limitations. Without getting too deep here, modern physics as well as practical concerns question assumptions of positivism. At the smallest (quantum) levels, prediction is at best uncertain. Nevertheless, at all levels of reality, the presence of the researcher changes what is being researched (Frey, 2018).

> **Reflection Questions**
> 1. What do you see as the greatest strength of quantitative methods? Why?
> 2. Do you agree that mathematics is a language? How well do you feel you understand the language?

This is a wonderful conversation for another day. For now, the overwhelming benefit of quantitative research is its efficiency. Numbers are easy to work with, while raw observations are not. Yet this also brings us to another limitation. Efficiency often ignores comprehensiveness. Qualitative analysis allows for very deep and rich descriptions (Chalhoub-Deville & Deville, 2008) and may well be much stronger for understanding depth of meaning.

Finally, mathematics is not everyone's strong point. Many students fear numbers (Kamentz, 2018) and experience anxiety about mathematics (Ashcraft, 2002) with consequences (Suárez-Pellicioni et al., 2016). Statistics are mathematics; it is a language with symbol and syntax. To understand statistics, you have to be able to translate what a number means into words or pictures.

GENERAL PROCESS

While there are general rules for using quantitative analysis, there are many possibilities. The possibilities are determined by the intent of the analysis and the statistics you choose. We recommend creating an analysis plan for your capstone research. The plan should include information on data management, variable definition, descriptive statistics, inferential statistics, and interpretation (O'Leary, 2020). Some of what follows was covered in Chapter 4 but is critical for understanding the choices you must make. We start with a definition of variables.

Variables

As a review, "variables" are the study-able manifestations of the concepts in your questions and theoretical/conceptual frameworks. Defined, a "variable" is some characteristic or attribute of members of a population whose values are changeable (Lavrakas, 2008), as opposed to a constant. Variables vary. They have categories—different possible amounts or kinds. Every observation of a variable should fit into one and only one of those categories. Thus, they must be measurable, discrete, and comprehensive.

> **Reflection Questions**
> 1. Are there any variables that you think are unmeasurable? What are they? Why?
> 2. What characteristics make for a good study population? What kinds of things make identifying a population difficult?

LEVELS OF MEASUREMENT

As stated, a variable differs in "amount or kind." This means that the variable has different possible categories. Sometimes, the different categories are conceptualized as discreet or continuous (Larson, 2006). For some variables, the categories differ in kind only (the categories are *qualitatively* different); for others, the categories differ in amount (the categories are *quantitatively* different). Sometimes quantitative differences are exact and sometimes approximate. The labels for how they differ are their *level of measurement*. The difference between categories strongly affects the choice of statistics. There are four levels of measurement:

- *Nominal.* Categories differ *qualitatively only* (meaning the categories differ in kind). Gender is an example. We name the categories for Gender, perhaps as Male, Female, or Sisgender. Indeed, these kinds of variables are called "categorical variables." The categories of the variable are represented by numbers for statistical purposes, but the number is just a symbol for the category and has no other meaning.
- *Ordinal.* Categories differ *qualitatively, but inexactly* (meaning categories differ in amount, but approximately). Sometimes people call these differences "rank order." So something like high, medium, or low, or first, second, and so on, apply. Statistics here assume the numbers themselves have some degree of meaning.
- *Interval data.* Categories differ *quantitatively and exactly, but no true, zero point exists.* Categories differ in amount and the difference between every category is always the same, or standardized. There is no "0" however.
- *Ratio data.* Categories differ *quantitatively and exactly, and a true zero point exists* (meaning categories differ in amount and the difference between every category is always the same).

> **Reflection Questions**
> 1. How can you determine the level of measurement of variables in a study that you are reading? What kind of information do you need?
> 2. How can you determine if a true 0 point exists in a measure? Consider the age? Do you agree that it does not have a 0 point? Why or why not?

■ The Function of Variables in Quantitative Analysis

The level of measurement affects statistics usage. Variables serve different purposes in the research process. Each purpose has a different name.

DEPENDENT VARIABLES

The variable that you hope to explain or understand is the *dependent* variable. Suppose your question is what do people think about the problem of race? What you are trying to explain is people's perceptions. Alternatively, suppose your research question is what is the most important social service need in your agency? Again, the definition of what you are looking for is very straightforward, the most important problem. Questions that are more complex look at relationships between two or more variables. You could also identify a number of potential variables that can help you understand why a problem is the most important. Each of these other variables, when used in certain kinds of equations, can give you some insight into the question of "why."

In this latter case, it is a cause and effect question. Here, the "effect" variable is the dependent variable. You might examine the effect of community racial attitudes on community violence. Here, the dependent variable (the effect) is community violence.

In either case, the dependent variable is what we want to explain. For your research, to be clear, the dependent variable must clearly be described? The statistics you choose are affected by how you choose to explain the variable.

INDEPENDENT VARIABLES

The factors or variables that help you to explain the dependent variable are the *independent* variables. If your question assumes cause and effect, this variable is the cause. The independent variable is what we believe makes the changes happen in our dependent variable. Now, often we do not really know cause and effect in advance. Many studies, particularly what we call "exploratory studies," may seek simply to identify important independent variables. Looking again at our example of community violence, we actually have many variables that could help us better understand the problem. Some may be unknown at the beginning of the study. Others may be known, but how they affect the variable is not known. Some methods and statistics may help us sort out the relationships.

INTERVENING AND CONTROL VARIABLES

Most problems are complex. Rarely does a single independent variable fully explain our dependent variable. A good research study, particularly with more complex research questions, will attempt to take some of these other variables into consideration. Thus, research studies may look at more than one independent variable. This also affects your statistics choices. These variables have different names depending upon what we believe their role is in the research problem. For example, if we try to remove or normalize the effects of a variable on both our dependent and independent variables through our methods of statistics, we call that variable a "control" variable. If we believe that the effect of a variable adds or detracts the effect between the dependent and independent variables, we might call them "mediating" or "moderating" variables.

EXTRANEOUS VARIABLES

One last type of variable that may be very important in your analysis is the extraneous variable. "Extraneous variables" are variables that appear to cause changes in the dependent variable, but in fact do not.

> **Reflection Questions**
> 1. What are some examples of intervening variables that would be important in a study of treatment outcomes? Why?
> 2. How might you know that you have identified all the important intervening variables in a study?

Sound complex? It may be. Some studies take into account dozens of variables. In extreme cases, only supercomputers can do the analysis. Weather forecasting or climate change research uses millions of data points and thousands of variables. This is why a theory or concept model surrounding your question is important. Your theory or model can help focus your variable choices. Generally, you want to have at least a very clear dependent variable and probably (though not necessary at the beginning) at least one independent variable. It is also possible that you know the dependent variable but you do not really know the independent variables. This research attempts to gather data about a large number of possible influences.

STATISTICS, PARAMETERS, AND VARIABLE DISTRIBUTIONS

Now, what will you do with your variables? Here, statistics begin. First, "statistics" actually refer to the mathematical manipulation of data from a sample. If your data are from a population, the term for the result of the calculation is a "parameter." You want to be clear about the difference. Similarly is the term *data*. "Data" are a group of observations or measurements of a variable. As a Latin word, the "a" at the end indicates a plural. A single observation would be "datum." In your capstone paper, you always want to say data *are*.

Distributions

Typically, the very first step in analysis, and part of your data management, is the organization of data in a logical manner. This organization can be done in any one of a number of ways, but conceptually you are creating a data "distribution" for each variable. Usually the distribution will apply the categories of the variable to group the observations. So rather than presenting your data in a write-up as the individual datum, you can apply and report summaries for the categories. This type of organization may, with the addition of a couple of very simple statistics, provide much helpful information. Data presented this way are useful visually, conceptually, and analytically.

What type of statistics might you offer along with the categories of the variable? Most typically, a visually useful distribution will include the count or frequency of each category (how many observations) and the percentage of cases in that category relative to the whole sample size. This type of distribution is called a "frequency distribution." You might plan to provide a frequency distribution for each important variable in your study.

TABLE 9.1 FREQUENCY DISTRIBUTION EXAMPLES

EXAMPLE 1: WHAT IS THE MOST IMPORTANT PROBLEM IN YOUR COMMUNITY? N = 173		
	N	%
Lack of jobs	89	51.4
Sense of despair	67	38.7
Housing decay	11	6.4
Police attitude	3	1.7
Other	3	1.7
Total	173	99.9
EXAMPLE 2: ARE THE LACK OF JOBS THE MOST IMPORTANT PROBLEM IN YOUR COMMUNITY? N = 170		
	N	%
Strongly agree	45	26.5
Agree	44	25.9
Neutral	74	43.5
Disagree	2	1.2
Strongly disagree	5	2.9
Total	170	100.0

■ **Reflection Questions**
1. What kinds of information can you glean from the visual presentation of data?
2. How might you handle a data distribution with lots of categories visually? Are there ways you can collapse data into smaller categories that might be useful? What are they?

In fact, it may well be that your research question can be analyzed with no other statistics than the frequency distribution. For example, a needs assessment might ask, What is the most important problem in your community? Table 9.1 shows different frequency distributions that might result.

■ Descriptive Statistics

You have just planned for your first statistical operation. The frequency distribution is an applied statistical method, particularly with the inclusion of percentages for a class of statistics called "descriptive statistics." Descriptive statistics are tools to describe the dataset. There are several types of descriptive statistics with different purpose and complexity. Descriptive statistics can summarize data, and other descriptive statistics can show relationships. Descriptive statistics that summarize a single variable are "univariate" statistics.

Descriptive statistics that show relationships imply more than one variable. These may be "bivariate" (if you have two variables) or "multivariate" (if you have many variables).

UNIVARIATE DESCRIPTIVE STATISTICS

"Univariate statistics" are the primary ways to describe distributions. The frequency distribution is one such tool. The "frequency distribution" provides information on the categories of the variable, along with frequencies and percentages.

Distributions can be summarized in other ways. The most common ways are *measures of central tendency* (MCT) and *measures of dispersion or variability* (MV). These statistics can summarize and describe even the largest datasets with just a couple of numbers. They provide information about the typical or common case and how spread out the distribution is overall. Much information can be described using *MCT* and *MV*.

Now we return to the levels of measurement. All statistics are selected based on the level of measurement. The mathematics associated with each statistic has different assumptions based on the type of relationship between the categories of the variable. Let us describe what MCT and a MV actually do.

The MCT tells you something about the average, typical, center, or most common case or category. The MV instead tells you how different most cases/categories in the distribution are from the center/typical case. Thus, the MCT tells you what is typical, and the MV tells you about how spread out or different the cases in the distribution are.

For both the MCT and MV, there are different kinds that are used under differing conditions. For the MCT, the choices are the *mean, the median, and the mode*. The "mean" is the average score of cases across categories, the "median" is the center case/category in a distribution, and the "mode" is the most common case or category (called the "modal category").

For the MV, choices include the *coefficient of variation, the range, and the standard deviation*. The "coefficient of variation" (not too commonly used) is the percentage of cases not in the modal category. The "range" is the difference between the high and low case scores or categories. The "standard deviation" is a mathematical formula that provides essentially the average distance away from the mean for cases in the distribution.

The most important deciding factor for both the MCT and MV are the level of measurement of each variable. Some of the MCTs and MVs are perfectly acceptable if the categories are *only* qualitatively different. On the other hand, some of the measures demand mathematical formulas to create and therefore require quantitative differences between the categories.

This is not a statistics book. So the mathematics for each of these statistics is not examined here. However, this is a book to help you choose the right statistics. Table 9.2 shows you the optimum choice for each level of measurement and can be a useful guide for making your decision.

Your capstone paper may actually include a table like this, with the first column presenting the names of your variables. You will also want to include the variable definition, categories (if known), and actual research questions getting at the variables. Typically,

TABLE 9.2 SELECTING THE APPROPRIATE MEASURE OF CENTRAL TENDENCY AND MEASURE OF DISPERSION

IF CATEGORIES OF THE VARIABLE ARE:	LEVEL OF MEASUREMENT	MEASURE OF CENTRAL TENDENCY (BEST CHOICE FIRST)	MEASURE OF DISPERSION
Categories are qualitative and names only (e.g., gender, diagnosis)	Nominal	Mode	Percentages on frequency distribution or (sometimes used) coefficient of variation
Categories differ *qualitatively,* but *inexactly* (may/may not be numbered by rank *or* name given like high, medium, low)	Ordinal	Median, mode	Range
Categories differ *qualitatively and exactly,* but no true zero point exists (number only given—e.g., age)	Interval	Mean is usually best, but mean, median, mode can all be used.	Standard deviation, range
Categories differ *qualitatively and exactly,* true zero point exists (number only given—e.g., number arrests)	Ratio	Mean is usually best, but mean, median, mode can all be used.	Standard deviation, range

this is a part of the methodology section, while the questions may be exclusive to your data collection instrument which is often an appendix.

BIVARIATE DESCRIPTIVE STATISTICS

Now, just as there are univariate descriptive statistics, there are also various "bivariate descriptive statistics." These statistics describe relationships. There are two primary types of measures, measures of association (often called "correlations") and measures of causality (many types, but many are called "regressions").

There is also a simple but powerful way to provide a visual representation of a bivariate relationship called a "cross tabulation." A cross tabulation is the merging of two or more frequency distributions. The addition of the second variable allows a visual analysis of how the categories of the variables affect each other. Table 9.3 shows a simple example of a cross tabulation. This is useful, if information is limited, but it may be appropriate for some studies.

TABLE 9.3 EXAMPLES OF CROSS TABULATIONS

HOW OFTEN DO YOU ATTEND HEALTH AND WELLNESS ACTIVITIES BY CENTER										
	CENTER 1		CENTER 2		CENTER 3		CENTER 4		TOTAL	
	N	%	N	%	N	%	N	%	N	%
Often	56	36.6	38	27.3	11	14.7	66	38.4	171	31.7
Sometimes	46	30.1	44	31.7	23	30.7	26	15.1	139	25.8
Rarely	16	10.5	15	10.8	13	17.3	18	10.5	62	11.5
Never	35	22.9	42	30.2	28	37.3	62	36.0	167	31.0
Total	153	100.0	139	100.0	75	100.0	172	100.0	539	100.0
I AM SATISFIED WITH THE HEALTH AND WELLNESS ACTIVITIES BY CENTER										
	CENTER 1		CENTER 2		CENTER 3		CENTER 4		TOTAL	
	N	%	N	%	N	%	N	%	N	%
Does not apply to me	51	29.5	32	21.9	36	44.4	90	45.0	209	34.8
Strongly agree	76	43.9	46	31.5	11	13.6	68	34.0	201	33.5
Agree	32	18.5	53	36.3	15	18.5	28	14.0	128	21.3
Neutral	7	4.0	11	7.5	11	13.6	10	5.0	39	6.5
Disagree	1	0.6	1	0.7	2	2.5	1	0.5	5	.8
Strongly disagree	6	3.5	3	2.1	6	7.4	3	1.5	18	3.0
Total	173	100.0	146	100.0	81	100.0	200	100.0	600	100.0

These examples demonstrate the relationship between the use of health and wellness services and different centers within an agency. In each example, note where the percentages in the top and bottom lines are similar or different across the centers.

As you review the two tables, what stands out to you? What information appears here? What questions would help to further understand the data?

Measures of Association-Correlations

Correlations are measures of covariation, or mutual influence of two variables on each other. This type of statistic reports the strength and sometimes the direction of the relationship. It may be difficult or impossible to identify true cause and effect, but you can instead measure the mutual effect of the variables. Most importantly, to argue cause and effect you must have proven time order between the variables. Changes in one variable must always precede changes in the other variable. There may also be a lack of good theory or explanatory models, or even any empirical research to successfully argue cause and effect.

Thus, the use of correlation measures relationships without worrying too much about cause and effect. Exploratory research that attempts to find the covariates of a problem is a common use for correlations. If several correlates are found, they can be rank ordered by the strength of each relationship. Further, more complex association measures, such as regression, depend on first demonstrating correlations.

There are several different types of correlations. Some of these measure the strength of relationship and some measure the strength *and* direction. Strength is typically measured on a scale from zero to one. Exactly what the number means depends upon the statistic chosen. For all measures of correlation, however, the closer to "one" the stronger the relationship. Conversely, the closer to "zero," the weaker. A correlation of 0.1 shows a weaker relationship than a correlation of 0.3. Likewise, a correlation of 0.42 is a much stronger relationship than a correlation of 0.11.

To what do these numbers ultimately refer? In many cases, they explain the percentage of *variance* one variable may account for by knowing the other. "Variance" is a mathematical concept—a way of measuring the aggregate difference from the center of the distribution for all the data in the distribution. This is one of those terms that cause headaches because it is a purely mathematical concept that we use to try to understand things that are not mathematical. Indeed, variance is an actual number that is calculated by an equation. This number becomes the target of many statistical operations. Explaining the variance is also a mathematical process. So translating this to the real world means finding a high correlation that allows you to understand much of what is affecting your dependent variable, while a low correlation means that very little of what causes changes in your dependent variable has been found.

Further, some, correlations also measure what is called "direction." Direction also sometimes confuses students because of the way it is reported. What direction actually refers to is whether the scale categories of the variables appear to get greater or smaller together, or if the categories of one variable increase while the other decreases. A positive relationship means that the scale direction of both variables is the same. The categories of both variables seem to increase or decrease together. A negative relationship is where the variables appear to be going in different directions at the same time.

Now here is where the confusion comes into this situation. The correlation statistics that use both strength and direction require the categories of the variables to be quantitative. However, when the statistics are generated, the coefficients are matched with a direction sign. If the direction is positive, it is sometimes designated by a + sign (but not always), while a negative direction is always shown with a − sign. Strength and direction are entirely different kinds of information. Yet they are reported together, and if we are not careful, we will interpret them as a single information point. When you select your correlation statistics, you want to understand what they will mean.

Because some correlations depend heavily on quantitative differences, and because the degree of these quantitative differences is important, please review Table 9.4 to

TABLE 9.4 SELECTING THE APPROPRIATE MEASURE
OF ASSOCIATION-CORRELATIONS

IF CATEGORIES OF THE VARIABLE ARE:	LEVEL OF MEASUREMENT	MEASURE	PROVIDES
Categories are qualitative and names only (e.g., gender, diagnosis)	Nominal	Non-parametric— Lambda Phi (for 2 × 2 tables) Cramer's v	Measure of strength (0–1). Lambda historically, not too commonly used (Glen, 2020)
Categories differ *qualitatively, but inexactly* (may/may not be numbered by rank *or* name given) (e.g., high, medium, low)	Ordinal	Non-parametric— Spearman *rho* or Kendall *tau* (see *Statistics Solutions* [2020] for partial discussion on optimum alternative)	Measure of strength (0–1) and direction
Categories differ *qualitatively and exactly, but no true zero point exists* (number only given—e.g., age)	Interval	Parametric— Pearson's *r*	Measure of strength (0–1) and direction
Categories differ *qualitatively and exactly, true zero point exists* (number only given—e.g., number arrests)	Ratio	Mean is usually best, but mean, median, mode can all be used	Standard deviation, range

determine which to use with a given level of measurement and what the information given will mean. Mukaka (2012) also provides a good overview of some selection criteria.

A large number of correlations between many variables may be computed and shown on a chart called a "correlation matrix." This shows the bivariate relationships between a number of variables. Such a matrix helps to order the relative impact of several independent variables. Such a matrix can also be used to rule out independent variables that have no or very little impact. This is a starting point for more complex statistical analysis.

Reflection Questions

1. What are some of the ways that you can demonstrate the time order exists to use a regression?
2. What is the difference between association and causality? How can you tell a difference?

Measures of Association-Regression

A second type of descriptive bivariate relationship is known as the "regression." Regressions give you all the information of the correlation, but with an important addition. With regressions, you can dive deeper into the specific contribution that one variable makes on another. One way you can think about this and interpret many of the regression coefficients is that they can show you the actual per-unit change in your dependent variable per-unit change in your independent variable. This is incredibly valuable. For understanding the direct contribution of change in your dependent variable can be useful for all kinds of service planning.

Differing types of data lead to a large number of possible regression statistics—at least 15 different by one count (ListenData, 2019)—most beginning students will use only one of a couple of types. For nominal dependent variables, logistical regression is appropriate. For ordinal data, ordinal regression is appropriate. For interval or ratio data, least squares regression is appropriate. Again, each type will provide a measure of the direct impact of one (or more) independent variable on your dependent variable.

MULTIVARIATE DESCRIPTIVE STATISTICS

Now, if you wish to examine the effects of more than one independent variable, many different statistical operations allow you to do so. These statistical operations begin with the same purposes and descriptions as the bivariate methods just described, but with increased complexity in the mathematical equations used to generate the statistics. However, so does the complexity in the kinds of questions you can ask and answer.

At the lower end of the complexity are found statistics such as partial correlation. "Partial correlation" provides all of the information of bivariate correlation but expands it to look at the effects of multiple variables. This can yield very specific amounts of influence given from one variable upon another. Such partial correlations are different from what might result in a correlation matrix as described earlier. The advantage of partial correlation over even a long list of bivariate relationships is that each partial correlation here controls the effect of other variables in the matrix.

Indeed, it is this issue of statistical controls that makes multivariate descriptive statistics very useful. Bivariate descriptive statistics are interesting, sometimes very useful, but limited. As has already been discussed, the world is a very complex place and very few relationships can be described by a single influencer.

This observation about the multivariate world we live in opens up many possibilities for interesting research. Most of the more complex statistical operations that are available to you help to parcel out the influence of multiple variables. Perhaps the simplest way to think about many of these statistical possibilities is to think about their use for modeling. There are, at a minimum, two major statistical types of model that you might think about. The simple list types of modeling attempt to look at the direct and additive impact of several variables on a target dependent variable. One of the most common examples here is what is known as "multiple regression." Multiple regression is a tool that takes many, sometimes very many, independent variables and attends to determine the individual and additive impact of these variables on a single dependent variable.

Somewhat more complex, but closely related to multiple regression, is what is known as "path analysis." Path analysis may include all the same variables that you could use in a multiple regression, but adds a visual and mathematical analysis of the interaction between the independent variables. By so doing, it acknowledges that independent variables influence independent variables as well as dependent variables. Consider, for example, the relationship between drinking, driving fast, and car accidents. Clearly drinking affects car accidents. So does speeding. However, drinking also influences speeding. Therefore, to get a better picture of the cause of car accidents it is necessary to look at the effect of several variables on each other.

Inferential Statistics

There is a serious problem in any research findings. Luck or chance may create the finding. How do you address this problem? In bivariate or multivariate relationships, or if you are comparing a sample statistic to the population, you should pair your statistical finding with an inferential statistic, typically called a "test of significance." Why? Descriptive statistics are computed with the data you have, which is primarily from a sample. Samples commonly differ from the population from which they come. Any sample that you draw from which you compute your statistics is only one of potentially an infinite number of samples, and by no means is every sample accurate and representative.

Chance alone can dictate results. This is the problem. For the demonstration of the relationship with a descriptive statistics does not mean the relationship is what really exists in the population. Indeed, we never really know if what we find from the statistical tests is real or just chance resulting from our sample.

What we are talking about is a problem of certainty. Without getting too deep, science seeks to understand universal laws. On one level, every scientific study we undertake hopefully moves us closer to finding these laws. The very act of generalizing data from a sample to a population is a step to the validation of these laws. More practically, suppose we find that there are differences between two groups in an experiment. Is that difference real, meaning reflective of the way the universe operates? Suppose that difference is looking at a treatment. We certainly hope that a finding that shows the treatment works is the real result, but not just in the chance sample that we studied.

The statistics called "inferential statistics" help us improve our confidence in results. Using tests of significance that is based in probability theory, inferential statistics are an essential tool for interpreting what we find. They do the following:

- Provide a degree of certainty in a given finding.
- Show if differences between two or more groups are real or random. This is the essence of a hypothesis test.
- Allow us to generalize from a sample to a population.
- Through such generalizations, help achieve the goals of positivism.

Unbelievably, all of these statements point to the same thing, although explaining how moves us beyond the scope of this chapter into deep mathematics and philosophy. What we are interested in is how these things may be useful in your capstone research. However, before we spend time talking about the application, there are some important caveats to the statements just made. First, probability theory is not itself certainty. Thus, the demonstration of a statistical difference that meets the requirements of a test of significance is not itself without the possibility of error. Random chance, even if controlled, still shows things that are not real sometimes. Second, findings of no relationship or no difference are still important. Findings that are not statistically significant are still findings.

INFERENTIAL TESTS OF SIGNIFICANCE

First, however, you should know some terms. The term "test of significance" is essentially the same as "inference test." While there are minor differences, usually associated with the function of the test, most people use the terms interchangeably. Also closely related is the term "hypothesis test."

A second term, and one that is critical, is the "significance level." When you choose an inference test, you must also choose the significance level. This is the point on a probability distribution at which you are willing to say your finding is probably not due to chance. Now what does the significance level mean? A few paragraphs back we said that you can draw many samples from the same population. If you run a relationship measure between two or more variables on each of those samples, the results might be different. It turns out that if you draw many samples from your population, each with its own result outcome, you can estimate the likelihood or probability that the given result will be found in the next sample you draw.

Many of you are familiar with a kind of probability distribution called a "normal distribution." In this distribution, the findings that are closer to the real relationship—the parameter—are more frequent and thus have a higher probability of being selected.

There is a simple example of this in the real world. Suppose you have a jar with several hundred marbles in it. If you ask 1,000 people to guess how many marbles are in the jar, and you graph out their results, you will have a distribution. The resulting distribution will show larger numbers at and around the correct answer, which will be at the center of the distribution. Increasingly smaller numbers will be found as you move farther and farther away from the correct answer (both higher and lower). Each point along the distribution can be calculated as a probability. High probabilities will be associated with answers closer to the real number of marbles, while lower probabilities will be associated with the wrong answers the farther you move from the correct answer.

This kind of distribution applies to different outcomes from a study. If you were to draw a large number of samples that looked at the relationship between two variables in two groups, for example, the difference between the average number of people who get better with a treatment versus the average number of people who get better without the treatment, you could chart the probabilities. Like the marbles, the closer the difference between the two groups is to the real difference, the higher the probability would be.

That seems simple enough. However, for logical reasons, you cannot confirm a positive, so you cannot directly test your finding to a probability distribution. Instead, logic rules allow you to disprove a negative. What tests of significance do is they set up an alternative probability distribution. Instead of trying to confirm what you hope to find, that a relationship is a HIGH-PROBABILITY event, you test an alternative possibility, that a relationship IF THE NULL WERE TRUE, is a low-probability event.

This alternative, in research, is a test of a hypothesis of *no* relationship between the variables. Since you cannot confirm your hypothesis that a relationship exists, you want to disprove the hypothesis that no relationship exists. This is called the "null hypothesis," which states that no relationship really exists. The null hypothesis assumes that there is no relationship between intervention and outcome. Moreover, for this test there is a theoretical probability distribution (a distribution of all possible "no relationship" outcomes). In this distribution, findings of strong relationships are rare events with low probability (out in the tails of the distribution), and nonexistent relationships or weak relationships are high-probability events.

Thus, a test of significance conceptually has two hypotheses. The hypothesis that you are actually testing is the hypothesis of no relationship—the null hypothesis. The research hypothesis (that a relationship does exist) just sits there until you complete the inference test. If you find a low enough probability of no relationship, you can reject the null hypothesis and instead accept your research hypothesis as a possible alternative.

Returning now to the significance level, you actually choose the probability level where you reject the null hypothesis. Traditionally, there are four standard significance levels. The four levels represent increasingly difficult challenges or hurdles to overcome to show the null hypothesis has been rejected. Which level you choose, and include in your proposal, depends primarily on the rigor of your study and your sample size. These four levels are 0.10, 0.05, 0.01, and 0.001. They are typically written with $p<$ the number selected (.10, .05, .01, or .001). The smaller the number you select the more difficult you make it for yourself to reject the null hypothesis. The harder you want to make rejecting the null, the smaller the p value. So a $p<.05$ might be appropriate for most survey research, but if you are really trying to examine the health effects of say a new treatment, you would want a more rigorous level, such as $p<.01$ or even $p<.001$.

Further, you might have a hypothesis that specifies a direction. In such cases, you want to worry about that direction as you think about your hypothesis test. These are one-tailed or two-tailed tests. The one-tailed test means that you have specified the direction and if the direction is different from that specified, you are unable to reject your null hypothesis. Two-tailed tests are more flexible, as you can accept either high or low findings.

One last concept to note before we discuss the various kinds of inference tests is the problem of error. Because your rejection of the null is based on a probability that is artificially selected, and because random error can always slip in, even a rigorous study can be wrong. There are two types of errors. Type I is accepting the false null hypothesis. This means your research finding is probably correct but you did not pass the null test. Type II error is rejecting a correct null hypothesis. This means you have a relationship shown by your research, but no relationship really exists. In your capstone paper you will want to discuss type I and type II errors.

TYPES OF TESTS

While there are a large number of tests with lots of nuances, the most common tests and some of the criteria you might choose for selecting your level are straightforward. The most basic kind of inference test is called the "chi-square test." This test may be used on variables of any level of measurement and samples of any size. It is most often used with crosstabs and two categorical variables. For studies that have two groups (e.g., a treatment and nontreatment group) for the independent variable and an interval or ratio-dependent variable, the choice is the *T* test, which compares means between each group. In addition, for studies that have multiple groups (e.g., a treatment group, a nontreatment group, and an alternative treatment group) and an interval or ratio-dependent variable, the choice is analysis of variance (ANOVA).

There are mathematically different distributions for each of these tests depending on sample size, and they all have important variants. You want to make sure you select the test that will yield you the most accurate information based on your research question and levels of measurement. The kind of information that tests provide, however, is reasonably similar across tests. All of the tests yield a point on the null distribution—a numeric value—and an associated probability. Other information is provided depending upon the test.

Data Management and Presentation

There are also two final important details that you need to think about for your research: data management and data presentation. "Data management" refers to what you do with the data as it is collected. "Data presentation" refers to your plan for the visual use of your data.

Data management can range from very simple to very complex procedures. Most often, because your data will be statistically analyzed, it makes sense to capture and store data in a form that can be quickly adopted by your statistics program. This often means the use of the database or spreadsheet program. Most such programs easily integrate into statistics programs. Further, many statistics programs provide simple spreadsheet-like formats. Thus, data can be entered directly into the spreadsheet for analysis. Conversely, many spreadsheet programs provide some statistical capacity. Simple descriptive statistics such as percentages, frequency distributions, and MCT and variation are available.

For more complex analysis, a statistical program should be selected. There are many available, and often your school makes them freely available to you. You should plan for a few contingencies by creating a codebook. A codebook keeps track of variable names and definitions. This is important for at least two reasons. First, with large datasets it is simple to forget what you are measuring. The codebook can provide the name of the variable, the definition of the variable, and the question used to collect the variable. Second, try to minimize the number of times data are transferred from one platform to another. The more often it is transferred, the greater the chance for error.

Other considerations are important. Think very carefully about all of the control variables in your analysis. It is difficult to return and expand the dataset after the analysis program is set up and data are collected. Understand the limitations of your statistical analysis program. Even simple things like the name of the variable may be important for your analysis.

Data presentation is also something to think about. Although you will not worry about this until the end of the project, planning is always a good idea. What tables might you want to present? Are there any charts or graphs that you think might be useful to describe important relationships? Again, however, there are a number of programs that will produce tables and charts for you. Many statistics and spreadsheet programs will create tables with varying levels of detail. Larson (2006) provides a variety of examples and templates to consider. At the same time, be mindful of the academic requirements of your school. These requirements might set the parameters that you must follow.

■ Your Analysis Plan

With all this information in mind, you are now ready to develop your research plan for analysis. There is no hard and fast rule for exactly what statistics should be included. The statistics depend upon your research question and the kind of information you hope to be able to provide. That said, the following are the components that commonly go into a plan.

- Clearly identify the purpose of your research. Is a description satisfactory or do you hope to describe and explain a relationship? If you have any formal hypotheses, what are they?
- Clearly identify each variable you intend to examine. Describe each variable, the level of measurement of each variable, and how you intend to capture that variable. This means, for example in a questionnaire, what questions or measures will be used to capture the information?
- Describe how you will manage the data. Where and how will you keep it organized?
- Describe the univariate descriptive statistics that you will use for each variable in your study. It is helpful to make the distinction between your independent, dependent, and other variables in this description.
- If you are examining relationships, describe the relationship measures that you will use. Will you use correlations? What kind? Will you use regressions? What kind? Will you be using any modeling programming? What kind?
- Describe the inferential statistics that you will use for the purposes of making your inferences, and/or testing relationships. If you have performed an operation to determine the optimal sample size—called a "power calculation"—include those results. Provide significance levels that you will use to determine the significance of your findings.
- If you plan to use any statistics programs as part of your analysis, identify the programs.
- Describe what your presentation will look like, including tables and charts.

PRACTICE ACTIVITIES

1. Develop a list of variables for the problem that you are interested in studying. By drawing lines between the variables, what do you think the relationships might be? Then, label each variable as an independent, intervening, or dependent variable.
2. For that same list of variables, think about ways by which you can measure them. Try and come up with three methods for each, one as a nominal variable, one as an ordinal variable, and one as an interval or ratio variable.

TECHNOLOGY EXERCISES

1. Think about the technology that you might want to use for analyzing your data. What computer programs are available at your campus that will help you with the analysis? Identify those programs and determine if there are any training opportunities at your school. Participate in the training if you can.
2. If your school has Statistical Package for the Social Sciences (SPSS), Statistical Analysis System (SAS), or a similar statistics program, access the program and its tutorials. Follow the tutorials and produce frequency distributions and cross tabulations.

REFERENCES

Asaduzzaman Fakir, A.N.M. (2016). *Quantative data analysis in social science research.* https://www.researchgate.net/publication/308647394_Quantative_Data_Analysis_in_Social_Science_Research

Ashcraft, M. H. (2002). Math anxiety: Personal, educational, and cognitive consequences. *Current Directions in Psychological Science, 11*(5), 181–185. https://doi.org/10.1111/1467-8721.0019

Bryman, A. (2012). *Social research methods* (4th ed.) Oxford University Press.

Chalhoub-Deville, M., & Deville, C. (2008). Utilizing psychometric methods in assessment. In E. Shohamy & N. H. Hornberger (Eds.), *Encyclopedia of language and education* (2nd ed., pp. 211–224). Springer Science + Business Media LLC.

Creswell, J. W. (2009). *Research design: Qualitative, quantitative, and mixed methods approaches* (3rd ed.). Sage Publications.

Frey, B. (2018). *The SAGE encyclopedia of educational research, measurement, and evaluation* (Vols. 1–4). Sage. https://doi.org/10.4135/9781506326139

Glen, S. (2020). *Lambda coefficient: Simple definition.* StatisticsHowTo.com: Elementary statistics for the rest of us! https://www.statisticshowto.com/lambda-coefficient

Kamentz, A. (2018). *Scared of math? Here's one way to fight the fear.* National Public Radio. https://www.npr.org/sections/ed/2018/07/16/619328200/got-math-anxiety-here-s-one-way-to-calm-it-down

Larson, M. (2006). Descriptive statistics and graphical displays. *Circulation, 114*(1), 76–81. https://doi.org/10.1161/CIRCULATIONAHA.105.584474

Lavrakas, P. J. (2008). *Encyclopedia of survey research methods.* Sage. https://doi.org/10.4135/9781412963947

ListenData. (2019). *15 types of data in regression science.* https://www.listendata.com/2018/03/regression-analysis.html

May, T., & Williams, M. (1998). *Knowing the social world.* Open University Press.

Mukaka, M. M. (2012). Statistics corner: A guide to appropriate use of correlation coefficient in medical research. *Malawi Medical Journal: The Journal of Medical Association of Malawi, 24*(3), 69–71. https://www.ncbi.nlm.nih.gov/pmc/articles/PMC3576830

O'Leary, Z. (2020). *The essential guide to doing your research project.* Sage. https://study.sagepub.com/oleary3e/student-resources/analysing-data/steps-in-quantitative-analysis

Shank, G. & Brown, L. (2007). *Exploring educational research literacy.* Routledge.

Suárez-Pellicioni, M., Núñez-Peña, M., & Colomé, À. (2016). Math anxiety: A review of its cognitive consequences, psychophysiological correlates, and brain bases. *Cognitive, Affective, & Behavioral Neuroscience, 16*(1), 3–22. https://doi.org/10.3758/s13415-015-0370-7

10

BEGINNING PHASES OF QUALITATIVE RESEARCH

This chapter reviews the first stages of the qualitative research study planning process by providing an introduction to qualitative data analysis. We begin with an overview of the three major approaches to qualitative data analysis (interpretive, social anthropological, and collaborative social). From there we present the fundamental components of content and thematic analysis, followed by descriptions of the different working phases of the qualitative data collection process (e.g., formulating research questions, identifying potential participants, sampling, using nonprobability sampling methods, data collection, and data transcription). This chapter concludes with a focus on the importance of transcribing one's own data (instead of using data transcription software) and sets the stage for the next phases of your research study: data coding, data interpretation, and data presentation.

By the end of this chapter, you will be able to do the following:

- Describe three major approaches to qualitative data analysis.
- Describe qualitative content analysis.
- Describe the three formal approaches to qualitative data analysis: conventional, directed, summative.
- Identify common challenges and limitations with content analysis.
- Describe the phases of the thematic analysis process.
- Formulate your qualitative research questions.
- Identify potential study participants.
- Discern between inclusion and exclusion criteria.
- Understand sample delimitations and limitations.
- Identify and understand a number of nonprobability sampling techniques (e.g., convenience, volunteer, quota, purposeful, homogeneous, snowball).
- Understand best practices for transcribing your audiovisual data.
- Determine sample size and understand the principle of saturation.
- Describe the process of data collection.
- Understand the process and importance of data transcription.

The Qualitative Research-Planning Stage

What you choose to study and how you do your analysis will shape your choice of methods. Before you can even think about collecting data, coding it, searching for themes, and then interpreting the results, you need to explore the kind of research project you are interested in pursuing. The external and internal resources that are readily available to you as you embark on your research adventure will impact the direction and quality of your study. There are a number of questions you should think about, try to answer, and prepare for before you begin your research project. What is the aim of your study? Is there an interesting problem you would like to explore and/or possibly address? After you have identified the problem, you will then need to conduct a thorough literature review on the topic. Who (i.e., study sample) can best answer questions that relate to your study's overall aim? How should the information from your participants be collected (e.g., by written or verbal questions, or by observations)? How should the data you collect be analyzed? And practically speaking, whose approval (e.g., institutional review board [IRB], field instructor, field supervisor, academic advisor, chair of your department) do you need to accomplish your research goals? After you have been able to provide yourself answers to those questions and have conducted a thorough review of the research literature relevant to your aim, it is time to begin formulating your research question(s).

FORMULATING QUALITATIVE RESEARCH QUESTIONS

In general, to begin any qualitative research project, your first priorities are to identify a research question and choose a sample(s) for analysis. Specifically, you need to decide what you are trying to explain. One of the most important components of a study is the quality of questions being asked of the participants. A research question guides and centers your research, should be clear and focused, as well as incorporate multiple sources to present your unique argument (Cuba, 1997). Research questions are interrogative sentences that clearly and succinctly state the major question or questions that your study aims to answer (Patten, 2002). Experienced and well-trained qualitative researchers know how to probe to elicit more nuanced answers from participants in their study group by asking questions containing words like "lived experience," "personal experience," "understanding," "meaning," and "story." Getting to the "how" and "why" is what makes qualitative research so useful. However, it is important to note that qualitative research questions can change and evolve as researchers conduct their studies.

In addition to considering what kind of problem you want to address, your qualitative capstone research should attempt to accomplish one of the following four goals (Porush, 1995):

1. Define or measure a specific fact or accumulate facts about a specific phenomenon.
2. Match theory and facts.
3. Evaluate and compare multiple theories, models, or hypotheses.
4. Provide evidence that a certain method is more effective than other methods.

While all research questions allow you to take an arguable position, they should not leave room for ambiguity. Social science research is required to have reliable data, meaning that if another researcher replicates your study and its methodologies, their results will be consistent with yours. Unreliable data in original research do not allow for a strong or arguable research question. Moreover, your research questions should address what the variables of your qualitative research study are, their relationships to each other, and should state something about how you will examine and provide explanations regarding those relationships.

Examples of research questions useful for the field of social work practice are:

- How do people who witness domestic violence understand how it impacts their current relationships?
- What is the experience of identifying as LGBTQ in the foster care system, in a drug rehabilitation program, or in any social service agency setting you identify?
- What does racial justice mean to residents of an urban neighborhood with high-income inequality? What does racial justice mean to residents of a racially diverse affluent suburban community?
- How do Asian Americans experience seeking help for mental health concerns? How do African Americans experience seeking help for mental health concerns?

After you have identified a question or questions like these, begin a thorough literature review of previous research that has explored your topic in some capacity. You may want to begin with the most recent research, perhaps the last 5 years or so, in order to get a current perspective on what other researchers have found. Often the most recent publications provide you not only with a great wealth of historical context woven into the literature review sections of their articles, but will also present you with neglected and/or recently identified areas of a phenomenon that needs further exploration. Your research project can help fill in those identified gaps of understanding and knowledge.

IDENTIFYING POTENTIAL PARTICIPANTS

Once you have formulated your research question(s) and you have had the chance to conduct a thorough review of the research literature related to your question(s), it is time to determine who your research sample will be. If it is a research-based undergraduate social work capstone project you are designing, you probably already have a good idea of who you would like your participants to be. Most likely your research sample(s) will consist of participants connected to your social work field practicum. For example, you may have identified a problem that deals with sexual health education and know that the participants of your study will be clients at a local methadone clinic. However, since most clinics serve patients with a variety of different demographics (i.e., age, ethnicity, race, sex, sexual orientation, gender and gender identity, socioeconomic levels) and other defining variables (i.e., housed or homeless, mental health diagnoses, related and nonrelated health issues, time in treatment, time since last visit), you will need to further identify the individuals to be included in your study. This process begins by determining the *inclusion* (participants to include) and *exclusion* (participants to exclude) criteria.

For example, let us imagine that the agency where you are placed provides services to children, teens, adults, older people, all ethnicities, and all genders, but your research question is very specific (e.g., what environmental factors increase violent behavior among adolescent boys?). You will need to draft an inclusion/exclusion plan. Inclusion criteria may include that your subjects are cisgender male, ranging in age from 13 to 19 years and who are currently receiving counseling and group therapy services due to their aggressive and violent behaviors. An example of an exclusion criterion may be that study subjects must have lived in the United States for at least 5 years.

DELIMITATIONS AND LIMITATIONS

Another area of the research process that you may want to consider are delimitations and your study's limitations. "Delimitations" are boundaries or parameters placed on a study by you, the researcher. Delimitations are very important since they are used to limit and clarify the scope of your study. Student researchers often want to take on large research efforts that are beyond the scope of their capstone research project. One way to address this is to narrow down and focus your research efforts using delimitations. Delimitations may involve delimiting a study by geographic location, population traits, time, or similar considerations (Cottrell & McKenzie, 2005).

For example, if you wanted to conduct a qualitative needs-assessment at a methadone clinic focusing on the sexual health needs of its clients (e.g., sexual health education, contraception use, sexually transmitted infections, intimate partner violence, transactional sex), you could limit your study to male patients from within the county where the clinic is located, who are employed but make less than $40,000 per year, are between the ages of 25 and 35, and who strongly identify with a religious practice. There needs to be a good rationale for any delimitations placed on your study, so whatever they may be they should be used because they make your study better, more practical, and not just for your interest or convenience. It is possible that you can delimit your study so much that the results have no value, or that you severely limit your potential subject pool because of the difficulty finding participants who meet all the inclusion or exclusion criteria stated in the delimitations you have set for your study.

"Limitations" are the parameters or boundaries of your research study that have been established by people or factors other than you, the researcher (Neutens & Robinson, 2002). Such factors are beyond the control of the researcher but may impact the results of the research, and as such, they should be identified for the future readers of your study report. For example, if you wanted to conduct a study using a sample of after-school youth programs from within the county where your field placement is located, you would have to obtain permission from each program for you to include their youth participants. Most likely, some programs will not grant you permission. And if a program does grant you permission, it is possible that a number of youth participants' parents may not grant you permission to include their child. Such refusals would be considered a limitation of your study.

Such limitations need to be documented and eventually communicated through your research report. By clearly identifying the limitations of your study, whatever they may be, you are essentially informing your reader that any potential methodological problems have already been considered but were not significant enough to prohibit you from conducting the study. In your final research report, you will need to communicate to your reader that any of your results should be viewed with consideration of your study's limitations.

SAMPLING FOR QUALITATIVE RESEARCH STUDIES

Once you have decided on your study's inclusion/exclusion criteria, you will need to decide how the specific participants or other units of analysis for your study will be selected. For example, you may not always be sampling people, but texts, pictures, video recordings, and so forth. If you will be working with people, depending on the number of potential participants and the resources available to collect data, you may want to attempt to collect data from all the participants within your established inclusion criteria (i.e., a census) or from just some of the participants (i.e., a sample). Each participant is referred to as a "sampling unit." A sampling unit is an aspect or set of aspects considered for selection to be part of a sample (Babbie, 1992). A sampling unit may be an individual, client records, program artifacts, text, and other units to be analyzed (Bowling, 2002). Your study population represents the total group of the study units that are actually accessible to you.

Even with a well-defined (i.e., delimited) study population, the number of potential participants may be so large that it makes it impractical to include everyone in your study due to a lack of resources to collect the data (i.e., not enough time to conduct interviews with everyone who fit your study delimitations). In such a case, you can take a sample from your study population (i.e., the people located at, or connected to, the field practicum location assigned to you).

Although it is not impossible, it is unlikely that as a social work student you will be given access to a potential subject pool large enough to warrant the use of probability sampling. "Probability sampling" employs random selection of participants to ensure that each person in a study population has an equal chance of being selected for involvement (Cottrell & McKenzie, 2005). Instead, due to the likely sampling limitations of your field placement site, employing nonprobability or nonrandom sampling (also known as "haphazard sampling" or "accidental sampling") strategies may be more practical for the purpose of conducting your capstone research project.

Nonprobability Sampling

Nonprobability sampling methods, also called "judgment" or "nonrandom sampling," are often used in qualitative studies. This style of sampling does not give everyone in a population an equal chance of being selected. It is a technique in which the researcher selects samples based on their own subjective judgment and academic expertise (Kohler et al., 2019; McKenzie et al., 2005). However, nonprobability sampling is a particularly useful methodology for student research projects since they are often quicker and less costly than probability sampling methods.

Nonprobability sampling is often used when a researcher (e.g., a field placement intern) does not have the resources to conduct a probability sample study due to constraints of time, finances, or personnel (Stall et al., 2020). A common example is when a student's research study is confined solely to their field placement location. In this case they may be able to recruit participants based only on convenience (e.g., because they attend group therapy at the agency, or they volunteered to be interviewed). Nonprobability sampling is well-suited for exploratory research designed to generate new ideas that can be systematically tested later. It is also a useful method for qualitative research aimed at developing an in-depth understanding of a specific population. The power of this research method lies in selecting information-rich cases that can provide researchers an opportunity to learn the most about the issues central to their study's purpose (Patton, 2002).

As mentioned, benefits to nonprobability sampling include being more cost-efficient and less time-consuming than random sampling methods. It is also great for gathering large amounts of data in a short time. There is often less effort needed for recruiting participants using nonprobability sampling, and it can ensure the presence of every subgroup of the population in the sample being studied. However, the major drawbacks to nonprobability sampling are that it is prone to systematic errors and sampling biases. The sample being studied and written about cannot claim to be representative of the population, and inferences and conclusions drawn from the sample are not generalizable to the population (Alvi, 2016). This is less of a problem with qualitative research since the purpose is often exploring "why" questions and not on generalizability.

Although there is a wide range of nonprobability sampling methods from which to choose, the following sections will highlight only a few. The methods chosen may be particularly useful for social work students limited with regard to sample pool, money, and time. The six sampling methods that may best fit a research-based social work capstone project are: convenience; volunteer; quota; purposive; homogeneous; and snowball (see Table 10.1).

Convenience Sampling

"Convenience sampling" is a type of nonprobability sampling in which members of a target population, who meet specific criteria, such as easy accessibility, availability at a given time, geographical proximity, or the willingness to participate, are included for the purpose of a research study (Dornyei, 2007; Saumure & Given, 2008). Convenience sampling is a popular qualitative data collection method because it allows a researcher to collect large amounts of data in a short period of time and for little money (McDermott & Sarvela, 1999; Neutens & Rubinson, 2002). A convenience sample is obtained by selecting any readily available participant from an intact group (Etikan et al., 2016). Examples of intact groups often used by social worker students and professionals are people who have to be at a certain place (e.g., participants in group therapy or clients living together in a domestic violence shelter), or people who voluntarily show up at a specific place for a specific reason (e.g., members of a support group like Alcoholics Anonymous or people who visit food pantries and/or soup kitchens).

TABLE 10.1 SUMMARY OF HIGHLIGHTED NONPROBABILITY SAMPLING PROCEDURES

SAMPLE	FUNDAMENTAL DESCRIPTIVE ELEMENTS
CONVENIENCE	Includes any available participant meeting some minimum criterion, usually being part of an accessible intact target group
VOLUNTEER	Includes any participant motivated enough to self-select themselves to be part of the study
QUOTA	Includes participants chosen in approximate proportion to the population traits they "represent" (e.g., gender identity, sexual orientation, age, ethnicity, socioeconomic)
PURPOSIVE	Not an exclusive sampling technique, rather a category of other nonprobability techniques which are purposive in nature (e.g., homogeneous and snowball)
HOMOGENEOUS	Includes participants chosen by a researcher due to a unique trait or characteristic (e.g., members of an Alcoholics Anonymous chapter)
SNOWBALL	Includes participants already identified by a researcher, who are then asked to refer other individuals who meet the same criteria for inclusion in the study

Volunteer Sampling

"Volunteer sampling" is a type of convenience sampling in which the decision to participate relies completely on respondents to an invitation (e.g., a general invitation to participate appearing in media, leaflets, posters, social media posts, tele-voting, self-selection in web surveys; Vehovar et al., 2016). The principle of this sampling type is self-selection, and its main advantage is the speed at which one can accumulate a sample (Alvi, 2016). However, primary disadvantages of this technique include the researcher having very little control over the sample, and participant motivation may be based on factors unrelated to their interest in a study's purpose (e.g., receiving money, food, or goods in exchange for participating).

Samples that include participants motivated enough to self-select for a research study are referred to as "volunteer samples" (McDermott & Sarvela, 1999). For example, a researcher who was interested in studying the self-care behaviors of people who have recently lost their jobs may have a hard time identifying a suitable study population. That researcher may place an ad in a local newspaper's classifieds section asking for volunteers to participate, or they may post a flyer in the Domestic Violence Agency in wich they are interning in order to recruit participants to examine the impact that intimate partner violence has had on their social networks. Because of the potential difficulty of getting people to volunteer, it is not unusual for researchers to offer an incentive (i.e., money, free services, t-shirts) to entice potential participants to volunteer. The resulting participants using this sampling method would include those who are really interested in the study, those just interested in the incentive, or both, and are probably not representative of those who do not volunteer (Cottrell & McKenzie, 2005).

Quota Sampling

When qualitative researchers want their sample to be representative of certain characteristics of a study population, but are unable to select a probability sample, they can employ quota sampling. "Quota sampling" is a methodology in which data are collected from a homogeneous population and then divided into mutually exclusive subgroups selected on the basis of a given proportion (McDermott & Sarvela, 1999). Suppose you know that the enrollment of adolescents attending an after-school youth development program is 50% female, 46% male, and 4% transgender, and you want to select a quota sample of 50 teens. In this example, you would select 25 female (50%), 23 male (46%), and 2 (4%) transgender participants. Using the same youth development program location, you could also select a quota sample based on the age, ethnicity, religion, or any other defined characteristic of the teen participant population you choose.

Purposeful Sampling

"Purposeful sampling" is a technique widely used in qualitative research in order to efficiently and effectively identify and select information-rich cases when resources are limited (Patton, 2002). Sometimes called "judgmental sampling" (Hagan, 2006), purposeful sampling involves researchers using their personal knowledge or expertise about some group to select subjects representative of that population. This process involves identifying and selecting individuals or groups of individuals who are experienced with or especially knowledgeable about a phenomenon of interest (Cresswell & Plano-Clark, 2011).

In addition to knowledge and experience, the purposeful sampling technique relies on the availability and willingness of individuals to participate, and their ability to communicate opinions and experiences in an expressive, articulate, and reflective manner. Despite some serious limitations (e.g., the lack of wide generalizability), purposive samples often provide qualitative researchers with data that enable a rich and textured description of the phenomenon being studied (Lune & Berg, 2018). Purposeful sampling strategies include homogeneous sampling and snowball sampling.

Homogeneous Sampling

"Homogeneous sampling" is when individuals are selected because of a unique factor or trait (Cottrell & McKenzie, 2005). Social workers may use this sampling method in qualitative studies when they want to study a specific subgroup of people in detail in order to reduce variation, simplify analysis, and facilitate group interviewing (Palinkas et al., 2015). This method of sampling is often used for selecting focus group participants. An example of such a study would be in-depth interviews with individuals who attend Alcoholics Anonymous meetings who have recently celebrated 5 years of sobriety.

Snowball Sampling

"Snowball sampling" (or "chain sampling") is a multiple stage method that literally "snowballs" (Neutens & Rubinson, 2002). It can be used when your target population is not readily available and/or difficult to identify and approach due to the sensitive nature of the research problem you are investigating (e.g., issues dealing with family-based violence or diseases and other health conditions that carry a social stigma). This sampling technique begins when participants with the specific characteristics you are looking for are identified and interviewed. You then ask these individuals if they know others with the same characteristics who may be willing to participate in your study (Palinkas et al., 2015). Once identified, you reach out to them, interview those who agree to participate, and then ask them if they know of others who would be willing to participate. This process is continued until you obtain the desired number of participants for your sample (Alvi, 2016; Cottrell & McKenzie, 2005). Table 10.1 summarizes the different types of nonprobability samples.

> **Reflection Question**
> Thinking about your social work practicum placement location, which of the nonprobability sampling techniques just reviewed (e.g., convenience, volunteer, quota, purposeful, homogeneous, snowball) would you consider to be the best fit for your purposes? Why?

SAMPLE SIZE AND THE PRINCIPLE OF SATURATION

The type of qualitative study you pursue will determine the best sample size for your research. Will your study require in-depth interviews, ethnographic research, or focus groups? Some studies blend all three and perhaps more. Depending on which method or methods are used will help determine the appropriate sample size for your project. Each methodology for gathering data will yield different outcomes.

In general, your sample size should be large enough to sufficiently describe the phenomenon of interest and address your research question(s). Too small of a sample and you may not be able to adequately describe a phenomenon or provide answers to questions, but a large sample size runs the risk of wasted time producing repetitive data. The goal of qualitative research should therefore be the attainment of saturation. "Saturation" occurs when adding more participants to your study does not result in obtaining additional information or perspectives. In qualitative research, larger samples often reach a point of diminishing returns; more data are collected that do not lead to more information (Mason, 2010).

As qualitative research aims to obtain diverse opinions from a sample size on a client's experiences, satisfaction levels, achievements, challenges, and outcomes, the goal of a qualitative study should be to have a large enough sample size to uncover a variety of thoughts and opinions, but to limit the sample size at the point of saturation (i.e., when no new data collection codes can be created). A general recommendation for in-depth interviews is to have a sample size of 20 to 30. However, in some cases a minimum of 10 is acceptable, particularly in cases where data saturation occurs among a relatively homogeneous population (Boddy, 2016).

Sampling in Qualitative Research Video
https://www.youtube.com/watch?v=z_w8Cl8LQds

DATA COLLECTION

Qualitative fieldwork can generate a vast amount of written or spoken data (aka, "corpus data") accumulated through hours of focus groups or interviews, stacks of observational notes, and the many documents retrieved during the data collection process. Therefore, one of the first steps in qualitative analysis is to organize and prepare the data. Typically, this involves scanning all the documents collected, converting handwritten field observation notes to digital format (e.g., Adobe PDF or Microsoft Word documents), and gathering all of the video- or audio-recorded interview files into one location (Lochmiller & Lester, 2017).

Lester et al. (2020) recommend that qualitative researchers create a structured naming protocol for each file, and also a master data inventory that lists each data source, the date of its collection, the person who created it, and its storage location. Through this data organization protocol, qualitative researchers are better able to begin applying their qualitative analysis to the copious amounts of information they have collected during their fieldwork. The collected, organized, and categorized qualitative data sets can then be more easily imported into any number of qualitative data analysis software packages, such as MACQDA, NVivo, or ATLAS.

DATA TRANSCRIPTION

Given that much of qualitative data collection is recorded through audio and video technology, qualitative researchers often need to dedicate considerable time to transcribing the data in preparation for analysis. There are a number of transcription options available to the qualitative researcher (e.g., verbatim transcription, gisted transcription, multimodal transcription). "Verbatim transcription" is perhaps the longest used and most common of all the transcription methods. Verbatim transcriptions aim to capture every single word and nonverbal auditory communication (e.g., sighs, laughing, snorts) from the participant in order to provide a comprehensive and accurate record of the conversation (Lester et al., 2020).

"Gisted transcription" is a type of summarization. Dempster and Woods (2011) describe gisting as creating a summary transcript that captures the essence (aka, "the gist") of the audio or video file's content without the time commitment required by a verbatim transcript. Evers (2011) explains gisting as a two-part process:

> *(1) Type detailed fieldnotes regarding my interviews and observations, based on my notes taken during the interview and my recollection of events and speech. For the typing of my fieldnotes, I divided a page in two columns and only typed in the front column. (2) Afterwards, I would listen to my tape, and in the left column, correct mistakes I may have made in the right column, or add things that were not in my detailed notes, and as such created some sort of gisted transcript. (p. 11, para 5–6)*

"Multimodal transcription" is a commonly used method when analyzing video recordings of interviews, focus groups, and other forms of social interaction. When conducting a multimodal transcription of a video-recorded qualitative interview, for example, all nonverbal communication (e.g., gaze, shake of a head, gestures, tapping fingers, fidgeting, eye-rolls, postures) and verbatim linguistic communication are transcribed (Bezemer & Mavers, 2011). Other variables that may influence participant responses and behaviors may also be noted (e.g., a loud sound from outside, a cell-phone ringing, the sound of furniture being moved in a room above). By recording all of the available data that can be seen in a video recording, the multimodal transcription process aims to produce a highly comprehensive set of analyzable data.

TRANSCRIPTION AND DATA FAMILIARIZATION

Transcribing many hours of audiovisual data can feel overwhelming. However, before outsourcing the job of transcribing to a professional transcriptionist, you should consider that one of the most beneficial aspects of transcribing your own data is that it familiarizes you with your data. Becoming familiarized with the data you have collected is a common practice in all forms of qualitative analysis. This familiarity helps to deepen your understanding of your participants' perspectives and supports you in understanding your data in a way that will likely speed up the analysis process later on (Lester et al., 2020).

During the familiarization phase, researchers immerse themselves in their datasets by repeatedly reading or listening to each and every item of data in order to develop a deeper understanding of the data they have collected. Familiarization also involves the process whereby the researcher begins to identify, and then notate, features of the data that are potentially relevant to the posited research question(s). Such notations assist the researcher in beginning the next phase: the coding process. It is important for new researchers to understand that although there are a growing number of automated transcription options (e.g., Transana, Temi, Trint) that are transforming how qualitative transcription is completed, there are significant benefits to becoming intimately familiar with one's collected data.

Once you have finished typing your fieldnotes and transcribing the interviews you have recorded, then comes the daunting task of taking the large amount of qualitative data you have painstakingly collected and transforming it into cohesive and comprehendible results. What exactly do you do now? Answering this question may feel a bit overwhelming. Fortunately, many experienced qualitative researchers know exactly what to do in this circumstance: step back and take a mental break. You may need only a few hours, a few days, or perhaps even a few weeks, but regardless of what time frame you choose, you absolutely need some time to rest your mind, time to dedicate to self-care, or do things that may have been neglected by the time-consuming tasks of conducting interviews and collecting data (Bogden & Biklen, 2006). Think of dedicating a portion of your time to self-care as a very small reward for all of your hard work! Once you have given yourself adequate time to do a cognitive reset, it is time to return to the data and begin the important process of developing and applying codes.

PRACTICE ACTIVITIES

1. Make a list of three qualitative research questions you would like to explore at your current or future social work field placement location.
2. Of the following types of sampling: nonprobability, convenience, volunteer, quota, homogeneous, and snowball, which method(s) do you think would generate an ideal sample for gathering data that would best enable you to answer the research question(s) you identified?

TECHNOLOGY EXERCISE

Using the internet, research the capabilities of the three transcription services mentioned in this chapter: Transana, Temi, Trint. Based on cost, capabilities, and ease of use, which of the three speech-to-text transcription software programs would you choose, and why?

REFERENCES

Alvi, M. (2016). *A manual for selecting sampling techniques in research*. Munich Personal RePEc Archive. https://mpra.ub.uni-muenchen.de/70218

Babbie, E. (1992). *The practice of social research* (6th ed.). Wadsworth.

Berg, B. (2007). *Qualitative research methods for the social sciences* (6th ed.). Allyn & Bacon.

Bezemer, J., & Mavers, D. (2011). Multimodal transcription as academic practice: A social semiotic perspective. *International Journal of Social Research Methodology, 14*(3), 191–206. https://doi.org/10.1080/13645579.2011.563616

Boddy, C. R. (2016). Sample size for qualitative research. *Qualitative Market Research, 19*(4), 426–432. https://doi.org/10.1108/QMR-06-2016-0053

Bogden, R., & Biklen, S. K. (2006). *Qualitative research for education: An introduction to theory and methods* (5th ed.). Pearson.

Bowling, A. (2002). *Research methods in health: Investigating health and health services* (2nd ed.). Open University Press.

Cottrell, R. R., & McKenzie, J. F. (2005). *Health promotion & education research methods: Using the five-chapter thesis/dissertation model*. Jones & Bartlett.

Cresswell, J. W., & Plano-Clark, V. L. (2011). *Designing and conducting mixed method research* (2nd ed.). Sage.

Cuba, L. (1997). *A short guide to writing about social science* (3rd ed.). Addison-Wesley.

Dempster, P. G., & Woods, D. K. (2011). The economic crisis through the eyes of Transana. *Forum Qualtative Sozialforschung/Forum: Qualitative Social Research, 12*(1), Art. 16. https://doi.org/10.17169/fqs-12.1.1515

Dornyei, Z. (2007). *Research methods in applied linguistics*. Oxford University Press.

Etikan, I., Musa, S. A., & Alkassim, R. S. (2016). Comparison of convenience sampling and purposive sampling. *American Journal of Theoretical and Applied Statistics, 5*(1), 1–4. https://doi.org/10.11648/j.ajtas.20160501.11

Evers, J. C. (2011). From the past into the future. How technological developments change our way of data collection, transcription and analysis [94 paragraphs]. *Forum: Qualitative Social Research, 12*(1), Art. 38, http://nbn-resolving.de/urn:nbn:de:0114-fqs1101381. Retrieved October 18, 2020, from http://www.qualitative-research.net/index.php/fqs/article/download/1636/3162

Hagan, F. E. (2006). *Research methods in criminal justice and criminology* (7th ed.). Allyn & Bacon.

Kohler, U., Kreutter, F., & Stuart, E. A. (2019). Nonprobability sampling and causal analysis. *Annual Review of Statistics and Its Applications, 6*, 149–172. https://doi.org/10.1146/annurev-statistics-030718-104951

Lester, J. N., Cho, Y., & Lochmiller, C. R. (2020). Learning to do qualitative data analysis: A starting point. *Human Resource Development Review, 19*(1), 94–106. https://doi.org/10.1177/1534484320903890

Lochmiller, C. R., & Lester, J. N. (2017). *An introduction to educational research: Connecting methods to practice*. Sage.

Lune, H., & Berg, B. L. (2018). *Qualitative research methods for the social sciences* (9th ed.). Pearson.

Mason, M. (2010). Sample size and saturation in PhD studies using qualitative interviews [63 paragraphs]. *Forum: Qualitative Social Research*, *11*(3), Art. 8. https://doi.org/10.17169/fqs-11.3.1428

McDermott, R. J., & Sarvela, P. D. (1999). *Health education evaluation and measurement: A practitioner's perspective* (2nd ed.). McGraw-Hill.

McKenzie, J. F., Neiger, B. L., & Smeltzer, J. L. (2005). *Planning, implementing, and evaluating health promotion programs: A primer* (4th ed.). Benjamin Cummings.

Neutens, J. J., & Rubinson, L. (2002). *Research techniques for the health sciences* (3rd ed.). Benjamin Cummings.

Palinkas, L. A., Horwitz, S. M., Green, C. A., Wisdom, J. P., Duan, N., & Hoagwood, K. (2015). Purposeful sampling for qualitative data collection and analysis in mixed method implementation research. *Administration and Policy in Mental Health*, *42*(5), 533–544. https://doi.org/10.1007/s10488-013-0528-y

Patten, M. L. (2002). *Understanding research methods* (3rd ed.). Pryczak.

Patton, M. Q. (2002). *Qualitative research and evaluation methods*. Sage.

Porush, D. (1995). *A short guide to writing about science*. HarperCollins.

Saumure, K., & Given, L. (2008). Convenience sample. In L. M. Given (Ed.), *The Sage encyclopedia of qualitative research methods* (pp. 125–125). Sage.

Stall, R., Dodge, B., Bauermeister, J. A., Poteat, T., & Beyrer, C. (2020). *LGBTQ health research: Theory, methods, practice*. Johns Hopkins University Press.

Vehovar, V., Toepoel, V., & Steimetz, S. (2016). Non-probability sampling. *The Sage handbook of survey methods* (pp. 329–349). Sage.

11

QUALITATIVE RESEARCH: DATA CODING, ANALYSIS, INTERPRETATION, AND REPORTING RESULTS

In this chapter, we explore a number of data-coding and analysis techniques. We discuss how to code text from your transcribed interviews and then create categories based on those codes. Also, we present methods to identify themes, patterns, and relationships based on their collected data and how to summarize your findings. This chapter provides a review of a standard qualitative research report, including some tips to ensure your readers of the validity and trustworthiness of your research. We also inform you about available qualitative data analysis software to assist in completing your qualitative capstone research project.

By the end of this chapter, you will be able to do the following:

- Describe the multiphased process of developing and applying codes.
- List general kinds of codes used in the coding process.
- Understand how to identify themes, patterns, and relationships among your data.
- Know the information needed to include in your data summary.
- Describe the sections of your written research report.
- Understand the importance of providing a detailed account of your qualitative methodologies.
- Identify, compare, and contrast three useful qualitative data analysis software programs.

Qualitative Research Data Analysis

Whether you are conducting a content analysis, thematic analysis, narrative, discourse or using a grounded theory approach, you will need to code your data. "Coding" is the process of selective reduction where transcribed interviews and other forms of text are "coded" into manageable content categories. By reducing text data into categories, you can focus on and code for specific words or patterns that inform your research question. Codes are short, descriptive phrases or words that help assign meaning to collected data or a meaningful label that captures something interesting and/or significant about the data in relation to the researcher's investigative interests (Elo et al., 2014).

Try to imagine an expansive warehouse floor covered with a large variety of fruits and vegetables. You are given the task of sorting all the fruits and veggies into piles according to an organizational strategy that you need to create. You pace around the warehouse floor, visually examining all of the fruits and vegetables on display, picking them up, feeling their textures, taking note of their colors, and smelling their scents. There are many ways to begin forming distinct piles. The produce can be sorted according to color, size, smell, taste, the seasons in which they naturally ripen, or where the produce was grown and harvested.

This kind of sorting activity is analogous to the approach a qualitative researcher uses during the first phase of developing a coding system for organizing the data they have collected. Unfortunately, unlike organizing a warehouse full of fruits and vegetables, the qualitative data collected for your research-based capstone project are likely to be a much more difficult process to undertake (Bogden & Biklen, 2006). Dissimilar to the more easily discernible characteristics of fruit and vegetables mentioned previously, the kinds of codes qualitative researchers classify data into can be more complex and/or abstract. The following are some examples of the general kinds of codes one can utilize for the first phase of the coding process.

SETTING/CONTEXT CODES

"Setting/context codes" are where the most general information about the setting, topic, or subjects can be located. Under these codes are where the collected material that allows you to place your study in a larger research-informed context is located (Bogden & Biklen, 2006). Material that can be categorized under setting/context codes include: descriptive literature about the research setting, subject(s), topic(s), sources (e.g., pamphlets, brochures, local newspaper articles, other media coverage); general and specific statements that people make about the subject, setting, and/or how the setting fits into their community; and descriptive statistics and other quantitative data describing the setting of your research subject (e.g., sets of data labeled: "Descriptions of human service agencies addressing homelessness" or "Local food banks and food pantries").

For example, the following statement made by a social work intern describing characteristics of the University Food Pantry at which they have been placed would be a setting/context code:

Our university has its very own Resource Pantry that is open to all undergraduate and graduate students and is staffed by dedicated and compassionate volunteers and interns. Some resources the Pantry offers is food, personal care items, school supplies, winter coats, and professional attire to anyone in need. It's located in the lower level of Commonwealth Court, in Student Services, room 108.

PROCESS CODES

"Process codes" are words and phrases that help you categorize sequences of events, passages from one kind or type of status to another or that change over time. In order to use a process code, you need to be able to view an individual, group, organization, or activity over time in order to perceive change taking place in a sequence of at least two parts. Common process codes indicate time periods, steps, phases, stages, and chronology. In addition, key points in a sequence (e.g., benchmarks, transitions, turning points) could be placed within the process code category.

Process coding strategies are commonly used in sequencing participation histories (or life histories). The coding categories include the participation in an activity or the periods in the life of the study participant that appear to separate important segments. A participation history of an individual that emphasizes their participation in a social service program might include categories such as (a) initial experience, (b) subsequent visits, (c) end of participation, and so forth (Bogden & Biklen, 2006).

The following is an example of data collected from a Food Pantry intern that could be assigned to the "process codes" category:

Each day during its operational hours of 8 am–4 pm, an average of 25–35 students visit the Food Pantry. On their first visit, everyone is given a brochure describing the Food Pantry's philosophy, goals, and community garden educational programs, and asked to complete a simple intake form before they shop. Students are then provided with a reusable bag to collect any food and other items they want. They take their bag to the front desk, their food is weighed, they're handed a satisfaction survey, and they're good to go!

ACTIVITY CODES

Codes that indicate regularly occurring forms of behavior are what are called "activity codes." Such behaviors can be relatively straightforward and lead to codes such as a "student smoking from a vape-pen," "joking," or "social justice conversation" or regularly occurring behaviors that are a formal part of a setting, such as "completing an intake," "breathing exercises at the beginning of each class," "12–1 pm university-wide lunch pause," "attendance taking," "cultural humility and awareness case conference," and "visits to the university's communal gardens." Units of data that might be coded under such headings should be fairly obvious. Again, using the Food Pantry study as the setting, information from a Food Pantry volunteer listed under "activity codes" could be:

After assisting a first-time visitor with their intake form, I provided them with a tour of the Pantry and helped them find items they were looking for. We had a wonderful conversation about different social justice issues needing to be better addressed, such as food insecurity. After talking and joking with one another for a while, she asked if I could walk her through the community gardens mentioned in the brochure she was provided with. I was more than happy to accompany her!

SITUATION CODES

Units of data that inform you how your subjects define a setting or particular topic can be placed in the "situation codes" category. Data under this type of code indicate a researcher's interest in their subjects' world views and how they see themselves in relation to your research topic or the setting in which your study is being conducted. Examples of questions that produce data that would be filed under this coding category could be: What do you hope to accomplish through your participation? How would you describe what you do here? What is important to you? How do you relate your role in this setting to your philosophy of life?. Questions that explore whether or not the subjects' participation is affected by a particular identity orientation (e.g., political orientation, religious affiliation, spiritual orientation, future career choice) also produce data that can be filed under the situation codes category. You may also find yourself collecting data on the views and experiences of various types of participants (e.g., paid staff, volunteers, student interns, upper administration) and, therefore, may want to create a separate file for each type of participant whose data you determine to belong under the situation codes category (Bogden & Biklen, 2006).

An example of data that fit in the situation codes family data is the following statement made by a social work field placement Intern, which can be coded under "*students'* views on their work":

For me, volunteering is a way of life. As a social work student, I'm growing increasingly aware of how systemic sexism and racism negatively impact most of the people I come into contact with. As a result, I find myself constantly thinking about how I can be a part of the change our society needs in order to create a better future for each other as U.S. citizens. In one of the wealthiest countries on our planet, people not having enough food to eat, or not being able to afford clothes, school supplies, or personal care items is a serious social justice issue. Being an intern here at our campus's Food Pantry provides me with the opportunity to serve members of my community by connecting them to the resources they need.

EVENT CODES

"Event codes" are directed at units of data related to specific activities that occur in the setting or in the lives of the research participants you are interviewing. Event codes indicate particular incidents that occur infrequently or only once. For example, in a dissertation study involving interviews with women about their experiences in school, the onset of menstruation was a one-time event mentioned by all of the women (Biklen, 1973 as cited in Bogden & Biklen, 2006). That event became a coding category.

In the course of participant observation studies, incidents that become event coding categories are those that cause a significant amount of attention and discussion by the participants in the study. Events that occurred prior to your research may be frequent topics of comment and discussion. If you were conducting a participant observation study during your field placement at the Food Pantry, the following events could become event coding categories: "the firing of a volunteer coordinator," "the domestic violence incident," and "the lantern fly infestation."

An example of a unit of data coded under the event code "the domestic violence incident" is cited next. It was taken from a conversation with a frequent visitor to the Food Pantry:

I was just minding my own business and collecting food for the week when two female students started yelling at each other. At first I thought they were just friends having an argument, but when one of the girls accused the other of cheating on her, I realized they were more than friends. All of a sudden they were attacking each other! They were grappling and punching each other when one lost her footing and tumbled back into a display full of office supplies. The display toppled over into a shelf of food, which fell over as well. An intern ran over to try and diffuse the situation, while the staff member at the front desk called campus safety. What a mess that was!

STRATEGY CODES

"Strategies" refer to the methods, tactics, practices, approaches, schemes, and other conscious ways people accomplish various things. Professors, for example, employ strategies to establish safety and mutual accountability in their classes, to get their students to complete the assigned reading, and to diffuse conflicts between students. Students may engage in tactics to get the classes they want, to approach professors about writing recommendation letters for graduate school admissions, to meet friends, or to negotiate conflicting demands. It is important to document the motives to people's behavior, including your own. If you perceive people's behaviors as tactics and strategies, be sure to distinguish between your judgment and theirs (Bogdan & Biklen, 2006). The following is an example of a quotation that might be coded under the strategy code "tactics to meet friends":

I'm a volunteer here at the Food Pantry. I'm also a beginning first year student, so I don't know many people on campus yet. My mother always tells me that volunteering is a great way to meet new friends, and after my academic advisor told me about all the good things the Food Pantry is doing for our campus community, I figured this could be an ideal location to make friends with kind-hearted people.

RELATIONSHIP AND SOCIAL STRUCTURE CODES

Commonplace patterns of interpersonal behavior among people not already defined by your previously established coding categories can be grouped under "relationships." Units of data indicating friendships, rivals, romances, alliances, enemies, and students/mentors are what is meant by "relationship codes." Relations that are more formally defined, what social scientists refer to as "social roles," "social role sets," and "positions," represent another branch of this coding family. The amassed description of interpersonal relations in any setting is referred to as its "social structure." Coding in this domain will help you develop a description of a particular setting's social structure (Bogdan & Biklen, 2006).

The following piece of data, including an example of a researcher's note to self, is related to relationships and could be coded under a relationship/social structure code like "student friendships":

The student volunteers returned from their lunch break during Bengal Pause (the time between 12–1pm when no classes are scheduled on campus). A group of three young men, Travis, Darnell, and Marcus, stood by the rack of suit jackets, talking and joking around with one another, while a fourth, Mike, sits by himself reading the campus paper. They did the same thing yesterday. Maripat and Zoe came in together and sat next to each other as did Guadalupe and Maria. (*Note: The three young men who hang out together after Bengal Pause are all African American, while the fourth, a Caucasian student is consistently by himself. Maripat and Zoe are both Caucasian, and Guadalupe and Maria are both Latinx. Is this racial segregation coincidental or a result of some unknown factor? I'll have to look further into this ...)

Additional pieces of data collected in the Food Pantry setting that could be related to relationship and social structure codes include information about how visitors are welcomed into the Food Pantry and how they are treated throughout their time there. Through observations of staff, volunteers, and interns, a pattern may emerge as the researcher documents the interactions they witness as a participant observer. Observations may begin to provide evidence that students are greeted and treated differently, dependent on a variety of superficial characteristics including the gender, race and/or ethnicity, age, physical size, and so forth of the visitors to the Food Pantry, as well as the staff, volunteers, and interns. Those observational notations may then be connected to anecdotal data from one-on-one and group interviews.

METHOD CODES

"Method codes" are those that separate material related to research procedures, challenges, dilemmas, insights, joys, and the like. Usually, the researcher's comments account for the bulk of the units of data that become coded under "methods." The following is an example of a researcher's comment from a study of a Food Pantry program previously mentioned that might be coded using this label:

Observer comment: I feel a little bit odd in this setting. Although I am surrounded by my peers, student volunteers, interns, and visitors to the food pantry, I often wonder if my presence as a participant/observer conducting research influences others' relations with me in any way. Sometimes I feel like people stop talking when I get close to them. I also wonder if those around me alter their behavior in my presence, being friendlier and less critical of others. Maybe I'm just being paranoid? I think I need to talk to my seminar professor about it.

THE THEMATIC ANALYSIS APPROACH TO CODING

When conducting a "thematic analysis" of your data, Lester et al. (2020) suggest that you think about coding as something that should be completed in no fewer than three cycles. In the first cycle, general codes are assigned to the entire data set. These codes are primarily descriptive in nature and should be directly related to the original research question(s) being investigated. This layer of coding assists in identifying important experiences, statements, and reflections found in the data. For example, in the "needs-assessment/program evaluation research" at the University Food Pantry described earlier, two general codes identified could be "Satisfaction with services provided" and "Consumer perceptions of treatment by service providers." Beyond providing a simple way to lump similar data together in preparation of a more focused examination later on, the researcher can also reduce data corpus (i.e., the total amount of data collected) by setting aside all data that do not denote experiences, statements, and reflections that are not related to the project's proposed research questions.

During the second cycle of coding, the researcher returns to the segments of data to which codes had been previously assigned in the first cycle and then proceeds to assign additional codes (Lester et al., 2020). In the first example provided about the Food Pantry study, the general code of "Satisfaction with services provided" can then further be separated into a range of codes representing different levels of satisfaction, whereas the "Consumer perceptions of treatment by service providers" can be further coded into whether consumers felt they were being treated positively, negatively, or some other category illuminated by the data. The goal of the second cycle of coding is to begin connecting experiences, statements, and reflections shared by participants to the focus of the study.

In the third and potentially final cycle of the coding process, researchers use the coded/amalgamated data, provided by their research participants, to emphasize explicit connections to their study's theoretical and conceptual ideas. In this cycle, coding typically leads to a set of conclusions based on the qualitative data, as well as on the educated reasoning of the researcher. For example, a comment or statement coded in prior cycles of the coding process may then be specifically highlighted as an example of a proposed conceptual idea, or to support or refute one of the researcher's original hypotheses (Lester et al., 2020).

THE GROUNDED THEORY APPROACH TO CODING

When utilizing a "grounded theory approach," coding is used to identify categories, which are then conceptually woven together into a grounded theory (Glaser & Strauss, 1967). The underlying goal of data analysis in the grounded theory methodology is theory development (Vollstedt & Rezat, 2019). In order to achieve this goal, you evaluate your collected data by applying different approaches to coding as the core process. Coding according to the grounded theory approach is a process of conceptual abstraction by assigning general concepts (codes) to particular incidences in your data. One of the challenges of understanding the grounded theory approach to data analysis is due to this abstract nature of its coding process (Gallicano, 2013). Three common approaches to grounded theory data analysis are Classic Glaserian (Glaser, 1978, 1992; Glaser & Strauss, 1967), Constructivist (Charmaz, 2006, 2014), and Straussian (Corbin & Strauss, 2008, 2015; Strauss & Corbin, 1990, 1998).

According to Classic Glaserian grounded theory, text data go through a two-stage process: substantive coding and theoretical coding (Glaser, 1978, 1992; Glaser & Strauss, 1967). Substantive coding is further divided into "open" and "selective" coding. Open coding results from immersing oneself in the data. This subphase is finished with the discovery of the core category. The selective coding subphase involves selectively coding data that relate to the identified core category. The theoretical coding stage integrates substantive codes, which may use a theoretical coding family, into a grounded theory (Rieger, 2018).

Constructivist grounded theory uses two coding stages: "initial coding" and "focused coding" (Charmaz, 2006, 2014). During the initial coding process, you study data fragments and label them with codes. During focused coding, you use your initial codes that frequently reappear and are the most relevant, in order to theoretically code all future data. However, being that it is one of the more understandable step-by-step approaches for beginning qualitative researchers to utilize, we focus on the Straussian grounded theory approach to coding. Straussian grounded theory involves three coding stages: open coding, axial coding, and selective coding (Corbin & Strauss, 2008, 2015; Strauss & Corbin, 1990, 1998).

Open Coding

"Open coding" involves coding your text data and discovering a category's properties and dimensions (Strauss & Corbin, 1998). During this initial phase of coding, you read through your data many times before you begin to create tentative labels for pieces of data that you feel summarize what you see happening (Gallicano, 2013). In essence, you will be coding pieces of data with line-by-line coding, identifying categories, as well as their properties or dimensions (Rieger, 2018). This process will provide you with the basic units of your analysis as you begin breaking down the data into first-level concepts, or primary headings, and second-level categories, or subheadings.

Researchers will often use different-colored highlighters (or different-colored highlighting on a word process platform) to distinguish concepts and categories. For example, if your interviewees consistently talk about staff training, each time an interviewee mentions training, or anything related to staff training, you would use the same color highlight. Staff training would become a concept, and other things related (types, in-person, virtual, etc.) would become categories, all highlighted using the same color. You would then use different-colored highlights to distinguish each broad concept and category. What you should have at the end of this phase are transcripts with three to five different colors in lots of highlighted text. Transfer these into a brief outline, with the concepts being your primary headings and the categories serving as subheadings.

Axial Coding

"Axial coding" involves assembling fragmented data back together through the use of questions derived from one of Glaser's (1978) coding families (see Table 11.1). Also known as a "coding paradigm," this framework of questions facilitates the identification of the relationship between structure and process, as well as the linking of categories and subcategories (Corbin & Strauss, 2015). For example, using the coding family "The Six Cs," a researcher groups code into six conceptual dimensions: causes, contexts, contingencies, consequences, conditions, and covariances (Corbin & Strauss, 2008; Glaser, 1978; Rieger, 2018; Thompson et al., 2006). Once the data have been grouped into these six conceptual dimensions, a core category is identified through selective coding, which is the final process where you (the researcher) conceptually relate all categories to a central, or core, category (Strauss & Corbin, 1990).

To reiterate, during the open-coding process, you are focused primarily on the text to define the concepts and categories that emerge, and then in the axial-coding process you reread your collected text while referencing back to your previously documented concepts and categories. You engage in this process for two reasons: (a) to confirm that the concepts

TABLE 11.1 GLASER'S CODING FAMILIES

CODING FAMILIES	CONCEPTS	EXAMPLES
The six Cs	Causes, conditions, contexts, contingencies, consequences, covariance	... of feeling discriminated against
Process	Phases, stages, steps, transitions, chains, passages, sequences, careers	Career of a person feeling discriminated against
The degree family	Extent, intensity, level, range, amount, continuum, standard deviation, statistical average	Extent of perceived discrimination
Type family	Types, genres, kinds, classes, styles, prototypes	Type of discrimination (e.g., overt, covert, individual, group, institutional, systemic)
The strategy family	Strategies, tactics, management, techniques, mechanisms	Coping with discrimination
Interactive family	Interaction, mutual effects, rituals, interdependence, reciprocity, symmetries, correlations	Interaction of perception of discrimination and coping strategies
Identity-self family	Identity, self-image, self-concept, self-evaluation, social worth, transformation of self	Self-concepts of subjects who feel discriminated against
Cutting-point family	Boundary, critical juncture, cutting point, turning point, tolerance levels, point of no return	Start of activist path for subject feeling chronically discriminated against
Cultural family	Social norms, social values, social beliefs	Social norms about tolerating discrimination
Consensus family	Contracts, definitions of the situation, agreements, uniformity, conformity, conflict	Compliance or disobedience of nondiscrimination policies

SOURCE: Adapted from Glaser, B. (1978). *Theoretical sensitivity: Advances in the methodology of grounded theory* (pp. 75–82). Sociology Press.

and categories you identified accurately represent your participants' interview responses and (b) to explore how your concepts and categories are connected and interacting (Gallicano, 2013). To investigate for possible connections, you might ask yourself, What conditions may have caused or influenced your identified concepts and categories? Are there social/political variables involved? or, Are there any associated effects or consequences?

Selective Coding

"Selective coding" entails a process of arranging and integrating categories and concepts to form a theoretical framework (Oliver et al., 2020). In this final phase of grounded theory coding, which Corbin and Strauss (2008, 2015) also refer to as "theoretical integration," you take all of the data into account (i.e., all the identified categories/dimensions) and then attempt to identify one core, or central, category that links everything together (Reiger, 2018). Once a selective code has been identified (e.g., "Wanting to make a difference"), you then reread the transcripts and selectively code any data relating to the core category you have identified (Gallicano, 2013).

Creating Tables

Regardless of the approach to qualitative data analysis you choose to employ, once you have identified all the distinct concepts and categories in your data, have reread all your text data while cross-checking your existing concepts and categories, and have explored for relationships among your concepts and categories, it is time to transfer your final concepts and categories into a data table.

If creating a data table for a study using a grounded theory approach, your table should consist of three columns, one for *Open Codes*, one for *Axial Codes*, and a third for *Selective Codes*. Regardless of the qualitative research method you choose to use, once all of your data have been coded and categorized, you will need to begin the often-satisfying process of analyzing and interpreting the data you have collected (Krippendorff, 2018).

Table 11.2 illustrates how Gallicano (2013) determined axial codes and a selective code based on the open codes collected from recorded answers to each of those three research questions. The information in Table 11.2 is adapted from a study by Gallicano (2013), where 50 participants contributed to asynchronous online Focus Forums. The Focus Forums centered on the topic of building relationships with the Millennial generation of employees working at public relation agencies. Gallicano's study was designed to answer three research questions: (a) How do Millennial practitioners who work at public relations agencies describe their generation of public relations practitioners?; (b) What can be learned about cultivating a long-term relationship with Millennial public relations agency employees based on their own perspectives?; and (c) What irritates or upsets Millennials when receiving feedback on their work?

THE GENERAL INDUCTIVE APPROACH

As a social work student, it is likely that you are just learning about many of the traditional approaches to qualitative analysis (e.g., grounded theory, phenomenology, discourse analysis, narrative analysis). It is also likely that your qualitative study will be confined to either a needs assessment or some kind of program evaluation. With this in mind, you may wish to learn a straightforward set of procedures to follow in order to complete your research-based capstone project. The following section introduces you to a strategy labeled as a "general inductive approach." Often without an explicit label assigned to it, this analysis strategy is evident in much qualitative data analysis (Bryman & Burgess, 1994; Dey, 1993; Thomas, 2006).

"Inductive analysis" refers to "approaches that primarily use detailed readings of raw data to derive concepts, themes, or a model through interpretations made from the raw data by an evaluator or researcher" (Thomas, 2006, p. 238). Unlike "deductive analysis," which refers to data analysis that aims to test whether data are consistent with prior

TABLE 11.2 AXIAL CODES AND SELECTIVE CODE BASED ON OPEN CODES

OPEN CODES	AXIAL CODES	SELECTIVE CODE
<ul><li>Wanting experiential learning</li><li>Constantly learning</li><li>Working in a good environment</li><li>Feeling entitled due to unique qualifications, as compared to previous generations</li><li>Possessing the personal skills and characteristics needed</li><li>Being groomed</li></ul>	Believing they are ready to be set loose on accounts	Wanting to make a positive difference
<ul><li>Craving immediate feedback and being motivated by feeling appreciated</li><li>Detesting getting called out</li><li>Receiving verbal encouragement and making observations</li></ul>	Seeking external validation	
<ul><li>Mind reading and expectations for a miracle worker</li><li>Getting called out</li><li>Not being heard</li></ul>	Silently blaming employers for failures	
<ul><li>Advocating a work–life balance</li><li>Being cared for as a whole person</li><li>Accommodating interests and preferences</li></ul>	Wanting a meaningful experience at work and outside work	

SOURCE: Adapted from Gallicano, T. (2013, June 22). *An example of how to perform open coding, axial coding and selective coding*. The PR Post. https://prpost.wordpress.com/2013/07/22/an-example-of-how-to-perform-open-coding-axial-coding-and-selective-coding

hypotheses, assumptions, or theories, inductive analysis begins with an area of study and allows the theory to emerge from the data (Strauss & Corbin, 1998). The primary purpose of the inductive approach is to allow research findings to develop from the frequent, consistent, or significant themes embedded in the raw data, without the methodological restraints imposed by more structured methodologies. For example, if you wish to describe the actual effects of a social service program and not just the planned effects, the inductive analysis approach enables you to conduct an objective goal-free evaluation (Scriven, 1991).

There are three elemental purposes in the development of the general inductive analysis approach (Thomas, 2006):

1. To condense large amounts of raw text data into a concise, summary format
2. To establish clear connections between the research objectives and the summary findings gleaned from the raw data and to ensure that these connections are both able to be clearly demonstrated to others (transparent) and justifiable, given the stated objectives of the research (defensible)
3. To develop a model or theory about the underlying elemental structure of processes or experiences evident in the text data

Descriptions from health and social science research provide illustrations of common data analysis strategies using a general inductive approach. It is important for researcher(s) to reread their data multiple times in order to create accurate codes and categories. According to Jain and Ogden (1999), if new codes emerge, the coding frame will need to be changed, and this will also impact the transcripts, which will then need to be reread and conceptualized into broader themes in order to maintain data accuracy. Once there is a thematic dispersion, relationships among the themes will be analyzed into identified relationship groups. In order to deepen the understanding of the data collected, these groups can then be explored through "similarities and differences across sub-groups (e.g., service providers vs. individuals, recent vs. long-term migrants)" (Elliott & Gillie, 1998, p. 331).

The utilization of an indicative approach is common in several types of qualitative data analyses, especially grounded theory (Strauss & Corbin, 1998). Three overarching tasks for qualitative data analysis are data reduction, data display, and conclusion-making or verification (Miles & Huberman, 1994). The general inductive approach, as outlined in this chapter, intends to clarify the data reduction process by describing a set of procedures that you can use to create meaning from complex raw data by developing summary themes or categories.

Analytic Strategies Using the General Inductive Approach

Examples of analytic strategies and principles fundamental for the use of a general inductive approach follow (McFarland & Waliczek, 2018; Miles & Huberman, 1994; Thomas, 2006).

1. Data analysis is guided by the researcher's evaluation objectives, which identify the topics of investigation. Through multiple readings and interpretations of the raw data, analysis is carried out inductively. Although the researcher's evaluation objectives and questions influence a study's finding, they arise directly from the analysis of the raw data and not from models or expectations from past research. The researcher's evaluation objectives provide a focus for conducting the analysis and do not impose expectations about specific findings.

2. The primary mode of the general inductive approach is the development of categories from the raw data in order to create a model or framework. The model includes key processes and themes constructed and identified by the researcher during the coding process.

3. Findings are produced from multiple interpretations gleaned from the raw data by the researcher (and other evaluators) who code the data. Ultimately, the findings are shaped by the experiences and assumptions of the researchers conducting the study and performing the data analyses. For the findings to be of use, the researcher(s) need to make decisions about what data are more or less important.

4. Different data evaluators may produce findings that are not identical and/or do not have overlapping components. In such cases, it is important for the evaluators to work together to see if there are commonalties they can both agree on, and if they may recruit others into the data evaluation process to gain further perspective.

Although researchers using general inductive analysis should not impose expectations about their findings, program evaluation and needs assessment projects often have specific objectives guiding data collection and analysis. Common objectives include identifying what is working well in a social service program, as well as where improvement is needed. If you are conducting a program evaluation, you may also be interested in collecting qualitative data that identify any unplanned positive or negative outcomes. Although incorporating specific objectives or evaluation questions will surely limit the range of possible interpretations and outcomes from a general inductive analysis by focusing attention on specific aspects of your data, this approach is unlike deductive investigations where specific hypotheses, theories, or models are being tested.

DEVELOPING CATEGORIES USING THE INDUCTIVE APPROACH

The general inductive analysis approach aims to use data categories to inform the creation of a framework or model that summarizes your raw data in order to highlight key themes and processes. The core of inductive analysis are the categories resulting from the coding process. Such inductively produced categories have five key features (Thomas, 2006):

1. Category label is a descriptive word or short phrase used to refer to the category.
2. Category description is a detailed description of the category's meaning, including key characteristics, its scope, and limitations.
3. Text or data associated with the category shows illustrative examples of text coded into the category that convey meanings, associations, and perspectives associated with the category.
4. Links show that each category may have relationships or links with other categories. In a hierarchical category system, these links may indicate subordinate, parallel, and subordinate categories (e.g., "client, intern," "volunteer, intern" or "intern, supervisor" relationships). Links are often based on assumed causal relationships or commonalities in meanings between categories.
5. The type of model in which the category is embedded allows the category system to then be incorporated into a model, framework, or theory. Examples of potential frameworks may include an open network (no sequence or hierarchy), a causal network (when a category creates changes in another), and a temporal sequence (change over time). To be consistent with the general inductive process, such frameworks or models represent an end point of the inductive analysis and should not be set up prior to the analysis being conducted. It is also possible that some identified categories end up not being fixed into any framework or model.

THE INDUCTIVE CODING PROCESS

Begin the inductive coding process by closely reading your collected text data and considering the multiple meanings that are implicit in the text. Then identify segments of the text that contain meaningful units and create a label for a new category to which the text segment will be assigned. Continue this process, adding text segments to relevant categories, until new segments of meaningful text no longer necessitate the creation of new categories. At some point, you may want to develop an initial description of the meaning of each category and write comments about the category (e.g., links, associations, implications). You may also want to note when you find that categories relate to other categories in various ways, such as a network, a causal sequence, or a hierarchy of categories (Creswell, 2002).

The following procedures are used for the general inductive analysis of qualitative data:

1. *Preparing raw data files (i.e., "data cleaning")*: Utilize a common format for your raw data files (e.g., font size, margins, highlighted questions, or researcher comments). Make a backup and/or print each raw data file (e.g., each written response or translated interview).
2. *Close reading of text*: Once you have prepared your text data, reread it as many times as needed in order to familiarize yourself with its contents. The goal is to gain a clear understanding of the themes and events documented throughout your raw text data.
3. *Creating categories*: At this point, you want to begin identifying and defining categories or themes. You can create general categories derived directly from the evaluation aims and/or the research question(s) of your study. More specific categories will be produced as you read and reread your raw data, a process sometimes referred to as "in-vivo coding." When using the generalized inductive coding method, the categories you create often come directly from meanings or actual phrases in specific segments of text. There are several ways in which you can do this. If you are using a program like Microsoft Word, notable text segments can be copied and pasted into your emerging categories. You also have the option of using qualitative analysis software to speed up the coding process when you have large amounts of text data (Durkin, 1997).
4. *Overlapping coding and uncoded text*: You may have segments of text that you determine need to be coded into more than one category (e.g., category 1 = negative statements about social service agency, and category 2 = negative statements about volunteers at social service agency), as well as the likelihood that you will have a considerable about of text that is not relative to the evaluation objectives and/or your study's research question(s).
5. *Continuing revision and refinement of category system*: Within each coding category you create, keep your eye out for subtopics, including new insights and contradictory points of view. Select relevant quotations that illustrate the essence of each category or its core theme. The categories created may be linked or combined under a superordinate category when their meanings are similar.

When you end up with many major categories (e.g., more than nine), you may have more work to do. In such a case, you will want to further analyze your identified categories and their contents to determine whether some of the categories need to be combined. You may also need to make some difficult decisions about which categories or themes are most important to your study and remove the ones of least importance and/or relevance.

ASSESSING TRUSTWORTHINESS

Due to the somewhat subjective nature of qualitative research, its trustworthiness is often questioned since the reliability and validity of qualitative findings cannot be addressed in the same way as most quantitative research methodologies. However, several authors on research methods have demonstrated how qualitative researchers can deal with these issues (Guba, 1981; Pitts, 1994; Shenton, 2004; Silverman, 2001). According to Guba (1981), there are four criteria that should be considered by qualitative researchers wishing to ensure the trustworthiness of their findings:

1. Credibility (to address internal validity)
2. Transferability (to address external validity/generalizability)
3. Dependability (to address reliability)
4. Confirmability (to address objectivity)

Among these procedures, the most applicable to performing qualitative data analysis includes assessing credibility and dependability by conducting peer debriefings and stakeholder checks in order to establish credibility and to compare the data with the research findings and interpretations. Other useful practices that can be used for assessing the trustworthiness of the data analysis process include checks of interrater reliability or consistency checks (e.g., asking another coder to take the category or theme descriptions and find the text that belongs within those identified categories) and stakeholder or member checks. Stakeholder checks involve people with a specific interest in the evaluation, (e.g., service providers, participants, and funding agencies), to offer commentary on identified categories or of the interpretations made from the data analysis performed by the researcher (Erlandson et al., 1993).

DATA CODING CONSISTENCY CHECKS

Checking the Clarity of Categories

Once you have completed coding your raw data, a second coder is provided with your study's objectives, your developed categories, and descriptions of each category. The second coder does not see the raw text you have assigned to each category; instead they are given a sample of the raw text (without any codes assigned) and asked to assign sections of that text to the categories you have previously developed. This process checks the extent to which the second coder designates the same text segments to the initial categories that you have created. Another way to do this kind of check is to give the second coder both your original coding categories and some of the text assigned to these categories. You then give the second coder a new set of text (that you have previously coded) without coding designations and ask them to assign sections of the new text into your original categories. You then check to see if they designated the same text segments to the coding categories that you have.

Independent Parallel Coding

After finishing an analysis of your preliminary findings and you have developed a set of coding categories, a second coder is informed of your study's objectives and some or all of the raw text that contributed to the development of your initial categories. You ask the second coder to create a second set of codes from the raw text (without seeing the categories you have previously developed). This new set of categories developed by the second coder is then compared with the first set to examine the extent that they overlap. These two sets of categories could then be merged into a combined set. If, however, you find that the overlap between the two categories is minimal, further analysis and discussion may be necessary in order to develop a more rigorous set of categories.

Stakeholder Checks

Promoting empowerment is one of the hallmarks of the social work profession. Stakeholder checks increase the credibility of your findings by allowing your participants and others who may have a vested interest in your research project to comment on or assess your research findings, interpretations, and conclusions. Stakeholder checks are an important part of establishing the credibility of your findings. For example, you can provide the participants in your study an opportunity to comment on whether the coding categories and outcomes described in your findings relate to their personal experiences. Stakeholder checks can be carried out on your initial documents (e.g., written responses on surveys, interview transcripts and summaries) and on your data interpretations and findings (Thomas, 2006). The following is a list of possible stakeholder checks during your study's evaluation process:

- After you have completed your interviews, you provide each interviewee with a summary and brief analysis of their interview data and allow them to correct errors or challenge your interpretations.
- You conduct a second interview with each of your participants in order to have them verify the accuracy of the data from the first interview and to elicit feedback on your initial interpretations.
- You can engage in informal conversations with members of the organization/agency in which your field placement internship is located who may have an interest in your study and its findings.
- Make copies of your preliminary research report, or specific sections of it, and provide them to stakeholder groups (e.g., clients, group therapy members, agency supervisors) in order to elicit oral and/or written commentary. In some cases, you may need specific stakeholders to approve and sign off on your data categories and interpretations. Ask your field supervisor and seminar professor about this.
- Before submitting your final report to your seminar professor, you can conduct a stakeholder check by providing a complete draft copy for review by your study participants or anyone else at your field placement location who may have an interest in your study's findings.

WRITING YOUR RESEARCH REPORT

After the arduous and time-consuming processes of data collection, transcription, coding, analysis, and interpretation have been completed, reviewed several times, and then cross-checked by others (e.g., field supervisor, seminar professor), it is time to write about your results. When completing your research-based capstone study report, you will want to start by presenting a fuller picture of the topic of your study by providing a written review of past literature regarding the topic. You will also want to provide a description of your qualitative research methods, a section that focuses on the results of your data analysis and interpretation, potential implications and/or applications of your study's findings, any identified study limitations and conclude your report with a concise conclusion (Taylor, 2017). A more detailed description of the standard format for your research-based capstone project report is as follows:

- An introduction to your research topic or the population you are studying, including a discussion regarding the purpose and relevance of your research
- A background or "literature review" section illustrating past research on the topic, including a discussion of any gaps in information highlighted by past research that might be addressed by your study
- A methods section detailing your sample, data collection, coding procedures, identified themes, analytic strategies, and any potential limitations/biases of your research
- A findings section (referred to as a "results" section in quantitative research reports) that details one or a few broad findings, as well as all of the specific and subtle distinctions in expression, meaning, and responses found within those findings (make sure you provide numerous examples of your original data in order to present and fully explain your findings)
- A discussion and/or conclusion section that summarizes what was found in your result as well as the implications of your findings, followed by suggestions for future research ideas, which may or may not be connected to your study's identified limitations
- The inclusion of an addendum section with tables, graphs, charts, or other appendices, that can make the discussion of your methods and findings clearer to your reader
- References to past research on your topic (i.e., a References page)

All of the sections just outlined may vary in length. For example, the methods section for any qualitative research report needs to be extremely detailed. In order to make your qualitative research analysis process as transparent as possible, you will need to inform your readers of each and every step of your process. Lester et al. (2020) suggest creating a detailed map of your study from beginning to end.

Mapping your entire qualitative research process will support you in being open about your choice of qualitative approach (e.g., phenomenological, ethnographic, grounded theory, narrative, action), your research question(s), your decisions related to sampling, your collection of data, and your development of codes, themes, and categories. Being open and transparent about the entire process will allow outside readers/evaluators of your research study to discern how you went about making key analytic choices. To support transparency, it is also recommended that you develop a detailed audit trail that clearly lays out the connections between data sources, codes, categories, and themes. This process may involve selecting a few representative sections from your data set, including which codes were initially applied to each section, and then articulating to which categories and themes the sections were connected.

By following the standard research-based capstone project report format provided, there is a greater likelihood that your qualitative research and analytic procedures will be considered trustworthy. This will be particularly important when presenting your research findings to people who value numerical results or explanation more than description and exploration (Taylor, 2017). More importantly, the research report just outlined will provide you with an easy-to-follow roadmap to complete your capstone research project paper.

Qualitative Data Analysis Software

Although there is the significant benefit of becoming familiar with one's data when you code, categorize, analyze, and interpret it manually, there exists software that you can use to help speed up your qualitative data analysis process, especially if you are short on time. Qualitative data analysis software reviews your interviews and participant data in bulk, saving you valuable time. By using software, you can input categories and have coding done automatically, efficiently, and quickly by the software program of your choice. Although most quality software programs come with a cost, the amount of time saved and the accuracy of the analyses provided may make it well worth your monetary investment. Free qualitative analysis programs such as FreeQDA, ConnectedText, and Visao provide basic analysis functions, but typically will not meet the needs inherent in a research-based capstone project. With this in mind, the following section describes three of the most highly ranked qualitative data analysis programs on the market: MAXQDA, NVivo, and ATLAS.ti.

MAXQDA is a pay-for-use (US$500+ for a single-user license) qualitative and mixed-method analysis software package designed for analyzing different types of data. This software allows researchers to import data from surveys, interviews, focus groups, videos, and even social media. MAXQDA makes it possible for you to review all of your qualitative data in a central location and is the only qualitative data analysis software to offer identical features on Windows and Mac (MAXQDA, n.d.). MAXQDA can be used for any type of qualitative research, including literature reviews, grounded theory, qualitative text analyses, and mixed-method approaches. Once your data are imported, you can then organize your data into groups or categories, mark specific data with tags, and leave notes for others to review your work (e.g., seminar professors, field supervisor, peers). The MAXQDA software even allows you to color code your data (Fontanella, 2020).

- MAXQDA 2020 User Manual: https://www.maxqda.com/help-mx20/welcome
- MAXQDA 2020 Video Tutorials: https://www.maxqda.com/maxqda-2020-video-tutorials

NVivo is also a pay-for-use (US$80+) software program used for qualitative and mixed-method research. Specifically, NVivo is used for the analysis of unstructured text, audio, video, and image data. Users of NVivo can use this software to code and analyze data from transcribed interviews, emails, focus groups, online surveys, spreadsheets, social media posts, web content, and peer-reviewed journal articles (NVivo: Qualitative Data Analysis, n.d.).

- NVivo Tutorial Pages: https://www.qsrinternational.com/nvivo-qualitative-data-analysis-software/support-services/customer-hub/getting-started
- NVivo Video Tutorials: https://www.youtube.com/playlist?list=PLNjHMRgHS4Fd7g4Q1BQuQgm-gLxy97FqY

ATLAS.ti is one of the most affordable qualitative data analysis software packages on the market. Students can choose subscriptions ranging from a one-semester license for US$51 to a 2-year license for US$99. Students can also test it out with a Free Trial Version. ATLAS.ti allows for the qualitative analysis of large bodies of textual, graphical, audio, and video data. Users can import data from a wide range of sources including PDFs, Microsoft Word, Evernote, Twitter, journal articles, and surveys. ATLAS.ti also supports collaborative work in a number of highly effective ways (ATLAS.ti, n.d.).

- ATLAS.ti Academy: https://atlasti.com/manuals-docs
- ATLAS.ti Qualitative Data Analysis YouTube Channel: https://www.youtube.com/user/ATLASti01

PRACTICE ACTIVITIES

1. Compare and contrast the three stages of the grounded theory and the thematic analysis approaches to data coding. Which of the two approaches to the data coding process do you feel would work best for you, and why?
2. Thinking about the kind of qualitative study you would like to pursue for your capstone research project, and referring to sections "Assessing Trustworthiness" and "Data Coding Consistency Checks," how might you ensure the readers of your research report that your data collection and coding processes are credible, dependable, and confirmable?

TECHNOLOGY EXERCISE

Imagine that you are beginning the initial phase of developing a coding system for organizing the qualitative data you have collected. Using the following web-link, choose one of the qualitative data sets provided (e.g., Weight & obesity focus group transcript; Body art focus group transcript; Views on pubic hair qualitative survey data set), and practice designating the data into as many of the following coding categories as you can:

    a. Setting/Context Codes
    b. Process Codes

c. Activity Codes
d. Situation Codes
e. Event Codes
f. Strategy Codes
g. Relationship Codes
h. Social Structure Codes

Qualitative Data Samples: https://studysites.sagepub.com/braunandclarke/study/qualitative.htm

REFERENCES

ATLAS.ti. (n.d.). *What is ATLAS.ti? ATLAS.ti: Qualitative data analysis.* https://atlasti.com/product/what-is-atlas-ti

Bogden, R., & Biklen, S. K. (2006). *Qualitative research for education: An introduction to theory and methods* (5th ed.). Pearson Publications.

Bryman, A., & Burgess, R. G. (Eds.). (1994). *Analyzing qualitative data.* Routledge.

Charmaz, K. (2006). *Constructing grounded theory: A practical guide through qualitative analysis.* Sage.

Charmaz, K. (2014). *Constructing grounded theory: The second generation* (pp. 127–193). Left Coast Press.

Corbin, J., & Strauss, A. L. (2008). *Basics of qualitative research* (3rd ed.). Sage.

Corbin, J., & Strauss, A. L. (2015). *Basics of qualitative research: Techniques and procedures for developing grounded theory* (4th ed.). Sage.

Creswell, J. W. (2002). *Educational research: Planning, conducting, and evaluating quantitative and qualitative research.* Pearson Education.

Dey, I. (1993). *Qualitative data analysis: A user-friendly guide for social scientists.* Routledge.

Durkin, T. (1997). Using computers in strategic qualitative research. In G. Miller & R. Dingwall (Eds.), *Content and method in qualitative research* (pp. 92–105). Sage.

Elliott, S. J., & Gillie, J. (1998). Moving experiences: A qualitative analysis of health and migration. *Health & Place, 4*(4), 327–339. https://doi.org/10.1016/S1353-8292(98)00029-X

Elo, S., Kaarianinen, M., Kanste, O., Polkki, R., Utrianen, K., & Kyngas, H. (2014). Qualitative content analysis: A focus on trustworthiness. *Sage Open, 4*, 1–10. https://doi.org/10.1177/2158244014522633

Erlandson, D. A., Harris, E. L., Skipper, B. L., & Allen, S. D. (1993). *Doing naturalistic enquiry: A guide to methods.* Sage.

Fontanella, C. (2020). *The best 10 qualitative data analysis software in 2020.* Hubspot. https://blog.hubspot.com/service/qualitative-data-analysis-software

Gallicano, T. (2013, June 22). *An example of how to perform open coding, axial coding and selective coding.* The PR Post. https://prpost.wordpress.com/2013/07/22/an-example-of-how-to-perform-open-coding-axial-coding-and-selective-coding

Glaser, B. (1978). *Theoretical sensitivity: Advances in the methodology of grounded theory.* Sociology Press.

Glaser, B. G. (1992). *Basics of grounded theory analysis: Emergence versus forcing.* Sociology Press.

Glaser, G. G., & Strauss, A. (1967). *The discovery of grounded theory: Strategies for qualitative research.* Aldine.

Guba, E. G. (1981). Criteria for assessing the trustworthiness of naturalistic inquiries. *Educational Communication and Technology Journal, 29*, 75–91. https://doi.org/10.1007/BF02766777

Jain, A., & Ogden, J. (1999). General practitioners' experiences of patients' complaints: Qualitative Study. *British Medical Journal, 318*, 1596–1599. https://doi.org/10.1136/bmj.318.7198.1596

Krippendorff, K. (2018). *Content analysis: An introduction to its methodology*. Sage.

Lester, J. N., Cho, Y., & Lochmiller, C. R. (2020). Learning to do qualitative data analysis: A starting point. *Human Resource Development Review, 19*(1), 94–106. https://doi.org/10.1177/1534484320903890

MAXQDA. (n.d.). *What is MAXQDA? Collect – Transcribe – Organize – Analyze – Visualize – Publish*. https://www.maxqda.com/what-is-maxqda

McFarland, A., & Waliczek, T. M. (2018). Understanding motivations for gardening using a qualitative general inductive approach. *Horticulture Technology, 28*(3), 289–295. https://doi.org/10.21273/HORTTECH03972-18

Miles, M. B., & Huberman, A. M. (1994). *An expanded sourcebook: Qualitative data analysis* (2nd ed.). Sage.

NVivo: Qualitative Data Analysis. (n.d.). *Powerful research, simplified*. https://www.qsrinternational.com/nvivo-qualitative-data-analysis-software/about/nvivo

Oliver, A., McCarthy, P. J., & Burns, L. (2020). A grounded-theory study of meta-attention in golfers. *The Sport Psychologist, 34*, 11–22. https://doi.org/10.1123/tsp.2019-0014

Pitts, J. M. (1994). Personal understandings and mental models of information: A qualitative study of factors associated with the information-seeking and use of adolescents. *School Library Media Annual (SLMA), 12*, 200–202. https://doi.org/10.1046/j.1365-2648.2002.2167b.x

Rieger, K. L. (2018). Discriminating among grounded theory approaches. *Nursing Inquiry, 26*(1), 1–12. https://doi.org/10.1111/nin.12261

Scriven, M. (1991). Pros and cons about goal-free evaluation. *Evaluation Practice, 12*(1), 55–76. https://doi.org/10.1177/109821409101200108

Shenton, A. K. (2004). Strategies for ensuring trustworthiness in qualitative research projects. *Education for Information, 22*, 63–75. https://doi.org/10.3233/EFI-2004-22201

Silverman, D. (2001). *Interpreting qualitative data methods for analyzing talk, text, and interaction*. Sage Publications.

Strauss, A. L., & Corbin, J. M. (1990). *Basics of qualitative research* (Vol. 15). Sage.

Strauss, A. L. & Corbin, J. (1998). *Basics of qualitative research: Techniques and procedures for developing grounded theory* (2nd ed.). Sage.

Taylor, R. R. (2017). *Kielhofner's research in occupational therapy: Methods of inquiry for enhancing practice* (2nd ed.). F. A. Davis.

Thomas, D. R. (2006). A general approach for analyzing qualitative evaluation data. *American Journal of Evaluation, 27*(2), 237–246. https://doi.org/10.1177/1098214005283748

Thompson, G. N., McClement, S. E., & Daeninck, P. J. (2006). "Changing lanes": Facilitating the transition from curative to palliative care. *Journal of Palliative Care, 22*(2), 91–98. https://doi.org/10.1177/082585970602200205

Vollstedt, M., & Rezat, S. (2019). An introduction to grounded theory with a special focus on axial coding and the coding paradigm. In G. Kaiser and N. Presmeg (Eds.), *Compendium for early career researchers in mathematics education*, ICME-13 (pp. 81–100). Monographs. https://doi.org/10.1007/978-3-030-15636-7_4

IV

WRITING AND PRESENTATIONS

12

WRITING YOUR CAPSTONE PAPER

In this chapter we explore writing a capstone paper. The structure and content areas of your capstone paper will be determined by your assignment guidelines and professor. The following describes what we believe should be included, since the components of a capstone paper are different from that of a standard research paper. The differences are a function of the different purposes of the two types of papers. The purpose of a standard research paper is to clearly communicate how the study was conducted and the research findings. Capstone papers share this purpose but also have the additional purposes of demonstrating your professional social work competencies and the integration of your classroom and field-learning experiences. Thus, there are components included in capstone research papers that are not included in a standard research paper. These additional components help tie your capstone paper to the Council on Social Work Education (CSWE, 2015) competencies.

By the end of this chapter, you will be able to do the following:

- Describe the purpose of the major sections of your capstone paper.
- Identify the content areas included in a section of your capstone paper.
- Complete a content checklist.
- Conduct a self-assessment on the extent each section of your capstone paper achieves its intended purpose.

■ INTRODUCTION

One of primary functions of the introductory section of your capstone paper is to clearly describe the topic your evaluation study addresses. Begin with a paragraph that in broad, general terms describes the issue or social problem addressed in your applied research study. You want the reader to have a clear idea about your study topic within the first few sentences of your paper. Table 12.1 lists the content areas to be covered in the introductory section.

Your introduction should also provide the reader with a brief review on the background of the issue or social problem. Again, this is done in broad, general terms. What is the scope of the problem? How big a problem is it? Who is most affected by the problem? What are the consequences of the problem for individuals, communities,

TABLE 12.1 INTRODUCTION SECTION

DESCRIPTION	CONTENT COVERAGE
The paper's introduction addresses the *why* question. It provides a rationale for the study, sets the context for the study, and specifies the study's purpose.	- Introduces topic being addressed - Provides background information on topic - Specifies purpose of the research - Lists hypotheses or research questions

and/or society? How long has it been an area of concern? What are the benefits of resolving the issue or social problem?

In addition to describing the scope and magnitude of the problem, information on gaps in the existing research on the topic should also be included in your introduction. A comprehensive review of the literature does not belong in your introduction. However, a brief summary of relevant research and how your study contributes to the existing body of knowledge is appropriate. Is there a lack of research on the topic? Are there gaps in the research on the topic? Are the research findings ambiguous or conflicting?

The summarizing of the background information and previous research on your topic sets the context for your study and provides a rationale for conducting the study. After reading your opening paragraph, background summary, and summary of prior research, your reader should have a very clear understanding of your study topic and why the study needs to be done. The goal for this part of your introduction is to develop a strong rationale for doing your applied research project. The reader should have a clear understanding of why your study is needed, why it is important, and how it will contribute to our understanding of the issue or social problem.

> **Reflection Questions**
> 1. What are the three main points that make up your rationale for your capstone project?
> 2. What is the purpose of your study?

The background information that establishes the context and rationale for your capstone research project is followed by a specific statement on the purpose of your research project. This is a very succinct statement that describes the objectives of your research. In one or two sentences, you should clearly define the specific purpose of your research. Your goal is to provide the reader with a clear statement that describes the focus of the research. Earlier in the introduction, you introduced your study topic in general terms. In this section of your introduction, you describe in very specific terms the study objectives (American Psychological Association [APA], 2020).

Table 12.2 provides an example of a broad, general statement of purpose that would be found at the beginning of the introduction and a specific study purpose statement that goes toward the end of the introduction. Both the general and specific statements of purpose should be part of the introduction section of your capstone paper. The general statement introduces your study topic and the specific statement of purpose tells the reader how the study will assess the identified topic.

TABLE 12.2 EXAMPLES OF GENERAL AND SPECIFIC RESEARCH PURPOSE STATEMENTS

GENERAL PURPOSE STATEMENT	SPECIFIC PURPOSE STATEMENT
Homelessness is a major social problem among LGBT teenagers in urban areas. This research study focuses on the impact a teen-support program has on the well-being of homeless teenagers.	This research examines the impact the Teens Together program has on the teenage participants' social, psychological, and physical well-being. Specifically, this research assesses change in the program participants' family relationships, peer relationships, self-esteem, and stability of their living arrangements.

TABLE 12.3 EXAMPLES OF QUANTITATIVE HYPOTHESES AND QUALITATIVE RESEARCH QUESTIONS

HYPOTHESES (QUANTITATIVE RESEARCH)	RESEARCH QUESTIONS (QUALITATIVE RESEARCH)
LGBT teenagers who complete the Teens Together program will have significantly higher levels of family support than nonparticipating teens.	How do LGBT teens view their family relationships and experiences?
LGBT teenagers' levels of informal peer support will increase significantly upon completion of the 10-week Teens Together peer support group program.	How has participating in the Teens Together program changed or affected LGBT teens' views of their family relationships and experiences?

Up to this point, everything in your capstone paper's introduction would be the same for both quantitative and qualitative evaluations. However, there would be differences in the final component of the introduction that lists the research questions or hypotheses examined in your study. Hypotheses are tentative predictions in statement form about the relationship between two or more variables. Research questions are essentially hypotheses in the form of questions. Quantitative studies use either hypotheses or research questions about the relationships between variables. The research questions used in qualitative studies are somewhat different. They tend to be phased more broadly than those used in quantitative studies.

The introduction ends with the specific hypotheses or research questions that are examined in your research. They have the highest level of specificity about your research. The introduction section of your capstone paper should be shaped like a funnel. It is very broad at the beginning and narrow at the bottom. Your study hypotheses or research questions represent the narrowest or most specific description of your research project. Table 12.3 provides examples of quantitative hypotheses and qualitative research questions. As shown in Table 12.3, qualitative research questions tend to be broader and more general than quantitative research hypotheses/research questions. The latter focus on relationships between the study variables, whereas the former tend to focus on exploring the study topic more broadly.

Literature Review

The literature review section of your capstone paper has three major subsections which are the same for both quantitative and qualitative capstone projects. They cover the following: (a) a description of the target problem, the study population, and their service needs; (b) a description of the policies and procedures impacting the program and service delivery; (c) a description of the program and/or services being evaluated.

TARGET PROBLEM AND POPULATION

As outlined in Table 12.4, this component of your literature review describes in detail the target problem being addressed in your capstone research project and the impact the target problem has on the client population served by the program or service. This section needs to clearly and comprehensively describe the available data and research on the target problem being addressed. It is here that you demonstrate the ability to summarize and synthesize the available literature on your topic. We suggest beginning with a detailed description of the problem with data on its size, frequency, and prevalence. Some of this was included in your introduction. Here, you should provide as much detail as possible on the target problem. Your description of the target problem should be followed with a description of the target population. Again, this should be as data driven as possible. You want to provide the reader with a clear picture of those impacted by the target problem. This includes a review of the available literature on the impact or consequences the target problem has on your client population. For example, if your capstone project is addressing teenage pregnancy, then you would have a section on how big a problem teenage pregnancy is and how prevalent it is among different racial and ethnic groups in the population. This description would be followed by a review of the literature on the short-term and long-term consequences of teenage parenthood.

> **Reflection Questions**
> 1. Why is your target problem something important to address?
> 2. What are the diversity issues related to your target population?

The target problem and population section of your literature review should also include a discussion of the social, economic, and environmental justice issues related to the target problem and experienced by your client population. Including this content provides you an opportunity to demonstrate your knowledge and understanding of justice issues related to your target problem and client population. Begin by identifying the various social, economic, and environmental justice concerns and how they impact your client population. Tie the justice issues to the professional social work values and the ethical principles and standards described in the National Association of Social Workers' (NASW) *Code of Ethics* (2017).

This part of your literature review should also include a discussion of any issues related to diversity and difference for your target population. How does diversity and difference shape the target population's experiences and perceptions? How do the different dimensions of diversity intersect in shaping their human experiences (CSWE), 2015)? This is an opportunity for you to demonstrate your understanding of how the intersectionality

TABLE 12.4 LITERATURE REVIEW SECTION

DESCRIPTION	CONTENT COVERAGE
Target Problem and Population This component of the literature review addresses the *who* question. It provides a detailed description of the target problem with data on the size and magnitude of the problem or issue. It also describes the target population, how they are impacted by the identified problem, and their service needs.	▪ Describes target problem ▪ Describes consequences of target problem ▪ Discusses social, economic, and environmental justice issues ▪ Discusses diversity issues ▪ Identifies the service needs of target population
Policies and Procedures This component of the literature review addresses the *how come* question. It provides a detailed description of the governmental and organizational policies that impact the program and service delivery. It also describes how organizational factors and procedures affect staff functioning and the delivery of the program services.	▪ Describes governmental policies that help fund the program/service ▪ Analyzes how governmental policies impact clients and service delivery ▪ Describes how organizational policies and procedures affect service delivery ▪ Analyzes how organizational policies and procedures impact clients and service delivery ▪ Assesses the impact governmental and organizational policies have on social, economic, and environmental justice for client population ▪ Assesses the impact governmental and organizational policies have on client diversity and difference
Program/Service This component of the literature review addresses the *what* question. It provides a detailed description of the program or service being evaluated.	▪ Discusses the program's organizational context and structure ▪ Describes the community setting ▪ Describes the program mission and goals ▪ Provides demographic information on program size, client population, length of service, and staffing ▪ Describes the program's/service's practice perspective and theoretical framework ▪ Describes the program's practice model

of diversity impacts the target population and their experiences related to the target problem. Your aim here is to increase the depth of understanding and appreciation of the life experiences of the target population. This discussion along with your social justice discussion will help highlight the complexity of the target problem and the challenges faced by the target population.

The final section of the target problem and population component of your literature review focuses on the service needs of the target population. What programs/services have been found to be helpful in addressing the target problem? What programs/services have not been helpful? What programs or services have been proposed in the literature?

If there is information on the type of program or service you are evaluating in your capstone project research, then you should provide a description and summary on its effectiveness in this section.

POLICIES AND PROCEDURES

A major purpose of this component of your literature review is to provide you with an opportunity to demonstrate your policy practice and organizational assessment competencies (CSWE, 2015). Begin by identifying all the governmental policies that govern the program being evaluated. These should include any federal, state, and/or municipal policies that fund or regulate the delivery of services. In your capstone paper, summarize your analyses of how each policy impacts the clients and service delivery. Your analyses should include both positive and negative consequences the various policies have on the target population and on the agency's capacity to deliver the program services.

The policy and procedures section of your literature review should also include an analysis of the impact the organization's policies and procedures have on clients and service delivery. At a minimum, this requires an identification of the program's policies and procedures as well as the identification of any organization-wide policies and procedures that impact service delivery. As with the governmental policies, summarize both the positive and negative effects the organizational and program policies and procedures have on the clients and service delivery.

> **Reflection Questions**
> 1. How do governmental policies impact your client population? Positively? Negatively?
> 2. How do organizational policies impact your client population? Positively? Negatively?

The final components of this section of your literature review focus on the impact governmental, organizational, and program policies and procedures have on social, economic, and environmental justice for the client population as well as their impact on diversity and difference considerations. Your aim is to help the reader understand how the various policies and procedures support or negate justice and diversity issues for the client population. Doing so provides you another opportunity to demonstrate your social justice and diversity competencies (CSWE, 2015).

PROGRAM/SERVICE

This component of your literature review section describes the organization and the program being evaluated. The aim here is to provide the reader with a detailed description of the organizational and community setting and the specific program being evaluated. We suggest beginning broadly with a description of the organization's community setting and communities served by the organization, if they are not the same. Is the organization embedded within the community or is it located in a different community? How accessible is the organization for community members? Does the organization participate in community coalitions with other service providers and neighborhood organizations? The purpose of this section is to provide the context for the program and/or services being evaluated. Programs do not operate in a vacuum. Understanding the community context is a critical component of understanding the program being evaluated.

After describing the community context, your next section should focus on describing the organization's mission, structure, and range of services offered. Typically, a program or service is part of a larger organization. If that is the case, then you need to provide the reader with a clear description of the organization. Sometimes, in smaller organizations the organization and the program are one. However, most human service organizations offer more than one program or service. Placing the program being evaluated within its larger organizational context helps the reader see the program's role and function within the organization.

Following your description of the organizational setting, we recommend that you provide a detailed description of the program being evaluated. This should include a description of the program's mission and goals, demographic information on the number and types of clients served, length of service, and descriptions on the size and qualifications of the administrative, supervisory, service delivery, and support staff. In addition, your program description should include a discussion of the program's practice perspective, theoretical framework, and practice model. All of this information helps the reader understand the program being evaluated and its approach to helping clients. This is a prerequisite for conducting a program evaluation. To conduct a program evaluation, you need to be able to describe the program. One cannot evaluate something that has not been defined. Creating a detailed description of the program or services being evaluated as part of your capstone research project is critical in terms of understanding your findings and for making recommendations for improvement.

Methods

The methods section is where you describe what and how you conducted your capstone research project. It describes what you did and is written in the past tense. The APA (2020) *Publication Manual* provides comprehensive descriptions of what to include in quantitative and qualitative research reports. What you include in your methods section will be determined by your capstone assignment guidelines. Here we describe, as shown in Table 12.5, the different components of the methods section that we believe, at a minimum, should be included in a capstone research paper. Research papers prepared for publication in peer-reviewed journals would need to follow the APA guidelines.

TABLE 12.5 METHODS SECTION

DESCRIPTION	CONTENT COVERAGE
The methods section addresses the *what* and *how* questions. The aim is to provide sufficient detail so that the study could be replicated.	- Study design - Participants - Measurement - Data collection - Data analysis - Protection of human subjects

STUDY DESIGN

We recommend that you begin this subsection with a restatement of the purpose of your capstone research along with a listing of your study hypotheses or research questions. Indicate whether you have done a quantitative or qualitative study, the type of applied research, and the data collection method. For quantitative research projects, the types of evaluations include program evaluations, community needs assessments, organizational needs assessments, or practice evaluations using single-subject designs. For qualitative research projects, the evaluation types also include program evaluations, community needs assessments, and organizational needs assessments as well as case studies, practice evaluations, and qualitative descriptive studies. Also, provide a brief description of the data collection method used in your evaluation. Indicate whether you used secondary or primary data. If you used primary data, describe your data collection method. For qualitative studies, that would be personal interviews, direct observation, or existing documents. For quantitative studies, it could be paper or electronic questionnaires, personal interviews, behavioral observation, or existing documents. Thus, this component of your methods section summarizes your study's purpose and hypotheses/research questions, the type of study you conducted, and your data collection method.

Reflection Questions
1. What are the strengths of your preferred study design?
2. What are the limitations?

PARTICIPANTS

This component of the methods section has two main parts. The first is a description of how you selected and recruited your study participants. Here you describe in detail how you identified potential participants, what your selection criteria were, and how the participants were selected. What were your recruitment procedures? What was your target sample size? What were your sampling methods? What was your response rate? Were participants assigned to different groups or conditions? If so, how were group assignments made? Your write-up should provide enough detail that someone else could replicate the process and procedures you used to obtain your study participants. Please note that if you are using agency records as your primary data source, you would use the same criteria to describe how the records used in your evaluation were selected.

Reflection Questions
1. What size sample will you need for your capstone study? Why?
2. What sampling method will you use? Why?

The second major part of the participant subsection is a description of the demographic characteristics of the study participants. At a minimum, you should provide breakdowns by age, gender, race and/or ethnicity, and level of education. For nominal and ordinal level variables, provide the number and percentage for each category of the variable. For interval and ratio level variables, provide the mean and standard deviation for each variable. The aim here is to provide a statistical summary of your study participants.

MEASUREMENT

This component of your methods section provides a description of the measures used in your evaluation. For quantitative research projects, provide detailed descriptions of how your independent, dependent, and control variables were measured. For standardized measures, provide a citation for the measure, a description of what it is intended to measure, its level of measurement, how it is scored, and any information on its reliability and validity. For nonstandardized ordinal measures created by you or someone else, describe what the measure is intended to measure, its scoring, and any information on its reliability. Internal consistency reliability can be computed from the study data. For all nominal type measures, specify the categories included in the measure. We recommend that you organize your quantitative measurement write-up into independent, dependent, and control variable groupings.

For qualitative research projects based on personal interviews, provide a listing of your study questions and briefly describe how you followed up your main questions with probing or elaborating questions. If your qualitative study is based on your observing your study participants, describe your process for documenting your observations.

> **Reflection Questions**
> 1. If you are planning a quantitative evaluation, how will you measure your dependent variable?
> 2. What control variable should you include in your evaluation? Why?

DATA ANALYSIS

This component of your methods section describes how you analyzed your data. For quantitative studies, identify the statistical software program you used and the various statistical methods used to analyze the data. Give the reader a very clear picture of how you conducted your analyses. Your aim is to provide enough information that the appropriateness of your statistical analyses can be accessed.

For qualitative studies, identify any qualitative analysis software that was used to code the data. Describe how the interviews were transcribed, your coding process, and the analysis approach you used. Provide a rationale for your data-analytic strategies and theoretical approach. Include information on the person(s) who did the coding, any coder training that was conducted, and information on intercoder reliability, if available. Describe any cross-checking of your coding categories and interpretation of data by independent researchers. Identify whether coding categories emerged from the analysis or were developed a priori (APA, 2020). Again, your aim is to provide sufficient detail to enable someone to replicate your data analysis approach.

> **Reflection Questions**
> 1. If you are planning on doing a qualitative evaluation, what coding method will you use? Why?
> 2. If you are planning a quantitative evaluation, what statistical methods will you use to address your research questions?

PROTECTION OF HUMAN SUBJECTS

The final component of your methods section provides a description of how you protected the rights of the study participants. Describe the procedures you used to obtain informed consent and reference the copy of your consent form that can be found in the appendices of your capstone paper. Also, describe how the confidentiality of your participants has been maintained, how you minimized risks, and addressed any harm or discomfort experienced by those who participated in your evaluation. If you obtained institutional review board (IRB) approval, indicate so along with your IRB approval number and date conferred.

Results

The results section of your capstone paper is written in the present tense and it contains information only on your study findings. Just present your findings. Do not interpret your findings or provide a discussion on the implications of your findings. For quantitative studies, provide tables, charts, and/or graphs to present your data and findings. Detailed guidelines on how to construct and format tables, charts, and graphs can be found in the APA *Publication Manual* (2020).

Your narrative should highlight key points presented in your tables or charts. Describe only key components of your graphic data. Do not discuss in the narrative all the data in a table or chart. Just focus on the highlights in your narrative discussion. We recommend that you use your study hypotheses or research questions as a way of organizing your results section. Include only data related to your hypotheses or research questions in your narrative. Do not discuss any findings that are not related to your study purpose or aims. It is tempting but limit your discussion to the results related to the identified purpose of your capstone project.

The results component for qualitative evaluations does not include any numerical graphs or tables. The findings are reported in terms of narrative themes. The themes may be organized into lists or charts with narrative descriptions. Typically, each theme is described and then verbatim quotes from the study interviews are presented as examples of the themes. Often, two or three quotes are presented for each identified theme. Unlike the quantitative results sections, the findings in qualitative studies in the form of themes, categories, and narratives are reported along with a discussion of the meaning and your understanding of the data. Thus, in qualitative research, the results section is a combination of describing the findings and a discussion of the meaning and interpretation of the findings.

Discussion

The discussion section of your capstone paper connects your results to your review of the existing literature and theories. How does your study support or contradict the research literature? How do your findings contribute to our knowledge about your research topic or social problem? This component of your applied research paper also addresses policy and program recommendations to improve client services and service delivery. Finally,

TABLE 12.6 DISCUSSION SECTION

DESCRIPTION	CONTENT COVERAGE
The discussion section addresses the *how come* and *what now* questions. How do the findings contribute to existing literature and theory? What are the policy and program recommendations? What are the unanswered questions?	▪ Summary and discussion of findings ▪ Policy and program recommendations ▪ Study limitations and future research

the discussion section outlines limitations of your study and provides suggestions for future research. Table 12.6 lists the content areas covered in your discussion section.

SUMMARY AND DISCUSSION OF FINDINGS

A common practice in both quantitative and qualitative research papers is to begin the discussion section with a summary of the major findings. The summary is then followed by a discussion and interpretation of the findings. How do the findings relate to previous research? Do they support or contradict other studies on the topic? If your findings were unexpected, what are the possible explanations for your results? It is in this section of your paper that you interpret your results and try to make meaning of your findings. To the extent possible, it is important to link your results to previous research and existing theories. Doing so provides a context for your results and how they contribute to the body of literature on your study topic. A note of caution about your discussion section: Do not reach conclusions that are not supported by your findings. In other words, do not go beyond your data when interpreting your findings or reaching conclusions.

POLICY AND PROGRAM RECOMMENDATIONS

Your capstone project paper should also include a discussion of your recommendations to change the governmental policies impacting the program or service being evaluated as well as recommendations to improve the program policies and procedures. Your recommendations should be based on your findings and not your impressions or antidotal evidence. In presenting your recommendations, tie each to at least one finding from your investigation. Often policy and program recommendations are presented in bullet format for ease of reading and to highlight each recommendation. We recommend that you have separate headings for your policy recommendations and your program recommendations.

STUDY LIMITATIONS AND FUTURE RESEARCH

This section should begin with a brief discussion of the limitations of your capstone research project. You need to acknowledge the limitations of your study.

The final component of this section of your paper should describe additional research that is needed on your target problem. The assumption is that no research answers all research questions, and, indeed, most raise more questions than were answered. Based on what you found or did not find, what additional research questions are raised by your research study? What research questions have not been significantly addressed? What new research questions have emerged? What research questions need further elaboration or investigation? The aim of this section is to provide the reader with a sense of your ideas on the next steps in investigating your study topic. Your suggestions can identify new research questions, replication of your research questions, and/or suggestions for different approaches to investigating the study topic.

■ Additional Components of the Capstone Paper

There are four additional components to your capstone paper. They are the title page, abstract page, references, and appendices. With the exception of your references, we recommend creating your title page, abstract, and appendices after you have completed the other sections of your capstone paper. Your reference page(s) should be worked on as you write the body of your paper. We recommend that every time you add a citation to the text, you immediately add the reference to your references. Conversely, when a text citation is removed from the text during the editing process, you should immediately remove the reference from your references. We have found that this approach helps minimize the occurrence of having a text citation missing from the references and vice versa.

TITLE PAGE

The APA *Publication Manual* (2020) lists the elements that are typically found on the title page of student papers. For your capstone paper, you should follow the guidelines of your instructor. The following are the elements identified in the APA *Publication Manual*:

Title

Your title should summarize the main topic of your capstone research project. Although there is no set limit on the length of your title, it should be focused and succinct (APA, 2020). We recommend that your title be no longer than 12 words. Your title should be centered and bold toward the top of your title page (three or four lines from the top). It should also be formatted with all the words beginning with a capital letter. Minor words, such as *of*, *the*, or *a*, that are three letters or fewer are not capitalized. Begin your page numbering on the title page.

Author Name and Affiliations

Put your name two lines below the title. If your paper is coauthored with equal contributions, then you are free to determine the order of the author names. If there have been agreed-upon unequal contributions to the paper, then the author names are ordered according to the relative contributions of the authors.

Two lines below your name(s), put the name of your university/college and department. Two lines below your school or department, put your course name and number followed by your instructor's name. And finally, below your instructor's name put the due date for your capstone paper.

ABSTRACT

Your title page is followed by an abstract page. Your abstract goes on a separate page and should be page two of your manuscript. The abstract is a brief description of all the major components of your paper (APA, 2020). All the major sections of your paper should be briefly summarized in your abstract. Typically, it is no longer than 250 words and the first sentence is not indented. The word **Abstract** centered and boldfaced is positioned above your study summary.

REFERENCE LIST

Your reference list follows your paper's discussion section. Include only references cited in the text of your paper. References are used to document and substantiate statements and interpretations made in the introduction, literature review, methods, and discussion sections of your paper. References may also have been used in the results section. The APA *Publication Manual* (2020) provides detailed instructions on the correct format of every conceivable type of reference. Start the reference list on a new page after the text of your paper. References are listed in alphabetical order by the first author's last name. Label the reference list **REFERENCES** with it capitalized, centered, and boldfaced. Double-space all references and use a hanging indent with the first line of the reference flush left and subsequent lines indented by 0.5 inches (APA, 2020).

APPENDICES

Appendices are used for materials that supplement your paper's content but would not be appropriate for inclusion in the text of the paper. Two items that we recommend being included with your capstone paper are your informed consent form and your data collection instrument. Include only items or materials that help your readers understand, evaluate, or replicate your study (APA, 2020). Each appendix begins on a separate page after the references. Give each appendix a label and title. If you have more than one appendix, label each appendix with a capital letter (Appendix A, Appendix B, etc.). The appendix title and label are bold and centered at the top of the page.

PRACTICE ACTIVITY

CAPSTONE PAPER CHECKLIST AND SELF-ASSESSMENT

Complete the checklist shown in Table 12.7 to ensure that your capstone paper includes all of the recommended sections and components. We recommend that you reread each section before completing the checklist and that you indicate the page numbers on paper where the identified content is located. We also recommend that you do a self-assessment of each section. Ask yourself to what extent you have achieved the specified purposes of each section of your paper. Have you made a strong and compelling presentation for each component of your paper? What needs to be added to strengthen each section? Is there anything in your paper that is not needed and should be deleted? Completing the checklist helps you identify any content areas of your paper that have

TABLE 12.7 CAPSTONE PAPER CHECKLIST

CONTENT	PAGES
Title Page	
▪ Title no longer than 12 words	
▪ Author(s) name and affiliation	
▪ Course name and number	
▪ Instructor's name	
▪ Capstone paper due date	
Abstract	
▪ 250 words or less	
Introduction	
▪ Introduces topic being addressed	
▪ Provides background information on topic	
▪ Specifies purpose of the research	
▪ Lists hypotheses or research questions	
Literature Review	
Target Problem and Population	
▪ Describes target problem	
▪ Describes consequences of target problem	
▪ Discusses social, economic, and environmental justice issues	
▪ Discusses diversity issues	
▪ Identifies the service needs of target population	
Policies and Procedures	
▪ Describes governmental policies that help fund the program/service	
▪ Analyzes how governmental policies impact clients and service delivery	
▪ Describes organizational policies and procedures that affect service delivery	
▪ Analyzes how organizational policies and procedures impact clients	
▪ Assesses the impact governmental and organizational policies have on social, economic, and environmental justice for the client population	
▪ Assesses the impact governmental and organizational policies have on client diversity and difference	

(continued)

TABLE 12.7 CAPSTONE PAPER CHECKLIST (continued)

CONTENT	PAGES
Program/Service	
▪ Discusses the program's organizational context and structure	
▪ Describes the community setting	
▪ Describes the program's mission and goals	
▪ Provides demographic information on program size, client population, length of service, and staffing	
▪ Describes the program's/service's practice perspective and theoretical framework	
▪ Describes the program's practice model	
Methods	
▪ Study design	
▪ Participants	
▪ Measurement	
▪ Data collection	
▪ Data analysis	
▪ Protection of human subjects	
Results (Quantitative)	
▪ Tables, graphs, and/or charts	
▪ Narrative highlights key findings	
Results (Qualitative)	
▪ Themes described	
▪ Quotes provided to support themes	
Discussion	
▪ Summarize and discuss findings	
▪ Policy and program recommendations	
▪ Study limitations	
▪ Future research	
REFERENCES	
▪ APA format	
Appendices	
▪ Informed consent form	
▪ Data collection instrument	

been omitted. Conducting a careful self-assessment will help you identify content that needs strengthening. We strongly recommend that you complete the checklist and self-assessment prior to submitting your final paper. An electronic copy of the checklist shown in Table 12.7 can be found on the publisher's Student Tools web pages at https://connect.springerpub.com/content/book/978-0-8261-8635-2

TECHNOLOGY EXERCISES

1. Conduct a literature search for qualitative research studies in social work. Compare the coding approaches of a study that used grounded theory and a study that used thematic analysis. How are the two approaches different? How are they similar?
2. Use the two qualitative studies retrieved from the that search and compare their results sections. How are the two write-ups different? How are they similar?
3. Conduct a literature search for quantitative research studies in social work. Compare the hypotheses/research questions of the quantitative study with the qualitative studies from the previous search. How do the hypotheses/research questions from the quantitative research differ from those of the qualitative studies? How are they similar?

REFERENCES

American Psychological Association. (2020). *The publication manual of the American Psychological Association: The official guide to APA style* (7th ed.). Author.

Council on Social Work Education. (2015). *Educational policy and accreditation standards for baccalaureate and master's social work programs.* https://www.cswe.org/getattachment/Accreditation/Accreditation-Process/2015-EPAS/2015EPAS_Web_FINAL.pdf.aspx

National Association of Social Workers. (2017). *Code of ethics.* https://www.socialworkers.org/About/Ethics/Code-of-Ethics

13

PRESENTING YOUR CAPSTONE PROJECT

This chapter focuses on a variety of methods you can use to present your capstone project and is organized into three main sections—electronic visual presentations, poster presentations, and oral presentations. The focus is on exploring the different electronic presentation options, as well as guidelines and tips for poster and oral presentations. This chapter is devoted to the presentation of your applied research capstone project.

By the end of this chapter, you will be able to do the following:

- Identify some of the current professional standards for technology in social work practice.
- Identify common features of quality electronic presentation apps.
- Describe a number of electronic presentation software options.
- Determine which presentation apps will work best for your needs.
- Locate sources of free images and videos to incorporate into electronic presentations.
- Identify components of a visually appealing and professional-looking poster presentation.
- Describe best practices regarding personal appearance and engagement with poster presentation audience members.
- Create an outline for an oral presentation.
- Recognize best practices for providing a quality oral presentation.
- Locate a number of online tutorials and videos that teach you how to use the various electronic presentation options available.
- Identify, compare, and contrast three useful videoconferencing platforms.

Project Presentations

Designing and completing a research-based capstone project is no small task. There are many steps involved, a lot of writing to do, and a great deal of time devoted to communication with professors, academic advisors, field directors and liaisons, institutional review boards (IRBs), placement supervisors, and peers. After completing all of the work that goes into making applied research happen, from the conception of the research study, to literature reviews, to designing the methodology, obtaining IRB approval (if required), connecting to participants, collecting and analyzing data, and writing about the results of the study, students are often then tasked with presenting their work. Whether it is an electronic slide show, an oral presentation like a lecture, a poster presentation as part of a departmental event, or an academic conference, it is important for the quality of the presentation to honor the time and effort it required of the student to complete it.

PROFESSIONAL STANDARDS FOR TECHNOLOGY IN SOCIAL WORK PRACTICE

Social workers' utilization of technology is increasing rapidly. Technology continues to transform the nature of social work practice and greatly enhances social workers' ability to address the needs of the people they serve. Social workers use technologies to access, gather, and manage information about clients and the social service agencies that provide them with assistance. Due to their increasing use and utility, social workers should always be on the lookout for new technologies that will benefit social work practice, explore those technologies, and then disseminate them with colleagues (National Association of Social Workers [NASW], 2017).

Social workers can now receive foundational and continuing education credits by attending their social work classes through videoconferencing applications, complete practicum placement work virtually, participate in live online webinars, and attend electronically transmitted lectures from remote locations. These significant developments require practice standards in the use of technology. The NASW (2017) divides these standards into the following main sections to address social workers' use of electronic technology:

1. Provide important and useful information to the public
2. Design, create, and deliver services
3. Accumulate, manage, store, and access information about clients

Providing Information to the Public

When you use technology to inform others about topics of interest to fellow social workers, to provide information to the public, or to engage in social advocacy, it is important that you uphold the values of the profession and adhere to the standards put forth by the NASW (2017). As an example, Standard 1.01: Ethics and Values informs us that when social workers use any technology to provide useful information to the public, reasonable steps should be taken to ensure that the information being disseminated is accurate, respectable, and congruent with the NASW *Code of Ethics*.

When providing a presentation about your capstone research project for example, you should always make sure that the information and the material you are sharing are accurate and appropriate. Not only should you be mindful of the credibility of the information sources you use in your literature review and discussion section, but you also need to ensure that all the information about your research project, from your methodology to your suggested implications and applications of your findings, are truthful and free of prejudicial biases (NASW, 2017).

Designing, Creating, and Delivering Services

According to the NASW, the Association of Social Work Boards (ASWB), the Council on Social Work Education (CSWE), and the Clinical Social Work Association (CSWA) Standards for Technology in Social Work Practice (NASW, 2017), technology is permitted for use in order to facilitate various forms of service, including case management, support, counseling, and other functions that social workers provide. Never has this been more important than during the nationwide response to the COVID-19 pandemic that necessitated the temporary end of in-person interactions throughout the world. All across the country, and at every level of education from kindergarten to graduate school, classes had to quickly transition their in-classroom curricula to various online videoconferencing platforms, most notably Zoom.

As people living in the United States and throughout the world continue to contend with the health and safety guidelines of social-distancing practices, and with the "new normal" of being prepared to quickly switch from in-person to virtual working and instructional modalities when mandated, the use of technology has become a vital skill to possess for social work students, educators, and practitioners. Although we have seen how technology is used to successfully create virtual classrooms, both synchronous and asynchronous, using technology to facilitate communication with clients, provide information to clients, obtain information from clients, and facilitate various interventions is becoming increasingly important (NASW, 2017).

Students responsible for designing, conducting, and presenting research-based capstone projects need to be prepared to use appropriate technology at every step of the process. Social work practicum placements may require students to provide case management and group counseling, and attend supervision meetings virtually. When conducting needs assessment and/or program evaluation research as part of a capstone project, students may need to meet with participants, collect data, and eventually present their research findings all in virtual settings. Although there are benefits in providing services electronically, there are also risks that social workers need to consider (NASW, 2017).

Accumulate, Manage, Store, and Access Information About Clients

According to Standard 2.01: Ethical Use of Technology, when delivering social work services using technology, the competence of social work practitioners and the well-being of clients are primary. When social workers use technology to provide services and present information, they need to reasonably ensure that the services they provide and the information collected and disseminated are kept confidential. For example, the data provided by a client should be accessible only by those who require access (e.g., the social workers assigned to the client, agency administration).

Social workers are permitted to use various forms of technology to gather, manage, store, and access information about clients. *Gathering information* refers to collecting information for the purposes of research, program evaluation, organizational or community needs assessments, social action, education, biopsychosocial assessments, progress notes, supervision, or other social work functions. *Managing information* refers to how information is organized after it has been collected, for example, how certain information may be shared with colleagues, supervisors, university or social work agency administrators, researchers, and others outside the social workers' practice settings. *Storing information* refers to how information is stored and managed electronically. When social workers, as well as social work students, use technology to gather, manage, and store information, they are required to adhere to ethical standards related to informed consent, research participant confidentiality, client confidentiality, boundaries, and providing research participants and clients access to their records (NASW, 2017). Student researchers need to keep these ethical standards in mind when designing and delivering their capstone project presentations.

ELECTRONIC VISUAL PRESENTATIONS

Slideshow presentations have come a long way since the world was introduced to McMillan's WordArt generator. Although spending hours tinkering with font sizes, images, and embedded videos and charts on PowerPoint is still commonplace, the latest presentation software and apps have made it easier than ever to create professional-looking slideshows.

Currently, in academia, one of the most commonly utilized programs is still PowerPoint; however, there are a number of apps available that are just as good as PowerPoint, if not better. Determining which software works best for you involves knowing what is available. The following sections explore what makes a great presentation app and provide descriptions and characteristics of some of the best free programs currently on the market.

FEATURES OF QUALITY PRESENTATION APPS

Presentation apps should make it easy for people to transform their research and policy practice into professional-looking and attractive presentations. Common characteristics of quality presentation apps include prebuilt templates that can easily be shared and used in collaboration, offer media support, contain graphic assets, have live-polling capabilities, and include presentation options. These useful tools are usually standard features of PowerPoint but can also be found in many free applications as well (Graw, 2020; Martinez, 2020).

- **Pre-built Themes and Templates:** The best presentation programs should have attractive, professional-looking templates to make building presentations in a hurry simple and straightforward. Themes and templates assist users in creating content that is not only attractive and consistent, but also help the user avoid lots of manual formatting. A "theme" is a predefined inventory of fonts, colors, and visual effects that can be applied to slides for a professional, unified appearance.

Using them gives presentations a congruous look with minimal effort. A "template" is a theme plus organizational formatting content designed for a specific purpose (e.g., a classroom lesson, to communicate research findings).

- **Presentation Options:** Quality programs should offer some form of presenter mode, as well as other presenter–audience interaction capabilities such as live polling. One kind of presenter mode most beneficial is Presenter View. Presenter View allows you to view your presentation with all your speaker notes displayed on your computer, while the audience sees only the notes-free version of your presentation displayed on a different screen or monitor(s). A few more useful presentation modes are ones that allow the presenter to rehearse timings and record their slide show. The Rehearse Timings option allows presenters to determine how much time is needed to cover the information on each slide. The Record Slide Show option allows the presenter to program their slide show to proceed along a predetermined path, allowing the presenter to move around, untethered to their computer.

- **Live-Polling Capabilities:** Live-polling systems allow a presenter to electronically solicit ideas and opinions from their audience in real-time. For instance, you might want your audience to choose the appropriate response to a question you have, to quiz them on some detail covered in your presentation, to gather opinions, or do an emotional check-in when covering sensitive topics. Although it is preferable for your presentation application to have built-in live-polling capabilities, there are a number of free polling programs that can easily be embedded into your electronic presentation. There are a number of low-cost polling programs available such as Vevox, Survey Monkey, Poll Everywhere, and Direct Poll, but one of the most utilized and free real-time polling systems is *Kahoot* and can be found at https://kahoot.com

- **Collaboration and Sharing Options:** With the option of being able to work remotely becoming an important part of many people's lives in the era of COVID-19, having a presentation app that facilitates this necessity is increasingly important for users. Whether you plan to share your presentation slides at a later date, or you just want to collaborate with a peer or colleague on a presentation, the program you use should make it easy to share files and cocreate in real time.

- **Graphic Assets:** Graphic assets are supplementary visuals that help presenters complement their presentation with additional creative artwork and visuals. When you need to create a presentation quickly, you often do not have time to scour the internet for visuals or animations to make your presentation more interesting. What is needed is an application stocked with graphic assets, like stock images, graphics, charts, and animations.

- **Media Support:** It is important that your chosen presentation app is able to incorporate a wide range of media files into your presentation. Whether you need to record a narration for your presentation, incorporate music, or insert a YouTube clip, the best presentation apps should support a wide variety of media types, like video, audio, images, and GIFs.

OPTIONS FOR FREE AND INEXPENSIVE PRESENTATION SOFTWARE

Presentation programs are an evolving and ever-expanding market. Most of the options for paid presentation programs have free (but limited) versions of their software, but there are a number of free high-quality options from which to choose as well. The following programs and applications are all useful for students to provide stimulating visual and multimedia presentations about their research projects. Based on the type of computer to which students have access (e.g., Mac or PC), some programs are better options than others.

- *PowerPoint Presentations* act as a visual aid for communicating information and/or media through a progressive series of slides (PowerPoint for Windows Training, n.d.). Along with regular text, PowerPoint slides can incorporate many types of content such as images, tables, charts, drawings, links, WordArt, audio, and video (Childress, 2019). Although PowerPoint is not free per se, it is often provided free of charge to university faculty and students.
    - PowerPoint YouTube Tutorial: https://www.youtube.com/watch?v=u7Tku3_RGPs
    - PowerPoint for Windows Training: https://support.office.com/en-us/article/powerpoint-for-windows-training-40e8c930-cb0b-40d8-82c4-bd53d3398787

- *Google Slides* does a good job of matching the capabilities of PowerPoint but is designed around collaboration. This free presentation software operates within student internet browsers and supports diagram creation, embedded videos, and adding animations to slides. There are a number of slide templates already built in, and students can easily download hundreds more for free. One of the best features of Google Slides is in its collaboration capabilities. Students can share a link to their presentation, allowing the recipient to add details to slides, write presentation notes, share feedback, and engage in live group chats (Martinez, 2020).
    - Google Slides YouTube Tutorial: https://www.youtube.com/watch?v=kYA6GLAzz9A
    - Google Slides Training and Help: https://support.google.com/a/users/answer/9282488?hl=en

- *Prezi* is a presentation tool that can be used as an alternative to PowerPoint and other traditional slide-making programs. Instead of a procession of information-packed slides, Prezi utilizes one large digital canvas, and allows users to pan and zoom to whatever part of the canvas where their ideas, information, activities, and multimedia files can be found. One of the key aspects of Prezi that makes it unique among its competitors is its ability to give audiences a sense of physical space and distance between canvas locations (Graw, 2020; Martinez, 2020).

- Prezi YouTube Tutorial: https://www.youtube.com/watch?time_continue=2&v=LRdbULX-abg&feature=emb_logo
- Prezi Tutorials: https://prezi.com/learn

- **Apple Keynote** is a presentation app that comes free with every new Apple device. Much like PowerPoint, Keynote is packed with typography, beautiful templates, and a library of smooth animations. It can be used online on a PC at iCloud.com, can be shared with others to view or edit, and gives users the ability to save their presentations to a PowerPoint file if needed. Presenters can use their iPhones to control their presentation remotely from their Mac, or they can present their work online free of charge with Keynote Live's presentation streaming service (Martinez, 2020).

  - Beginner's Guide to Apple Keynote YouTube: https://www.youtube.com/watch?time_continue=20&v=tphW6ajNjCI&feature=emb_logo
  - Apple Keynote Support: https://support.apple.com

- **LibraOffice** contains a PowerPoint equivalent called *impress* and is a free alternative to Microsoft Office. The reason LibreOffice is free is because it is open source software created by a large group of free software advocate volunteers. Although LibraOffice lacks an ability to integrate and collaborate with Microsoft OneDrive, it has some unique advantages. LibreOffice can import files from Keynote, offers hundreds of free downloadable templates, and has no limit on what fonts you can use, something that PowerPoint lacks (Graw, 2020).

  - How to Make a Presentation in LibreOffice YouTube: https://www.youtube.com/watch?v=ekMNTktguik
  - LibreOffice Presentation Guide: https://libreofficehelp.com/create-your-first-presentation-using-libreoffice-impress

SOURCES FOR FREE DIGITAL IMAGES

The electronic presentation sources just described represent some of the best free software presently on the market. However, if you are willing to pay subscription fees, there are many more. Regardless of the presentation software one uses, it is likely that you will also need to know where to find images for your presentation. Fortunately, there are a number of free image sources available. Three of the most well-known are Pixabay, Unsplash, and WikiMedia Commons.

- **Pixabay.** Over 1.7 million high-quality open-access stock images and videos: https://pixabay.com
- **Unsplash.** The internet's source of freely usable images powered by creators everywhere: https://unsplash.com
- **Wikimedia Commons.** A collection of over 60 million usable media files anyone can use and contribute to: https://commons.wikimedia.org/wiki/Main_Page

Poster Presentations

Poster sessions in classes and at conferences are an effective way to visually convey research projects. Poster presentations communicate a student's research or their understanding of a topic in a short and concise format. There are three basic components to a poster session: (a) you (the student), (b) your poster, and (c) a handout. All three components should complement one another without being too repetitive. Poster presentations can be created by hand using printed components arranged on a trifold or poster display board, but most professional poster presentations are designed through Microsoft PowerPoint and Publisher.

TIPS FOR POSTER DESIGN

The first task a student has, before beginning to actually create their poster presentation, is to thoroughly review the guidelines and instructions provided by the event or conference. Every conference and academic event will give presenters instructions and guidelines outlining important information such as size requirements, space limitations, and/or other restrictions that are important for students to know. The next aspect to consider is the audience at the event.

There are typically three types of audiences—general audiences, those in related fields or areas, and specialists in your discipline (e.g., social work). Students may want to tailor their poster and presentation for the type of audience attending their poster session. For example, if presenting to a group of professional social workers (i.e., specialists), you may want to include technical details and connections to industry standards, such as the NASW *Code of Ethics* or the CSWE core competencies. Conversely, if the poster presentation will be attended by a general audience (e.g., at a university student research event), simplifying the content of a poster in order to avoid overwhelming people with technical jargon would be a better tactic.

Research posters should be designed to provide a general idea or the most important points of your research, so do not feel pressured to provide every single detail of your study. When creating your poster, you need to think about the message you want to convey to your audience, so it is important to decide what key information should be included. Presenters should brainstorm about what essential information needs to be included and what they want to highlight. This can be accomplished by creating a clear outline of the information to be included. Often, the required abstract submission can be used as a guide to develop such an outline. The following are general elements of qualitative and quantitative research posters:

- **Title:** Titles for research posters should summarize your project as a whole with particular emphasis on your results. A line with your name and university should follow your title.
- **Abstract:** An abstract succinctly summarizes your entire research project. The abstract should not repeat information stated in other sections but should highlight features of all the other elements on your poster.
- **Objectives/Hypothesis:** This section of your poster needs to clearly state the objectives, research question(s), and/or hypothesis of your study (a bullet list will work well).
- **Introduction**: Your introduction should provide a brief background of the topic. The reader needs to be able to quickly understand why you chose this particular topic to study (why is it important?) and be provided with general background information (bulleted list or maximum length of around 200 words).
- **Materials and Methods**: This section should be simple and to the point (bulleted list or maximum of around 200 words). For complex procedures, you may want to have a handout describing the materials and detailing the research methods used in your study.
- **Results:** This section of your poster should briefly describe qualitative (descriptive) and quantitative results using limited text or a bullet list. Use figures with figure legends, tables, and graphs to enhance the presentation of your results. If you are presenting qualitative research, you may want to provide examples of specific quotes from your data that support your findings. Do not just provide a textual description. People are far more likely to stop at posters that include colorful, high-quality images.
- **Conclusions/Future Directions**: This section is where you remind your readers about the objective(s), research question(s), and/or hypothesis of your study. State if your hypothesis was correct (if appropriate), discuss the relevance of your findings, and provide suggestions for future research (bulleted list of around 200 words).
- **References:** This section should be limited to no more than 10 citations.

The poster itself should be consistent, have a clean layout that provides a balance of visuals and text, outline the student's research with interesting commentary about what was learned along the way, and be easily readable from about 10 feet away. In summary, the title should be concise and draw people's interest. The total word count should be between 300 to 800 words with text that is large print, clear, and to the point. Using bullets, numbering, and headlines that make it easy to read are important as well. Effective use of graphics, color, and fonts should also be done to enhance the poster's visual attractiveness. Importantly, student poster presentations should include acknowledgments, the student's name(s), and their institutional affiliation(s). To examine a list of downloadable PDF research poster templates, visit:

- Designing Conference Posters by Colin Purrington: https://colinpurrington.com/tips/poster-design
- Undergraduate Research Poster Presentation Examples from University of Maryland, Baltimore County: https://ur.umbc.edu/poster-presentation-examples

TIPS FOR STUDENT PRESENTERS

You should prepare and rehearse a 1- to 2-minute oral overview of your research. Your overview should highlight unique experiences and/or insights gained by the research in simple, easy-to-understand language. Those viewing your poster presentation will likely have questions, so it is important for you to prepare to answer questions about your research.

Presenting a poster for the first time can be a daunting and intimidating prospect. Small audiences, at times just a single person, can ask many questions, interrupt the presenter, and may even grill you about your research. However, giving a poster presentation is a great way to receive feedback and interact with other social workers and social scientists, and can boost your confidence when others show interest in your research.

You should plan to arrive early on the day you are scheduled to present your poster. Extra pushpins, a black marker, and white out are always good supplies to bring. Even if you have not made any mistakes, a fellow researcher in need may be grateful for them. Arriving early allows the presenter ample time to make sure their poster is properly mounted and gives them time to meet their neighbors (Block, 1996; Miller, 2007). Once the poster is mounted and has been given a final inspection, it is a good idea for you to practice a 1- to 2-minute oral overview and prepare to answer questions (Wilson, 2012). Some common questions asked at poster presentations include the following: Why did you choose this particular research question? What is the most interesting thing you learned through your research? Did you learn anything unexpected? How do you plan to apply your findings to your future practice as a social worker? Do you have any plans to continue this line of research? What would you like to research in the future?

An important component of a student research poster presentation is how a student's appearance represents themselves and their supporting institutions. The clothing that a student wears should convey confidence and professionalism (Miller, 2007; Wilson,

2012). Business casual (e.g., contemporary slacks or a skirt, a button-down blouse or shirt) will help the presenter look and feel professional. It is also advisable to wear comfortable shoes since poster presentations often involve standing for a significant amount of time. Presenters should also make sure their name badge is always visible and easily readable for their audience members (Block, 1996).

While presenting, you should stay close to your poster, just off to the side, in order to avoid blocking the view of audience members. It also gives passers-by the opportunity to quickly step in and look at an interesting table or graph, or to read the abstract to help them decide whether or not they want to learn more. When people begin to gather, do not focus on only one person. The presenter should use their eyes and body language to draw people into the conversation. This can be accomplished by smiling, looking into the eyes of and greeting everyone who walks by, while asking if they would like to know more about the research; doing so increases the chance of having a well-attended poster session (Wilson, 2012). In addition, remember to have a stack of handouts available. Providing handouts to those who show interest in your poster helps you connect with others after the poster session ends. Finally, even if your poster is not well attended, or if things seem slow overall, stay until the time slot is over (Miller, 2007).

TIPS FOR POSTER-RELATED HANDOUTS

The following are some best practices for poster-presentation handouts. Avoid printing your entire capstone research paper since event participants often need to carry around what they collect for extended amounts of time while going from one presentation to another. Instead, try to design your handout to fit on one double-sided sheet of paper. The front side of the paper should include a picture of the poster, and the back side a condensed literature review, cited references, further information about the topic, and contact information. By designing the handout to be short and concise, and by providing contact information, those who attend your presentation can later contact you to ask more about your research or request a full copy of your research paper (Block, 1996; Miller, 2007; Wilson, 2012).

Oral Presentations

In some classes, writing a research paper is only part of what is required of students. A professor may require or a field supervisor may request that a student provide an oral presentation of their study. An oral presentation is much more than simply reading a research paper or showing a set of slides to an audience. How you deliver your presentation is as important in effectively communicating your message as what you actually say. Here are some points to consider before giving an oral presentation.

WHAT SHOULD YOU SAY?

If a professor or field supervisor does not explicitly state what the content of your presentation should focus on, it is best to think about what you want to achieve and what you feel are the most important things that the audience should know about your study. Think about the following: Do you want to inform your audience, inspire them to think about your research beyond your presentation, or convince them of a particular viewpoint? Thinking about what you want to accomplish will help you frame your approach to your presentation topic.

Oral Communication Is Different From Written Communication

In an oral presentation, your audience has only one opportunity to hear what you have to say and cannot simply reread your words if they do not understand something the first time. Focus on being clear and concise, especially if the audience members are unable to ask questions during your talk. There are two well-known methods for communicating points effectively. The first is a design principle introduced by the U.S. Navy in 1960 referred to as the KISS ("keep it simple stupid") method (Dalzell, 2009; Partridge et al., 2007). The KISS principle asserts that most systems work best if they are kept as simple as possible, and that unnecessary complexity should be avoided. With this principle in mind, students should focus on getting two or three key points across to the audience when presenting their capstone research project. A second approach is to forecast, explain, and summarize. Communicate to the audience what you are going to tell them (forecast), then talk about it (explain), and then tell them what you just told them (summarize).

Know What is Expected of You and Your Oral Presentation

When presenting your research in a class, your professor will likely provide you with a list of expectations and requirements for your presentation. You may even be provided with a grading rubric that will assist you in designing your oral presentation. When presenting at an academic conference on the other hand, it may be assumed that you have read all the guidelines and expectations provided by the conference (Adler, 2010).

When planning a conference presentation, there are a few questions you need to answer: (a) Who will potentially attend the conference and my presentation? (b) What can I assume my audience will know? (c) What can I assume that I will need to explain to my audience? (d) What is the typical method for presenting at the conference (e.g., Do people read a paper out loud? Do they incorporate a slideshow? Do presenters typically engage with their audience by asking questions or asking for feedback?)? (e) How much time will I have to present? (f) Will I even be able to present a slideshow?

Think About Your Audience

One of the most important questions that needs to be answered before your oral presentation is: Who will my potential audience be? Different audiences have different expectations and information needs (Stuenkel & Rauch, 2018). The needs of your audience depend on where you are presenting your research. If you are providing an oral presentation in one of your college classes, your audience is your professor and your peers. However, if you are giving an oral presentation at a student research event or an academic conference, your audience will be more diverse demographically, as well as in background and in expertise (Adler, 2010).

In a classroom setting, you and your audience have likely spent weeks or months together studying the same topics and reading much of the same materials. Logically, you might assume that your peers and professor know what you know, so you might not need to spend a lot of time covering background information. At a student research event or an academic conference, however, you might be presenting to a generally diverse audience that does not share your background and academic frame of reference, necessitating that you spend more time communicating background and explanatory information to your audience.

HOW TO BEGIN PREPARING FOR YOUR ORAL PRESENTATION

Reducing an entire research project down to a 10-, 20-, 30-, or even a 40-minute oral presentation can be quite a challenge. It also takes time and focused care to design a slideshow that will supplement your presentation. The best way to get started is to outline your presentation. Begin by doing some research or asking around to determine what is customarily done among practitioners in your field of study.

After familiarizing yourself with your academic field or research area's general outline for presentations, you can begin populating your outline. A helpful method for beginning to fill in the details of your oral presentation is to focus on what, who, how, and why (Stuenkel & Rauch, 2018). The following are questions you should address in preparing your presentation:

- What is the issue or problem your research addresses?
- Who is affected, impacted, involved, and so forth?
- Why is this issue or problem important for social workers?
- How does your research fit into the research already available?
- How did you research and/or analyze the issue or problem?
- What are your research findings?
- What do your findings communicate about the identified issue or problem?
- What are the theoretical and/or practical implications of your findings?
- What conclusions can be drawn from your research?

All of the "what, who, how, and why" details just listed can be annotated onto note cards or pages to help you stay on track throughout your oral presentation.

CREATING EFFECTIVE NOTES

Without notes to refer to as you speak, you risk forgetting something important. Not having notes also increases the chance of losing your train of thought and begin relying on reading directly from your presentation slides. Nothing is more distracting to an audience than watching a speaker fumbling around with their notes as they try to speak. Witnessing such an occurrence gives the impression that the presenter is disorganized and unprepared. Therefore, it is important to create notes that can be easily referred to as you are giving an oral presentation. One good strategy is to dedicate a page of bulleted notes for each slide or talking topic, so that you are reminded to move on to the next slide or topic when all your notes have been addressed. This also creates a natural pause, allowing your audience to contemplate what you just presented. Some useful strategies for creating effective notes include the following (Genard, 2016; Stewart & Fulop, 2019):

- Use a large, readable font.
- Use bold text, underlining, or color-coded text to highlight elements of your speech that you want to emphasize. Highlight only the most important elements of your presentation.
- Leave space on your note pages/cards to write additional thoughts or observations before and during your presentation (e.g., thoughts about a question posed by an audience member, or to remember a multipart question). Remember to have a pen or two with you during your presentation.
- Place a visual cue in the text of your notes indicating when to move to the next slide or topic, or to take some other action, such as clicking a link to a video clip. You may also use cues to remind you when you want to communicate a specific point, ask the audience a question, or when you want the audience to refer to a handout you have previously provided.
- Spell out challenging words phonetically and practice saying them before you have to do so in front of an audience. This is especially important for accurately pronouncing technical scientific terminology, accurately pronouncing people's names, unfamiliar words, or words in a foreign language.

BEST PRACTICES FOR PROVIDING QUALITY ORAL PRESENTATIONS

Delivering a high-quality, engaging, and memorable presentation can be considered an art form. Take a minute or two to think about some of the best presentations or the best speakers and presenters you have seen, such as a professor who captivated you with their lectures, or someone who gave an excellent Technology, Entertainment, Design (TED) talk you watched online or in person. How did they capture and maintain your attention? What exactly (e.g., format, techniques, visual aids) did they do to deliver such a great presentation? In general, experienced oral presenters focus on three important parts of their presentations: their introduction, the body of their talk, and their conclusion.

The Introduction

Most seasoned presenters tend to have a strong opening, one that captures the listeners' attention. They sometimes start with a question, tell an amusing story, or a provocative statement related to what inspired them to conduct their research (Zivkovic, 2014). Good presenters clearly communicate their purpose with statements like "I'm going to talk about . . ." and "This afternoon I want to explain how . . ." It is also good practice to present your audience with an outline of your talk. For example, "Today, I will focus on the following points: First off . . . Then . . . Which will lead to . . . And in conclusion . . ." It is also common for experienced presenters to utilize the complementary techniques of "telling" and "showing." Having the ability to share information by *telling* people about their research, while simultaneously *showing* their research through charts, graphs, photos, audio clips, short videos, or other media are hallmarks of the seasoned and effective presenter (Adler, 2010).

The Body

When delivering a talk to an audience, it is good practice to present your main points one by one in a logical order. Give your audience members time to take notes, or to think about what you are telling them, by pausing at the end of each point (Genard, 2016). When you are moving to another point, make it clear to your audience with statements like, "Now on to the next point, which is that . . ." "Of course, it's important to remember that . . .," and "However, it's important to understand that . . ." Also, work to incorporate examples that clearly illustrate your points and/or significant findings. Finally, when appropriate, provide visual aids to make your presentation more interesting (e.g., charts, graphs, maps, pictures, links to videos).

The Conclusion

Before concluding your oral presentation, provide your audience with a clear summary of everything you have communicated, and then summarize the main points of your talk again (Genard, 2016). For example, you may use phrases such as: "To recap the most important aspects of my project …," "In conclusion …," "In summary, it is important to understand …" Follow that up by restating the purpose of your oral presentation and communicate how you have achieved your objective with statements such as "My intention for this presentation was …, and it should now be clear to all in attendance that …"

One of the most important techniques of good presentations is to end on a high note. You should never let your talk just fizzle out. Instead, make it obvious to your audience that you have reached the end of your presentation. A common way to do this is to try to end your talk with a bang. In other words, try to conclude your presentation with one or two sentences that sum up the importance of your research, and of how the world is better off as a result of your work. Conclude by thanking your audience and inviting them to ask questions (Stewart & Fulop, 2019).

GENERAL TIPS FOR ORAL PRESENTERS

A common characteristic of good presenters is that they exhibit mastery over their material. They are comfortable and appear at ease while talking about who they are, what they do, what their research is about, and what they achieve or want to accomplish through their work (Stuenkel & Rauch, 2018). Good presenters tend to look like they are having a great time and communicate through their body language that they are comfortable presenting in front of audiences. They do not stand with their hands in their pockets, looking at the floor, or stand with their shoulders hunched. They make frequent eye contact with audience members, and often use hand gestures and facial cues as they speak, holding their palms up to convey a problem they faced, covering their face with their palm to express embarrassment, or smiling to convey a funny point they have made (Stewart & Fulop, 2019).

The most effective way for you to become a good public speaker is through repetitive practice. The sense of comfort and ease that is a hallmark of great presenters comes from practice. Practicing talking about their work and sharing their personal stories is part of what makes their presentations so smooth and clear. The more you do or talk about something, the easier it becomes for you. For example, using the "what, who, how, and why" list and the supplemental slideshow previously reviewed as guides, you can practice rehearsing for your presentation by reading aloud everything you wrote down. The more you do this, the less you will need to rely on reading from slides or note cards, as you are increasingly able to communicate the information in your presentation from memory (Genard, 2016).

Try to anticipate what questions may arise during or after your presentation (Adler, 2010). Imagine questions that you might have a hard time answering, focus on finding answers to those questions, and then rehearse communicating your responses out loud. Rehearse imaginary question-and-answer exchanges as if you were actually in front of your audience. This may involve some creativity and a willingness to feel uncomfortable, and perhaps even silly, as you pretend to be looking at and talking to your imagined audience members.

As your comfort with your material grows, and as you get accustomed to hearing your own voice communicating the details of your research and answering potential questions that may arise, your confidence will increase, and your stress level will lessen. You may even want to videotape yourself so that you can watch it from the vantage point of your audience members (Kessler, n.d.). Watching your presentation is a great way to take note of your body language, the volume of your voice, and to see if there are any areas you can revise and improve. Or, you may even want to gather friends and family together to serve as a test audience (Stewart & Fulop, 2019).

SOME TIPS ON AVOIDING PRESENTATION DIFFICULTIES

There are a few things you will want to avoid when presenting your research project. No one is born an expert presenter, but all masterful presenters practice every chance they get. They also know what to expect at the location where they are presenting. For example, you do not want to show up to the room in which you are presenting with a flash drive containing your electronic presentation if there is only a podium and a dry-erase board available. Likewise, you will not want to show up with only a link to your online presentation (e.g., a PowerPoint slide show saved on Google Drive or a Prezi) if the room to which you have been assigned lacks an internet connection.

It is a good idea to contact conference organizers with questions prior to your presentation (Stuenkel & Rauch, 2018). For example, you could ask them what technology will be available in your room, if the internet is Wi-Fi or accessible only through a direct connection, if there are computers available or you need to bring your own, and if there *are* computers for use by presenters, whether they have USB ports for a flash drive. Often, presenters need to arrange or request technology ahead of the conference. You may also be required to register for Wi-Fi access, create a profile, username, and password.

You should also practice your timing to ensure that you have prepared an appropriate amount of information for the time you are allotted (Kessler, n.d.; Stuenkel & Rauch, 2018; Zivkovic, 2014). Also remember to leave some time at the end of your presentation for questions and answers! At professional conferences, 30 minutes means exactly 30 minutes. If you surpass your time limit, you are effectively stealing the presentation time of those who are scheduled after you.

Finally, be prepared for things to go wrong. If your electronic presentation is on a flash drive, make sure to email your presentation to yourself as well. If the computer, the projector, or the internet stops working, it is good to have a backup plan so you can still present your research through other means, such as on a dry-erase board or poster paper. Although it may be a little cumbersome to bring emergency supplies like poster paper, dry-erase markers, handwritten note cards, or a printed outline of your electronic presentation, knowing that you are prepared if anything does go wrong will help ease your presentation jitters and may even bolster your confidence.

UTILIZING VIRTUAL AND DISTANCE TECHNOLOGIES TO PRESENT YOUR RESEARCH

The COVID-19 pandemic necessarily changed the way education is delivered when social distancing or stay-at-home orders are in effect. Although there are options (e.g., fully online instruction, synchronous/asynchronous, staggered in-person instruction), knowing how to utilize virtual platforms to watch class lectures, engage in group discussions, participate in live polls, and knowing how to present your projects and/or research will likely remain important skills to learn. This section begins with an overview of the most widely utilized virtual meeting platforms (Zoom) and then provides information about similar, albeit lesser known, alternatives.

Zoom

Zoom is a cloud-based communication software program that allows users to set up virtual video and audio classrooms, conferencing, webinars, screen sharing, live chats, breakout room discussions, polling surveys, and other collaborative capabilities. To enhance user privacy, a virtual background feature blocks others from seeing what is in the room behind you while participating. The Zoom app can be accessed on a desktop computer, a computer tablet, or through a mobile phone with or without video. This software offers quality video, audio, and wireless screen-sharing features across Mac, Windows, Linux, iOS, Blackberry, and Android systems.

Users can join an instant meeting through an instant messaging or email invite, from an internet browser, from the mobile application or the Zoom desktop, from a mobile phone or even through a landline. Before joining a Zoom meeting on a mobile device or computer, users will need to download and install the Zoom app from an App Store, or by clicking a "join" link attached to their Zoom meeting invite. Each member of a Zoom meeting will be assigned a unique 9- to 11-digit number called a "meeting ID" that will be required in order to join. If users can join only via telephone, they will need the "teleconferencing number" provided in the invite.

Fortunately, Zoom provides a lot of resources to help people become adept at using their software. Although Zoom is not free, only the hosts of Zoom meetings have to pay a fee. If you are invited to a Zoom meeting, by a professor, supervisor, friend, or anyone else, your participation is *free*, provided you download and install the Zoom app.

- Zoom Video Tutorials: https://support.zoom.us/hc/en-us/articles/206618765-Zoom-video-tutorials
- Zoom Technical Support and Resources Page: https://zoom.us/docs/en-us/covid19.html#training-resources

SKYPE MEET NOW

Most people are familiar with the Skype videoconferencing application. It has been the place to go for face-to-face videoconferencing since it was released in 2003 (Weisbein, 2020). Skype's new Meet Now feature (accessed by clicking on the *Meet Now* button on the left side of the app) offers videoconferencing for free. Meet Now in Skype allows you to easily set up virtual collaboration spaces and invite colleagues, friends, and family. A convenient feature of Meet Now is that participants can easily join virtual meetings whether they have a Skype account or not. In addition, you can also create a free conference room through the Skype website ("What Is Meet Now," n.d.).

There are a few more features that makes Skype's Meet Now a useful alternative to Zoom. Just like with Zoom, you can record your meetings and save them to review later. Skype's Meet Now stores your recording for up to 30 days. Although Meet Now does not offer a virtual background option like Zoom, you can blur your background before entering the call and keep it blurred throughout your meeting. However, just like with Zoom, Meet Now allows you to easily share slide presentations, documents, and video clips on your screen whenever necessary. Users can then collaborate and review their work with others in the chat feature (n.d.)

- Skype *Meet Now* Tutorial YouTube Video: https://www.youtube.com/watch?v=441lx7CFQY0&t=219s
- Skype *Meet Now* Tutorial Help Page: https://support.skype.com/en/faq/FA34926/what-is-meet-now-and-how-do-i-use-it-in-skype

GOOGLE MEET

You may already know about "Google Hangouts," an application that allows you to have a video chat with up to 10 participants, and conversations with up to 150 participants. However, due to the popularity of Zoom and other video-conferencing rivals, Google recently announced that it is making its professional video-conferencing tool, "Google Meet," free for all. The free version allows up to 100 participants to videoconference for up to 60 minutes but requires an upgrade if you want your virtual gatherings to last longer. The only requirement is for users to have a gmail account (Weisbein, 2020).

One of the primary concerns when Zoom became the must-have application software at the beginning of the COVID-19 pandemic was security issues such as Zoombombing. The mandatory Google account is aimed at providing a higher level of user security, but there are also a number of additional safety measures built in. Like Zoom, Google Meet mandates all meeting attendees to enter a virtual waiting room until they are let in by the host(s). In addition, since Google Meet can function without any add-ons in the user's internet browser, Google claims that it is less vulnerable to security threats than Zoom (Agarwal, 2020).

- Google Meet Tutorial YouTube Video: https://www.youtube.com/watch?v=wGXI0KpkR50
- Google Meet Help Page: https://support.google.com/meet/?hl=en#topic=7192926

PRACTICE ACTIVITIES

1. Of the electronic presentation programs reviewed in this chapter, write about which ones you would most want to use and why.
2. Do you know of any other quality presentation programs and/or sources of free images and videos you would recommend? If so, create a list.
3. Imagine yourself as a presenter of a poster at a national conference. Referring to the information presented in this chapter, list some of the ways you would prepare for your presentation.
4. Referring to the "General Tips for Oral Presenters" section in this chapter, write a list of ways you could best prepare for an oral presentation about your research.
5. What are your thoughts about in-person presentations versus virtual ones? Do you think one is better than the other? Fill out Table 13.1 to weigh what you feel are the positive and negative (pros vs. cons) aspects of each.

TABLE 13.1 PROS AND CONS OF IN-PERSON AND VIRTUAL PRESENTATIONS

IN-PERSON PRESENTATIONS		VIRTUAL PRESENTATIONS	
Positives	Negatives	Positives	Negatives

TECHNOLOGY EXERCISE

Zoom is one of the most used and well-known virtual conferencing software packages on the market. Using the following link, join a test meeting in order to familiarize yourself with Zoom: https://zoom.us/test. Once you are set up, explore Zoom's capabilities by clicking on all the available buttons (e.g., Mute + audio settings, Start Video + options such as choosing a virtual background, Participants, Chat, Share Screen, Record, and Reactions) and test out what you discover.

- Zoom Test: https://zoom.us/test

REFERENCES

Adler, A. (2010, April). *Talking the talk: Tips on giving a successful conference presentation. Psychological Science Agenda.* American Psychology Association. https://www.apa.org/science/about/psa/2010/04/presentation

Agarwal, S. (2020, April 29). *To take on Zoom, Google Meet goes free for everyone.* Digital Trends. https://www.digitaltrends.com/web/google-meet-free-update

Block, S. M. (1996). Do's and don'ts of poster presentation. *Biophysical Journal, 71,* 3529–3527. https://doi.org/10.1016/S0006-3495(96)79549-8

Childress, A. (2019, January 18). *How to learn PowerPoint quickly (complete beginner's guide).* EnvatoTuts+. https://business.tutsplus.com/tutorials/how-to-learn-powerpoint--cms-29884

Dalzell, T. (2009). *The Routledge dictionary of modern American slang and unconventional English.* Taylor & Francis.

Genard, G. (2016). *How to give a speech: Easy-to-learn skills for successful presentations, speeches, pitches, lectures, and more!* (2nd ed.). Cedar & Maitland Press.

Graw, M. (2020, February 27). *The best free presentation software 2020: Free alternatives to PowerPoint.* Techradar. https://www.techradar.com/best/free-presentation-software

Kessler, S. (n.d.). *How to improve your presentation skills.* Inc. https://www.inc.com/guides/how-to-improve-your-presentation-skills.html

Martinez, K. (2020, May 22). *The best presentation software in 2020.* Zapier. https://zapier.com/blog/best-powerpoint-alternatives

Miller, J. E. (2007). Preparing and presenting effective research posters. *Health Service Research, 42,* 311–328. https://doi.org/10.1111/j.1475-6773.2006.00588.x

National Association of Social Workers. (2017). *NASW, ASWB, CSWE, & CSWA standards for technology in social work practice.* NASW Practice Standards & Guidelines. https://www.socialworkers.org/Practice/Practice-Standards-Guidelines

Partridge, E., Dalzel, T., & Victor, T. (2007). *The concise new Partridge dictionary of slang.* Psychology Press.

PowerPoint for Windows Training. (n.d.). *Microsoft.* https://support.microsoft.com/en-us/office/powerpoint-for-windows-training-40e8c930-cb0b-40d8-82c4-bd53d3398787?ui=en-us&rs=en-us&ad=us

Stewart, J. P., & Fulop, D. (2019). *Mastering the art of oral presentations: Winning orals, speeches, and stand-up presentations.* Wiley.

Stuenkel, D. L., & Rauch, L. A. (2018). Communicating practice scholarship through oral presentation. In M. P. Murphy, B. A. Staffileno, & M. D. Foreman, (Eds.), *Research for advanced practice nurses: From evidence to practice* (3rd ed., pp. 357–370). Springer Publishing Company.

Use full potential of Skype's features during your video conference. (n.d.). *Skype*. https://www.skype.com/en/free-conference-call

Weisbein, J. (2020, April 29). *The best zoom alternatives for videoconferencing*. Digital trends. https://www.digitaltrends.com/computing/best-zoom-alternatives-video-conferencing

What Is Meet Now and How Do I Use It in Skype? (n.d.). *Skype*. https://support.skype.com/en/faq/FA34926/what-is-meet-now-and-how-do-i-use-it-in-skype

Wilson, J. H. (2012, November). *Student presenting research posters: Helpful tips for teaching students on how to construct and present research posters. Psychology Teacher Network: American Psychological Association*. American Pyschology Association. https://www.apa.org/ed/precollege/ptn/2012/11/research-posters

Zivkovic, S. (2014). The importance of oral presentations for university students. *Mediterranean Journal of Social Sciences*, 5(19), 468–475. https://doi.org/10.5901/mjss.2014.v5n19p468

INDEX

ACA. *See* Affordable Care Act
action research, 16–18
activity codes, 199
Affordable Care Act (ACA), 88
American Psychological Association (APA), 25, 30–31, 33–36, 39
APA (2020) Publication Manual, 227
APA. *See* American Psychological Association
Apple Keynote, 243
applied research 15–18
applied research studies, 62, 65, 67, 69, 75
Association of Social Work Boards (ASWB), 239
ASWB. *See* Association of Social Work Boards
ATLAS.ti, 215
axial coding, 204–205

behavioral health rehabilitation services (BHRS), 151
behavioral observation form, 72
BHRS. *See* behavioral health rehabilitation services
bias-free writing, 32–37
    age, 34
    bisexual, 36
    disability, 34–35
    gay and lesbian, 36
    gender, 35
    key components, 34
    queer, 36
    race and ethnicity, 35–36
    sexual orientation, 36
biases in research
    analysis and interpretation, 47
    controlling, 47–48
    epistemological, social, and economic context, 45
    implementation, 46–47
    methodologies, 46
    sources, 45
    study design, 46

capstone competency log (CCL), 18–21
capstone projects 3–4. *See also* writing strategies
    abstract, 233
    additional components, 232
    appendices, 233
    author name and affiliations, 233
    checklist and self-assessment, 233–236
    cognitive and affective processes, 10
    competency model, 10–11
    core social work values, 12
    data analysis, 230
    discussion section, 230–231
    ethical standards, 12–13
    future research, 231–232
    human subjects, protection, 230
    introductory section, 221–224
    IRB approval, 13–14
    knowledge, values and skill dimension, 9
    literature review, 224
    measurement, 229
    methods section, 227
    participants, 228
    policies and procedures, 226
    program recommendations, 231
    program/service, 226–227
    reference list, 233
    results section, 230
    study design, 228
    summary of major findings, 231
    target problem, 224–226
    technology exercises, 236
    title page, 232
capstone project approval
    obtaining agency permission, 52
    writing a problem statement, 52–54
CCL. *See* capstone competency log
Clinical Social Work Association (CSWA), 239
closed-ended questions, 75–76
COA. *See* Commission on Accreditation
Code-of-Ethics/Code-of-Ethics-English, 12
COEP. *See* Commission on Educational Policy

Commission on Accreditation (COA), 4
Commission on Educational
    Policy (COEP), 4
community needs assessment 113
    boundaries and membership, 114–115
    data collection issues, 116–117
    focus groups, 119
    mixed methods, 119
    questions and variables, 115–116
    secondary analysis, 117–118
    surveys and interviews, 118
    types, 113–114
competency log: capstone project, paper, and
        presentation 18–21
    sample log, 21
    technology exercises, 22
competency model of social
    work practice 10–11
continuous recording approach, 72
convenience sampling, 188–189
conventional content analysis, 133–134
Council on Social Work Education
    (CSWE), 239, 244
COVID-19 pandemic, 239, 241, 253, 255
CSWA. *See* Clinical Social Work
    Association
CSWE. *See* Council on Social Work
    Education

data coding consistency checks, 211–212
data collection, 59, 192
    methods 63–64
    nonprobability samples, 65–66
    practice exercises 78
    primary data, 61–63
    probability samples, 65
    qualitative methods, 75
    quantitative methods, 66–75
    sampling, 64–65
    secondary data, 59–61
    sources of data, 59
    technology exercises 79
data familiarization, 193
data set, 59–60, 79
data sources, 59, 62, 78

data transcription, 192–193
directed content analysis, 134

Educational Policy and Accreditation
    Standards (EPAS), 4, 19
elaboration skills, 63–64
EPAS. *See* Educational Policy and
    Accreditation Standards
ethical standards 12–13
event codes, 200–201
evidence-based approach, 79

FBI. *See* Federal Bureau of Investigation
Federal Bureau of Investigation (FBI), 100
Feminist Memory Work (FMW), 124, 140
FMW. *See* Feminist Memory Work)
formative evaluations 89–91
free digital images, 243–244

general inductive approach, 206–209
Google Meet, 254–255
Google Slides, 242
grounded theory approach, 203–204

holistic competency 9–10
homogeneous sampling, 190

ICPSR, 60–61
in-depth information, 63–64
inductive coding process, 209–210
information technology. *See also specific*
    software
    role in research, 44–45
informed consent, 14–15
Institutional Review Board (IRBs),
    3, 13–15, 43, 49
Interrupted time-series analysis (ITSA), 153–154
interval data, 165
IRBs. *See* Institutional Review Board
ITSA. *See* Interrupted time-series
    analysis

LibraOffice, 243
literature review, 47–48
    components, 48–49
    sources/quality of information, 49
    theoretical or conceptual framework, 50–52
    useful tips, 50

MAXQDA, 214
method codes, 202

narrative analysis approach, 136–138
NASW Code of Ethics, 238, 244
NASW. *See* National Association of Social Workers
National Association of Social Workers (NASW), 32, 39, 143, 147, 160
needs assessment 103
    comparative analysis, 105–106
    expressed analysis, 105–106
    normative analysis, 105–106
    practice activities 119
    prevalence and incidence, 107
    purpose identification, 103–104
    services utilization, 105–106
    severity studies, 107
    technology exercise, 120
    variable selection and measurement, 108
needs, definition, 104–105
nominal measurement, 165
nonprobability sampling, 187–188
notes, use of, 249–250
NVivo, 214

open coding, 204
oral presentations, 247–253
ordinal measurement, 165
organizational needs assessment 108
    capacity, 109
    focus groups, 112–113
    qualitative and quantitative methods, 111–112
    questions and variables, 109–111
    secondary analysis, 112
    service assessments, 110–111
    surveys and interviews, 112
personal interviews, 63–64, 75
Pixabay, 244
policy evaluation 85
    description frameworks, 87
    historical and legislative analyses, 87–88
    outcome and effectiveness analysis, 88–89
    purpose of analysis, 86–87
    values and concept analysis, 88
poster presentations, 244–246
PowerPoint presentations, 242
Practice Activities 22
Prezi, 242–243
probability, 59, 65, 78
process codes, 199
professional social work competencies 4–9
program evaluation, 89
    commonalities and differences, 85
    context, 89
    definition, 84
    formative evaluations, 91–93
    practice activities 100
    purposes, 84
    purposes, 89–90
    summative evaluations 93
    technology exercises 101
    types, 89
project presentation, 238
    Apple keynote, 243
    collaboration and sharing options, 241
    designing, creating, and delivering services, 239–240
    electronic visual presentations, 240
    free digital images, 243–244
    Google Meet, 254–255
    Google Slides, 242
    graphic assets, 241
    LibraOffice, 243
    live-polling capabilities, 241
    media support, 241
    NASW code of ethics, 238
    notes, use of, 249–250
    options, 241

project presentation (*continued*)
   oral presentations, 247–253
   poster presentations, 244–246
   PowerPoint presentations, 242
   practice activities, 255
   pre-built themes and templates, 240–241
   Prezi, 242–243
   providing information to the public, 238–239
   Skype videoconferencing, 254
   technology exercises, 256
   tips for poster-related handouts, 247
   tips for student presenters, 246–247
   use of technology, 238
   virtual and distance technologies, 253
   Zoom, 253–254
purposeful sampling, 190

qualitative data analysis approaches 130
   collaborative social research approaches, 131–132
   content analysis, 132–135
   interpretive approaches, 130–131
   social anthropological approaches, 131
   thematic analysis, 135–138
qualitative data analysis software, 214–215
qualitative data collection
   challenge with silences, 77
   focused listening, 78
   minimal prompts, 76
   open-ended questions, 75–76
   reflective empathy, 78
   seeking concreteness, 76–77
   summarizing, 77
qualitative descriptive studies 121
   alternative methods, 121–122
   case study approach, 123–125
   eight characteristics, 122
   grounded theory, 125–128
   phenomenological approach, 128–130
   practice activities 138
   research approaches, 122–123
   technology exercises 138
qualitative research
   convenience sampling, 188–189
   data collection, 192
   data familiarization, 193
   data transcription, 192–193
   delimitations and limitations, 186–187
   exclusion criteria, 183, 186
   homogeneous sampling, 190
   nonprobability sampling, 187–188
   overview, 184
   participants' identification, 185–186
   practice activities, 193
   purposeful sampling, 190
   question formulation, 184–185
   quota sampling, 190
   sampling, 187–191
   saturation principle and sample size, 191
   snowball sampling, 190–191
   technology exercises, 194
   transcription, 193
   volunteer sampling, 189
qualitative research data analysis
   activity codes, 199
   assessing trustworthiness, 211
   ATLAS.TI, 215
   axial coding, 204–205
   coding, 197–198
   creating tables, 206
   data coding consistency checks, 211–212
   event codes, 200–201
   general inductive approach, 206–209
   grounded theory approach, 203–204
   inductive coding process, 209–210
   MAXQDA, 214
   method codes, 202
   NVIVO, 214
   open coding, 204
   practice activities, 215
   process codes, 199
   qualitative data analysis software, 214–215
   relationship and social structure codes, 201–202
   research report writing, 212–213
   selective coding, 205–206
   setting/context codes, 198
   situation codes, 200
   strategy codes, 201
   technology exercises, 215
   thematic analysis, 202–203

quantitative data analysis
    advantages and disadvantages, 163–164
    association-correlations, 171–173
    association-regression, 173–174
    bivariate descriptive statistics, 170–171
    data management and presentation, 178–179
    definition, 163
    dependent variables, 166
    descriptive statistics, 168–169
    extraneous variables, 167
    general process, 164
    independent variables, 166
    inferential statistics, 175–176
    inferential tests of significance, 176–177
    intervening and control variables, 166
    levels of measurement, 165
    multivariate descriptive statistics, 174–175
    practice activities, 180
    research plan analysis, 179
    statistics, parameters, 167
    technology exercise, 180
    test, types, 177–178
    univariate descriptive statistics, 169–170
    "variables", 164–165
    variable distributions, 167–168
quantitative methods, 66–75
    behavioral observations, 71–72
    client log, sample, 71
    levels of measurement, 66–67
    measurement tools, 70
    participant logs, 70–71
    rating scales, 73–74
    relevance, 68
    reliability, 68
    sensitivity, 68
    standardized measures, 74–75
    types of variables, 67
    validity, 69–70
question formulation, 184–185
quota sampling, 190

ratio data, 165
relationship and social structure codes, 201–202

research report writing, 212–213
researcher, 43–47
research topic, 41
    application of knowledge, 42
    bias, prevention research, 45–47
    ethics, 43
    feasibility. 42–43
    importance, 44
    interest and purpose, 42
    practice activities 54
    scientific soundness, 43–44
    technology exercises, 54

SAM. *See* Short Anger Measure
sampling, 187–191
SAS. *See* Statistical Analysis System
saturation principle and sample size, 191
selective coding, 205–206
setting/context codes, 198
sexually transmitted infections (STIs), 127–128
Short Anger Measure (SAM). 156–157, 159
single-subject design (SSD), 143, 147, 149, 157
situation codes, 200
Skype videoconferencing. 254
snowball sampling, 190–191
social work competencies
    assessment and decision-making, 7
    diversity and difference in practice, 5
    ethical and professional behavior, 4–5
    evaluating outcomes and practice effectiveness, 8–9
    evidence-informed interventions, 8
    human relationships, 7
    human rights protection, 5–6
    policy practice, 6
    practice-informed research and research-informed practice, 6
social work practice, evaluation, 143
    client feedback, 145–146
    clinical significance, 150
    designing the evaluation, 146–147
    ethical and social justice issues, 155–158
    formal practice evaluation, single-system designs 146
    informal methods, 144

social work practice, evaluation (*continued*)
    overview, 143–144
    practice activities 159
    single-system designs, 146–149
    statistical significance, 153–155
    supervision and self-reflection, 144–145
    technology exercises 159
    visual significance, 150–152
social work values and ethics, 12
SPSS. *See* Statistical Package for the Social Sciences
SSD. *See* single-subject design
standardized measures, 70, 74–75, 79
Standards for Technology in Social Work Practice, 239
Statistical Analysis System (SAS), 153, 180
Statistical Package for the Social Sciences (SPSS), 153, 180
STIs. *See* sexually transmitted infections
strategy codes, 201
summative content analysis, 134–135
summative evaluations
    analytical assumptions, 97
    available data sets (secondary analysis), 99–100
    goals and objectives, 94–96
    pretesting and posttesting, 98–99
    purpose, 93–94
    qualitative/mixed methodologies, 100
    quantitative methodologies, 97
    surveys, 98

tables, 206
target problem, 59, 63, 68, 70–71, 73–75
thematic analysis, 202–203
transcription, 193

Unsplash, 244

validity, 68–70, 74–75, 79
variables, 60, 66–67, 78–79
virtual and distance technologies, 253–254
volunteer sampling, 189

Wikimedia Commons, 244
writing strategies
    bias-free writing, 32–37
    citation guidelines, 37
    concise and clear sentences, 30–31
    cultural competence, 32–33
    cultural humility, 33
    dos and don'ts of writing, 29
    getting organized, 25–26
    headings and subheadings, 31–32
    intersectionality, 33
    outlining, 26–27
    plan development, 27–28
    practice activities 38
    printed version, 38
    proofreading tips, 37–38
    read backward, 38
    read out loud, 38
    references and hyperlinks check, 38
    short paragraphs, 29–30
    spellchecker, 37
    style norms, 29
    technology exercises 39
    time and space, 26
    transitional words, 31
    use of "I", 29

Zoom, 253–254

Printed in the USA
CPSIA information can be obtained
at www.ICGtesting.com
CBHW081913120824
13074CB00006B/296